Ed,

Best Wishes!

Mike Benoit

Bill Schneider

Bob D

The Practical
Guide to
Managing
Nonprofit
Assets

The Practical Guide to Managing Nonprofit Assets

WILLIAM A. SCHNEIDER,

ROBERT A. DIMEO,

MICHAEL S. BENOIT &
ASSOCIATES

WILEY

John Wiley & Sons, Inc.

For general information on our other products and services, or technical support, please contact our Customer Care Department within the United States at 800-762-2974, outside the United States at 317-572-3993 or fax 317-572-4002.

Wiley also publishes its books in a variety of electronic formats. Some content that appears in print may not be available in electronic books.

For more information about Wiley products, visit our web site at www.wiley.com.

Library of Congress Cataloging-in-Publication Data:

ISBN-13 978-0-471-69233-1
ISBN-10 0-471-69233-6

Printed in the United States of America.

10 9 8 7 6 5 4 3 2 1

To my wife, Caren, and children: Erik, Laura, Chris, Katie, and Jamie for their love and support.

William A. Schneider

To my wife Adriane and sons Chris and Danny for providing enormous joy in my life and to my partners and associates for being truly great teammates in building a wonderful firm.

Bob DiMeo

To my wife, Mary Alice, and family for their encouragement and patience in putting up with me while working on this book. Also, thanks to my associates Julie and Katie for their help in deciphering and organizing many of my cryptic notes.

Mike Benoit

To my wife, Jeannie, for her ever lasting love, devotion, and support. Also, to my beautiful daughters, Mira and Petrea, who bring way too much joy to my life. Lastly, to my loving mother, Sandy, and to my late father—I miss you, Lee.

Doug Balsam

To my wife, Kristin, my inspiration, whose love and support has meant everything. Also, to my parents, Carrie and Jay, for their guidance and encouragement.

Matt Porter

I would like to thank my wife and partner, Jennifer, for her endless patience and understanding during all the evenings and weekends spent at the local coffee shop working on this book.

Matt Rice

I would like to thank my husband, Jeff Rondini, for his constant encouragement, confidence, and support in all of my endeavors.

Jackie Rondini

To my wife, Kelli, whose constant support and encouragement is so very appreciated. Also, to my parents, Polly and Frank, for their friendship and guidance through the years.

Steve Spencer

To my husband, Todd, who patiently listened to the countless readings of my drafts and offered well-timed words of encouragement. Also, to my dogs, Bobby and Max, who eagerly participated on long walks through the streets of Chicago to clear my writer's block.

Trina Sweet

About the Authors

William A. Schneider, CIMA, is a Managing Director of DiMeo Schneider & Associates, L.L.C., a Chicago-based firm that provides advisory services to sponsors and financial institutions. He currently advises several hospitals, university endowments, and private foundations as well as not-for-profit organizations, corporate plans, several leading Midwest law firms, and Fortune 500 companies. He holds the title Certified Investment Management Analyst, awarded through the Investment Management Consultants Association (IMCA) accreditation program at the Wharton School of Business. He is the coauthor of *Asset Management for Endowments & Foundations* (McGraw-Hill) and *Designing a 401(k) Plan* (Probus).

Robert A. DiMeo, CIMA, CFP, is a Managing Director of DiMeo Schneider & Associates, L.L.C. Bob is an Advisory Board member for Catholic Charities of Chicago, on the Governance Board for Notre Dame High School, and a former member of the Board of Directors for the IMCA. He is the coauthor of *Asset Management for Endowments & Foundations* (McGraw-Hill) and *Designing a 401(k) Plan* (Probus).

Michael S. Benoit, CIMA, CFP, is Managing Director, Private Client Services at DiMeo Schneider & Associates, L.L.C. He is a cofounder of the firm. As a Certified Financial Planner he provides investment counseling services to corporate executives, family trusts, and private foundations. He has addressed national conferences on subjects including professional money management, financial planning, and estate planning. Mike is a member of the Financial Planning Association. He received his bachelor's degree from Bradley University in Peoria, IL and has completed the College for Financial Planning's CFP Professional Education Program. Mike is a Certified Investment Management Analyst.

Douglas M Balsam, CIMA, AIFA, is a Principal and Director of Institutional Consulting at DiMeo Schneider & Associates, L.L.C. Prior to joining the firm, he was a Communications/Education Consultant at Scudder, Stevens & Clark. He earned his bachelor's degree at Miami University in Ohio, and his MBA, with honors, from Loyola University in Chicago. He is a Certified Investment Management Analyst and Accredited Investment Fiduciary Auditor.

Mathew P. Porter, CIMA, is a Principal at DiMeo Schneider & Associates, L.L.C. Matt chairs the firm's investment committee. Prior to joining the firm, he was a Trust Officer, Wealth Management Trust Administrator at the Northern Trust Company. He is currently a member of the Investment Management Consultants Association (IMCA). Matt received a Bachelor of Science degree in Finance from the University of Illinois in Urbana-Champaign, IL. He obtained the title Certified Investment Management Analyst (CIMA) from IMCA's accreditation program at the Wharton School of Business.

Mathew R. Rice, CFA, CIMA, CIMC, is a Senior Consultant at DiMeo Schneider & Associates, L.L.C. and member of the firm's investment committee. Prior to joining the firm, he was a Trust Officer, Institutional Investment Services at Old Kent Bank. Matt has performed extensive research in the areas of asset allocation, portfolio optimization, best-practice portfolio rebalancing methods, and alternative investment strategies. Matt earned his Bachelor of Arts degree in Economics from Northwestern University where he was Co-Defensive Most Valuable Player on their 1996 Rose Bowl Team. He is a Chartered Financial Analyst, Certified Investment Management Analyst, and Certified Investment Management Consultant.

Jacqueline A. Rondini, CFP, CMFC, is a Senior Investment Analyst at DiMeo Schneider & Associates, L.L.C. and member of the firm's investment committee. Prior to joining the firm, she was the Managed Accounts Coordinator at Rodman & Renshaw, Inc. She earned her Bachelor of Business Administration degree from Iowa State University in Ames, IA. She is a Certified Financial Planner and a Chartered Mutual Fund Counselor.

Stephen W. Spencer, CIMC, is a Senior Consultant at DiMeo Schneider & Associates, L.L.C. and a member of the firm's investment committee. Prior to joining the firm, he was a Financial Representative at Scudder Kemper Investments. Steve earned his Bachelor of Arts degree in Economics from the University of New Hampshire. Steve is a Certified Investment Management Consultant and a member of the Investment Management Consultants Association (IMCA).

Trina M. Sweet is Director of Investment Research at DiMeo Schneider & Associates, L.L.C. and a founding member of the firm. She previously worked at Franklin Mutual Fund Company, Securities Counselors of Iowa, and Kidder, Peabody & Company. Trina has advanced training in performance monitoring. She received her bachelor's degree from Northeast Missouri State.

ABOUT THE CONTRIBUTORS

Joseph S. Adams is a partner in the international law firm of McDermott Will & Emery LLP based in the Firm's Chicago office. As a member of the Employee Benefits Department, Joe concentrates his practice on employee benefits and executive compensation matters for private, public, and tax-exempt organizations. A frequent speaker and writer on employee benefits and executive compensation issues, Joe currently serves as the contributing editor for the *Pension Plan Fix-It Handbook* and for *Executive Compensation Strategis*. He has previously served as the contibuting editor for the *Guide to Assigning and Loaning Benefit Plan Money* and co-authored the first and second editions of *Domestic Partner Benefits: An Employer's Guide*. Joe received his law degree, *cum laude*, from Cornell Law School, where he served as an editor for the *Cornell Law Review*. Joe received his undergraduate degree from the University of Chicago's Honors Economics Program.

Richard S. Gallagher is a partner in the Milwaukee office of Foley & Lardner. As chair of the firm's Tax and Individual Planning Department and a member of the Taxation Practice Group, his practice focuses on business and tax matters for family-owned companies; corporate planning and reorganizations; trust and estate administration; the qualification of tax-exempt organizations; unrelated business income and private inurement matters; and tax, estate, and gift planning for philanthropists, foundations, and charitable trusts.

Mr. Gallagher is the former chairman of the Exempt Organizations Committee of the American Bar Association (ABA) Section on Taxation, the past chairman of the Committee on Administration of Estates and Trusts of the Real Property, Probate, and Trust Law Section of the ABA, and a fellow of the American Law Institute, the American College of Tax Counsel, the American College of Trust and Estate Counsel, and the Milwaukee Bar Association Foundation, over which he presided as president from 1977 until 1983. He is listed in *The Best Lawyers in America* under Tax Law and Trusts and Estates.

Mr. Gallagher graduated from Harvard University Law School (J.D., 1967) and from Northwestern University (B.S. in business administration, with distinction, 1964). He was admitted to the Wisconsin Bar in 1967.

Contents

## CHAPTER 1

Introduction

A CRYING NEED

"It was the best of times; it was the worst of times." That's how Charles Dickens began *A Tale of Two Cities*, a novel about another turbulent era. Our own is more challenging. Information can travel around the globe at the speed of an electric current, but the ancient scourges of ignorance, disease, poverty, and hatred are far from banished. An optimist can find cause for gratitude: new advances in agriculture allow fewer and fewer farmers to feed the world. Biotechnology has changed the face of medicine. The fall of Communism has already freed millions of workers and is beginning to create more vibrant economies around the globe. But change creates turmoil. Some lives improve, others get worse.

Not-for-profit institutions (charities, hospitals, schools, and religious organizations) face a growing need for their services. Simultaneously, governments in the United States and around the world have been forced to cut back some of their traditional support. The money simply is not there.

Demographics have changed and will continue to change dramatically. Medical science makes it possible to live longer, but at a cost. An aging population taxes the infrastructure. Promised entitlements such as Social Security and Medicare will ultimately be cut back. Who will pick up the slack?

The extended family structure that served mankind for centuries has broken down. Millions of children are now raised by single parents. Even in the "traditional" family, if both parents need to work, the odds are the kids will be shipped off to a day-care center rather than to loving relatives. Many grandparents now live halfway across the country rather than around the corner. Incapacitated grandparents themselves face the prospect of ending up in a nursing home or assisted-care facility rather than in a spare room at their son's or daughter's home.

Increased globalization also creates serious challenges. On the one hand, society profits from free trade. Goods and services become more affordable and ultimately more jobs are created as entrepreneurs find ways to profit from the new economy. Think of all the people employed in importing, distributing, and retailing a portable compact disc player made in China. And since the player is so cheap, almost every teenager has one. The teens, in turn, become voracious consumers of compact discs, thus employing musicians, singers, artists, producers, sales people, and so forth. On the other hand, try explaining all that to an unemployed factory worker whose assembly line job will never return to the United States.

Our educational system has produced uneven output. Although our colleges and universities train the best and the brightest as future doctors and scientists, an alarming percentage of high school students fall through the cracks. Math and reading scores have fallen, and drop-out rates have increased over the past 30 years. In the mid-20th century, those failing students could still join the workforce as unskilled laborers or find a job on an assembly line—boring jobs to be sure. But it's exactly those boring or repetitive jobs that are being lost to automation or exported to countries with cheap labor.

SHOCKS TO THE SYSTEM

Other disturbing trends are afoot around the globe. First and foremost, the spread of AIDS may overwhelm all other forces. Sub-Saharan Africa provides an example. Just as the great plague threw Europe into the Dark Ages, AIDS has already destroyed the fabric of society in certain areas. Tens of thousands of orphans have been left to raise themselves. With no parents to teach them how to farm, even the basics of food production lie in jeopardy.

The world has become more polarized. The rise of Islamic fundamentalism has led to new levels of intolerance and barbarism. We live in a time when some parents and "religious leaders" train their own children to become suicide bombers! Even in the United States, politicians seek to exploit class warfare and partisanship for their own political ends.

Billions of dollars worth of illegal drugs and alcohol are consumed each year. By some estimates, the underground drug trade may be the third or fourth largest sector of the economy. The social challenges are enormous. Government attempts to stamp out the drug trade have been a spectacular failure. We have, however, succeeded in creating the largest prison population of all time.

In short, there is a crying need for all of the services provided by not-for-profit organizations. It does not matter whether your mission is extremely broad or quite narrow, the challenges are enormous.

FINANCES

Although the challenges are abundant, money is not. The 21st century began with a three-year bear market in stocks. This downturn (the worst in 100 years) devastated many nonprofit organizations. Even a strong market recovery in 2003 and 2004 hasn't restored financial health.

In the 1980s and 1990s, fund fiduciaries became accustomed to equity returns of over 15% per year and double-digit bond returns as well. Nonprofit investment committees debated whether to spend part of the "extra" return they had earned. Sometimes they did. Many universities issued bonds to finance new stadiums or other facilities, counting on return from the portfolio to help pay the debt. By 2003 some of the loan covenants were in jeopardy.

To put the magnitude of the equity decline into perspective, if returns on the Standard & Poor's (S&P) 500 index average 15% per year from 2004 through 2009, then the average annual return for the entire *decade* will be just 6.9%! And most experts doubt that the S&P 500 will return anywhere near 15% per year for that period.

There are only three possible components of stock return: dividend yield plus earnings growth plus (or minus) multiple expansion (or contraction). The dividend yield of the S&P 500 is currently under 2%. Assuming that analysts are not wildly optimistic, nominal earnings growth might be in the 5% to 6% range. This produces a 6.7% to 7.8% return— *unless* you expect multiples to rise.

Earnings multiples (the price-earnings ratio, or P/E) reflect the price investors are willing to pay to acquire a dollar's worth of earnings. The S&P 500's current multiple is around 21 times earnings. Unfortunately that number is near the high end of its historic range. The long-term P/E ratio average for the index is 16 times earnings. Bearish investors argue that P/E ratios are more likely to contract than to expand. Non-U.S. stocks seem more reasonably priced, but one can't build a portfolio of only foreign equities.

Bonds don't seem to be a compelling bargain either. With interest rates near a 45-year low and the threat of inflation increasing, rates may continue to rise. That is a problem for bond investors. Bond prices, of course, move in the opposite direction from interest rates, like the opposite ends of a teeter-totter. When rates go up, bond prices fall and vice versa.

We've heard the argument that "if we hold the bonds until maturity, we'll get all our money back." That may be true, but prior to maturity, one would not be able to sell without realizing a substantial loss. This means the investor would be locked into lower-yielding bonds and unable to replace them with higher yields available in the marketplace. This is still an opportunity cost. Investors who use bond funds rather than directly owning the bonds themselves do not even have this option. Bond *funds* never mature.

CONTRIBUTIONS

One additional component of this "perfect storm" for nonprofit organizations has been the effect on giving. There used to be a substantial incentive for wealthy donors to gift appreciated stock to charities. Not only did the donors avoid paying capital gains tax on the stock, but they also received a tax deduction for the full amount donated. After the bear market, highly appreciated stock may be in short supply. Additionally, the tax code now provides more favorable capital gains treatment than it did a few years ago. In any case, donations have dropped considerably.

THE PENSION PROBLEM

Some not-for-profit organizations face an additional challenge. Organizations that offer a defined benefit (DB) pension plan to employees may find their resources squeezed even further. Because of the way pension liabilities are calculated, DB plans face a double whammy. The lower interest rates act as a multiplier for pension obligations while lower asset values mean that there is less money to pay for those liabilities. This has forced some institutions to make required pension contributions instead of funding important programs.

ENVIRONMENT OF MISTRUST

Fund fiduciaries are also uneasy about their financial vendors. Corporate America is sporting a black eye. It now seems that a number of companies were cooking the books so that insiders could reap huge profits in the form of rising prices on their stock options. In some cases, auditors who were supposed to safeguard the public were in on the scam. Andersen, one of the oldest and most respected accounting firms, was driven out of business for its role in the Enron scandal.

Wall Street analysts in many cases were shown to be nothing more than shills for the investment bankers. E-mails revealed that certain analysts privately labeled stocks "dogs" that they publicly touted as strong buys. Several of the largest brokerage firms were forced to pay huge fines.

Even mutual funds, long considered to be the champion of the small investor, were tainted by the probes. A significant number of fund companies allowed certain hedge funds to trade in ways that harmed the rest of their investors. "Late trading" and "market timing" abuses led to hundreds of millions of dollars in fines. Some fund CEO's lost their jobs, and in one case the founder of the fund company was forced to resign.

In this environment, board members of not-for-profit organizations feel the added pressure of scrutiny themselves. The Senate Finance Committee has been reviewing the financial practices of public charities. Not-for-profit funds are categorically different from most other investment pools. (In most cases, there are no "beneficiaries" who have a claim on the funds—hence less chance of litigation.) However, in some cases dissatisfied donors have demanded refunds. Maybe board members are just feeling less confident then they did in the late 1990s. In any case, there is a clear increase in fiduciaries' desire for prudence. See Chapters 18 and 19 for more information on regulatory requirements.

THE GOOD NEWS

The bleeding stopped, at least temporarily, in 2003 and 2004. Virtually all of the capital markets performed well. Stocks and bonds, both domestic and international, turned in solid years. Furthermore, even the substyles (large-cap, mid-cap, and small-cap—both growth and value) did well. In addition, Congress has provided some legislative relief on pension funding requirements.

Perhaps the most important developments have come in the form of advances in investment theory. These should lead to improved risk-adjusted (and absolute) return. These advances will be presented later in the book. To take profit from these new techniques, fund fiduciaries will need greater knowledge and analytical capabilities. But the payoff from new investment strategies and asset classes will be substantial.

One outgrowth of the Wall Street scandal is that investment organizations are much more concerned with compliance. The treatment of investors should become much more even-handed. Mutual funds, in particular, will be working hard to avoid any hint of future scandal. Nothing focuses attention on governance issues more than a few highly public firings.

Finally, costs are coming down. Some of the mutual fund settlements have involved fee reductions. Also, the Securities and Exchange Commission (SEC) and other regulators are focusing on expenses. 12b-1 fees and trading costs will likely shrink dramatically. The use of "soft dollar" payments is coming to a screeching halt. *Soft dollars* are commissions (usually above market rate) awarded to compensate broker/dealers for other services, such as research and marketing.

THE FUND-RAISING CHALLENGE

Entire books are written on the subject of fund-raising, and it has become an industry unto itself. Here, rather than present fund-raising ideas, we wish to briefly address the important role that investment strategy and structure has in aiding the fund-raising effort for nonprofit organizations.

All fund-raising—whether a significant capital campaign or a single request for an individual gift—will have a better chance of success if you can articulate well-conceived gifting strategies and investment policies. Sure, potential donors want to know "what their donation will buy"; however, they also need to understand:

1. What gifting options or strategies are available to them; and,
2. How the money will be managed (investment policy).

GIFTING STRATEGIES

Nonprofit organizations that expand the ways in which donors can make gifts receive more contributions. Successful institutions move beyond year-end checkbook campaigns to offer donors true value-added gifting strategies.

To increase your raise, be flexible in how you'll accept gifts. Create mechanisms that allow you to accommodate and even encourage nontraditional gifting.

Noncash Gifts. Make it simple for individuals to donate appreciated securities, real estate, or other assets. It is important to have policies in place regarding the disposition of such assets. Also, and this is critical, be sure that appropriate acknowledgement and appreciation procedures are in place. There is perhaps nothing that will harm your fund-raising efforts more than not thanking donors on a timely basis. Too many nonprofit organizations tolerate sloppy procedures. Weeks or even months pass between the day a donor ships securities to the broker of record and when the charity is notified of the gift (Exhibit 1.1). Obviously the lack of a prompt "thank you" discourages future gifts.

INVESTMENT STRATEGY

The more that donors and potential donors know about your investment program, the better. Donors gain confidence when they see a well-conceived strategy that is clearly articulated. As a result, they are likely to give more.

EXHIBIT 1.1   KEYS TO WORLD-CLASS DONOR SERVICE

- Be committed
- Be properly resourced
- Be consistent
- Be quick
- Be personal
- Be known
- Be meticulous
- Be there
- Be honest

Source: CharityVillage.com/Ken Burnett, author of *Relationship Fund Raising-Based Approach to the Business of Raising Money.*

Consider the University of Notre Dame Endowment. At over $3 billion, it is among the 20 largest educational funds in the United States. A visit to the investment office link at www.nd.edu reveals a nonprofit organization that is serious about communicating investment strategy.

The site is flush with general information on the purpose of the fund, but, for those interested, they provide specific details on topics including:

- *Basic Objectives of the Fund:* Specific rate-of-return targets.
- *Investment Policy:* Long-term asset allocation targets by asset class.
- *Investment Management Strategy:* Selection criteria for hiring and evaluating managers.
- *Performance Results:* Historical results compared to key benchmarks.
- *Spending Policies and Trends.*

In attempting to raise money, nonprofit organizations must use every available resource. This book can help an institution create an outstanding investment structure. The key is to be sure to communicate this structure to donors and potential donors.

EXPECT TO FIND

In this book the authors will:

- Examine fund-raising challenges.
- Explore special issues facing hospitals, colleges, and religious orders.

- Examine spending policy and its impact on the health of the organization.
- Explore investment theory, including some of the new insights of *behavioral finance.*
- Discuss fiduciary issues, including the evolving state of the various uniform investment acts, as well as the impact of the Employee Retirement Income Security Act (ERISA).
- Provide a framework for evaluating and selecting consultants, brokers, vendors, record keepers, and other resources for the fund.

Most importantly, we will outline a systematic approach for the prudent steward. The coming chapters explore, in depth, each of these important steps:

- Goal setting
- Asset allocation
- Developing a written investment policy statement
- Selecting managers
- Portfolio rebalancing
- Performance evaluation
- Cost control

HOW TO USE THIS BOOK

Of course one could read the book from beginning to end. But the book is designed to be modular. That is, each section is self-contained. So if, for example, your immediate concern is manager selection, you could turn to that section. One important note: to create the optimal systematic approach, you need to follow all the steps listed above. If you skip any of them, you will do your fund and yourself a great disservice.

We have attempted to make this resource as user friendly as possible. Wherever possible, we have included checklists, forms, sample documents, and worksheets. We also list sources for information, software, and services. These lists, while not exhaustive, should provide helpful direction.

We examine the roles and responsibilities of various providers and vendors to the fund. Fiduciaries are often confused about the function of consultants versus money managers versus brokers versus custodians. We explain what you should and should not expect from each. We also provide a framework to help you select providers in each area.

WHO SHOULD USE THIS BOOK?

This book is written, first and foremost, as a practical guide for fiduciaries of nonprofit funds—board members and internal business managers. We hope to convey the best practices of the marketplace as well as current academic research. We try to keep this as readable as possible so that it can be a pragmatic guide. Wherever possible, we attempt to tell you "what time it is" rather than "how the watch is made." Some technical explanations are necessary from time to time, but we will stick to plain English as much as possible.

A second group that may find this book useful are the various advisers to nonprofit organizations. This group includes accountants, attorneys, and even consultants. Hopefully, this book will enable professionals and their client (the not-for-profit organization) to better communicate. It should also provide tools that can help add even more value for your client. In some cases, it may provide ammunition to persuade your client to take needed action.

Money managers, brokers, custodians, and other vendors will find this book useful. It may give you an enhanced sense of how your service fits into the client's world-view. It may even be a sales tool to help clients understand how your services benefit them.

Finally, anyone who is interested in the oversight of nonprofit funds should gain new insight. This group includes legislators, teachers, students, community activists, reporters, and others.

## CHAPTER 2

Special Issues

HOSPITALS—THE RETIREMENT PLAN MESS

Regardless of how large or small a hospital might be, retirement plans are a big issue. Pension plans cover a growing number of retirees, and defined contribution plans have almost become a requirement for attracting and retaining quality employees. In this chapter, we discuss several topics, including underfunded pension plans, 403(b), 401(k) plans, and capital campaigns.

UNDERFUNDED PENSIONS

During much of the 1980s and 1990s, pension funding was an afterthought. Consistent double-digit returns from the equity markets kept the coffers full for most plans. Plan sponsors were not as interested in true asset allocation strategies as they were in just being "in the market." As we've noted, the bear market of the early 2000s changed all of that. Steep declines in the equity markets coupled with low interest rates helped create the current mess, but ill-conceived investment policies compounded the problems. For the first time in nearly two decades, pension plan committees are looking at hefty funding requirements. Hospital administrators face a serious challenge in dealing with underfunded pension plans.

Because government regulations require pension plan balances to stay within a certain percentage of outstanding liabilities (the amount owed to current and future retirees), organizations must ratchet up contributions to their plans if the ratio slips. Corporations face similar problems, but the cost of pension plan liabilities shows up in lower corporate earnings. When hospitals or other not-for-profit organizations are forced to make extra contributions to pension plans, important organizational goals may be jeopardized. If budgets are tight, a contribution to a pension plan may take the place of a new piece of much-needed medical equipment.

The pension quandary forces you to make sure that you have a full and real understanding of your pension plan. What does the demographic profile of the plan look like? Has an asset/liability study been done recently? Is there too much risk embedded in the plan's asset allocation? Too little? Do you properly monitor the investment managers? Although these questions are extremely important for all pension plans, they are crucial for not-for-profit organizations that may rely on donations or special funding for their success. In addition to pension problems, not-for-profit organizations face challenges with their other retirement vehicles.

403(B) VERSUS 401(K)

Since its inception in 1958, the 403(b) has been the primary retirement savings plan available to not-for-profit organizations. Historically, most 403(b) vendors have been insurance companies. Some have been top-notch vendors, but many are secondary or tertiary players. Mutual fund companies have traditionally avoided this market, even though their record keeping, investment prowess, and educational materials make them the dominant providers in the 401(k) arena.

401(k) plans had their inception in 1981. They quickly grew to become the dominant retirement plan type. Competing vendors, mostly mutual fund companies, engaged in a kind of "arms race" of service offerings seeking to increase their share of this exploding market. Daily valuation, on-line account access, 24-hour call centers, robust educational capabilities, and almost complete investment flexibility became hallmarks of the 401(k) arena. Vendors commit millions of dollars each year for hardware, software, systems, and people to enhance their ability to service participant-directed plans. Simultaneously, competition has driven prices down.

Superficially, 401(k) and 403(b) plans look very similar. Both are sponsored by the participants' employer. Both allow participants to save their own money on a tax-deferred basis. Both allow for investment choice. However, there were small but significant differences in testing, record-keeping, and eligibility requirements. Maybe, more importantly, assets in 401(k) plans were showing enormous growth while 403(b) plan assets were not. Part of the problem for 403(b) plans has been that they have been just different enough that the mutual fund companies abandoned the field to the insurers.

With the passage of legislation in 1996, nonprofit organizations (including hospitals) now have more options. Some of the "one-off" reporting and record-keeping requirements were modified to make 401(k) and 403(b) plans more similar. Not-for-profit organizations are able to offer 401(k) plans in lieu of or alongside 403(b) plans. Plan sponsors can look outside the insurance industry for providers. The ability to access 401(k) plans and vendors has been a significant upgrade for both not-for-profit plan sponsors and participants.

Traditional 403(b) plans have several inherent problems. Two of the biggest are the issues of "retail" (as opposed to institutional) pricing and the lack of adequate participant education. Historically, each 403(b) participant has been treated as an individual investor rather than as part of a sizable retirement plan. Competing vendors often set up tables in the cafeteria and tried to sell individual participants their product. Any "education" was typically a thinly disguised sales pitch. Of course, this inefficient delivery system required sizable commissions to incent the sales force. Commissions as high as 5% to 7% of invested assets are common! In addition, there are often trailers, ongoing commissions paid as long as the policy is in force.

ANNUITIES

The overwhelming majority of investment options in 403(b) plans are variable or fixed annuities. Exhibit 2.1 shows the breakdown of assets within the 403(b) marketplace.

As an investment vehicle, annuities are qualitatively different from mutual funds. An annuity is a contract with an insurance company. Annuities can be either *variable* or *fixed*. Variable annuities do not pay a stated rate of return but rather a variable rate depending on the market returns for the underlying investments. In essence, they are mutual funds within the umbrella of an annuity contract. Fixed annuities operate in a similar fashion to a certificate of deposit (CD), paying a stated rate of return.

There are typically added layers of expense attached to the variable contracts; sometimes this added layer is called a *wrap fee* (because it wraps around the usual mutual fund expenses). The wrap fee is used to pay administrative fees, mortality (these are insurance contracts), and commissions. An additional expense often associated with both types of annuity contracts is the *surrender charge*, or deferred sales charge. This is a fee that is paid out of the fund balance if the investment is sold within a defined period after the contract's purchase. The surrender charge schedule may extend as long as 10 years, with charges declining each year until the surrender period is over. Excessive fees and onerous contracts are the biggest problems with annuity investments. In response to competitive pressure, some in-

EXHIBIT 2.1 403(B) PLAN ASSETS AND SHARE OF TOTAL 403(B) PLAN ASSETS BY
INSTITUTION, 1996-2003

| | Life Insurance Companies | | Variable Annuity Mutual Funds | | Non–Variable Annuity Mutual Funds | |
	Assets (billions)	Share* (percent)	Assets (billions)	Share* (percent)	Assets (billions)	Share* (percent)	Assets (billion)
1996	208	58	103	29	45	13	356
1997	238	56	129	30	59	14	425
1998	205	47	158	36	75	17	437
1999	236	45	191	36	98	19	525
2000	252	49	174	34	90	17	516
2001	205	46	150	34	88	20	443
2002	235	54	120	28	79	18	435
2003	269	50	158	30	105	20	532

*Percentage of total 403(b) plan assets.
Source: Investment Company Institute.

surers have upgraded their offerings to bring them in line with current best practices. But far too many are still sold the old-fashioned way.

Why is the annuity still so prevalent in the 403(b) marketplace? Until 1974, they were the only approved investment for 403(b) plans. Over many years, they became entrenched and, until recently, were thought of as an appropriate investment vehicle for participants. As mentioned, traditional 403(b) plan investments are sold directly to employees. A large, commission-based sales force has focused on these plans for decades. Of course, they have a strong incentive to defend their market share.

403(b) plans that make no employer contributions are not subject to the Employers Retirement Income Security Act (ERISA). Such plans do not face discrimination testing requirements and do not have to file a form 5500. This flexibility will likely keep certain sponsors in the 403(b) fold. Plans that do make a match have either already moved or are considering a switch to 401(k). However, many of the major 401(k) vendors are now beginning to service 403(b) plans as well.

MUTUAL FUNDS

Why should a plan sponsor consider mutual funds instead of annuities? There are several reasons, starting with fees. Mutual funds in 401(k) and "updated" 403(b) plans are available with no front-end or back-end loads to participants. Their overall expense ratio will generally be low as well (if the plan sponsor is prudent in the selection process). A retirement plan has an enormous advantage over an individual investor … sheer size. Defined contribution (DC) plans have access to institutionally priced funds that are unavailable to individual investors. These institutional funds often have expense ratios that may be half of those in retail share classes.

Access to superior money management is the second major advantage of mutual funds. With the number of mutual funds nearing 9,000, there is an abundance of quality money management firms from which to choose. In the mutual fund world, if a fund underperforms significantly, investors leave. As you can imagine, competition for top talent is fierce and money managers who succeed are rewarded handsomely. There are few back-end loads or contracts to keep investors in place. Fund companies recognize this and go to great lengths to maintain a competitive performance record.

A final advantage of mutual funds is name recognition. It comforts participants and may raise their level of interest in the plan. Name brand mutual funds are more likely to generate water cooler conversation about investing.

Because of these advantages, a number of insurers have begun to offer well-known mutual funds either as subadvisers to their annuities or as stand-alone offerings within the plan.

EDUCATION AND COMMUNICATION

Average participation rates in 403(b) plans are near 60%, whereas the average participation in 401(k) plans is 70% (Exhibit 2.2).

Why is there such a significant difference, particularly among the non–highly compensated group? One major reason is the lack of access to effective participant education. With investment options often scattered across several insurance vendors and a lack of a central record keeper providing statements, it is exceedingly difficult to communicate a consistent message to employees. And a consistent message is crucial. With multiple vendors and multiple statements, participants may become victims of information overload and simply quit trying to understand it all. To exacerbate the problem, when it comes to the number of investment choices, 403(b) plans have operated under the assumption that "more is better." Recent research shows that as the number of plan investment options increases, participation rates actually decline. Exhibit 2.3 details the number of investment options that hospitals offer by plan type.

Academic research shows that asset allocation is the prime determinant of investment success. In other words, a participant needs to be able to effectively diversify among several asset classes (see Chapter 7). But with roughly half of hospital-sponsored 403(b) plans offering in excess of 20 investment options, participants are overwhelmed! It is tough enough to help participants understand the

EXHIBIT 2.2 PARTICIPATION AND DEFERRAL RATES BY PLAN TYPE

	403(b)	401(k)
Rates of participation		
Median for all employees	60%	70%
Median for HCE	95%	100%
Median for NHCE	55%	66%
Employee deferral rates		
Median for all employees	5%	5%
Median for HCE	7%	7%
Median for NHCE	4%	5%

HCE, highly compensated employees; NHCE, non–highly compensated employees.
Source: American Hospital Association, Diversified Investment Advisors: *Retirement Plan Trends in Today's Healthcare Market,* 2003.

EXHIBIT 2.3 NUMBER OF INVESTMENT OPTIONS OFFERED
BY PLAN TYPE (HOSPITALS ONLY)

	403(b)	401(k)
1–5	8%	4%
6–10	12%	27%
11–15	21%	24%
16–20	13%	22%
More than 20	47%	24%

includes multiple provider situations.

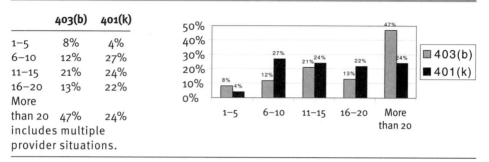

Source: American Hospital Association/Diversified Investment Advisors.

difference between large-cap and small-cap stocks or value and growth styles. It is too much to expect them to sift through a list of 30 choices, several of which overlap. Ill-informed participants either invest in something they have heard of, or they are frightened of making a bad decision so they invest in the safest option. Keeping it simple is the most effective way to communicate. Participants need to learn why they should save for retirement, why the plan is the best place to save, and how to invest.

Participants in defined contribution plans all have the same needs and concerns. The goal of a plan sponsor should be to put them in the best position to succeed. A 403(b) plan or a 401(k) plan is by far the best tool to help them save for retirement. A quality DC plan should offer low-cost, high-quality investments, state-of-the art services such as Web access and call centers, high-quality communication materials, and in-person employee education. Often the best way to have these benefits is to move away from the traditional 403(b) model (multiple annuity investments from multiple vendors) to a consolidated environment.

CASE STUDY

A Midwest-based hospital sponsored a traditional 403(b) plan, a smaller 401(k) plan, and several nonqualified plans. There were three 403(b) vendors, each offering its own investments, each with its own contact people, and each providing individual statements to participants. The client wanted to consolidate both qualified plans but was unsure of how to proceed. Our firm drafted a request for proposal. The goals were to consolidate the investments, find a provider who excelled in communication and education, and to offer state-of-the-art technology and participant services.

One major obstacle arose. There was a huge deferred sales charge (back-end load) attached to the annuity investments. This multi-million dollar liability would be owed by participants. The hospital was very sensitive to the impact that a move away from these annuities would have on their employees' balances. The vendor who was ultimately selected agreed to buy out these sales charges and allow participant balances to transfer to the new platform without shrinkage. The vendor did not do this for free (a large, up-front hit makes it tough to have a profitable relationship), but they did allow participants to "pay back" the sales charges over a period of three years in the form of a slightly higher expense ratio until the liability was erased. That expense was netted from performance. Of course, our firm made certain that the fees were reduced after the three years. So, there are creative ways to exit a difficult situation.

When the process was completed, the new vendor administered their 403(b), 401(k), 457(f), and 457(b) plans as well as their COBRA (Consolidated Omnibus Budget Reconciliation Act) and HIPAA (Health Insurance Portability and Accountability Act) plans. All the plans were structured to use the exact same investment line-up. Communication materials and education campaigns were uniformly presented to all participants, regardless of which plans they participated in. Participants could now check their funds in the newspaper and could see all of their balances on one statement. Both participation and satisfaction rates increased. Simply put, the move created a much better environment for participants and the hospital.

ENDOWMENT AND OPERATING FUNDS

Pension and 401(k) plans are governed by ERISA—but what are the guidelines for running non–ERISA funds? Section 404 of ERISA sets a standard often referred to as the *prudent expert rule*. Plan fiduciaries must act in the manner of "a prudent person, familiar with such matters." It only makes sense to apply the same standard of prudence to the oversight of endowments and operating funds. What does this mean? If your board is not expert in these areas, hire someone who is! Setting goals, writing an investment policy statement, asset allocation, manager selection, and performance monitoring and evaluation are crucial components in the oversight of your fund. This book will explore each of those areas in coming chapters. In addition, fund-raising is likely to take on greater and greater importance.

CONTRIBUTIONS

As most board members and trustees know, contributions are the lifeblood of any successful endowment. Just how important might contributions be in the coming years? Credit rating agency Standard & Poor's (S&P) on June 10, 2004, wrote "a variety of emerging or intensifying factors threaten the future performance and credit quality of the nation's not-for-profit health care system." In a new report on the midyear outlook for the U.S. not-for-profit health-care sector, the agency said "growing concerns include: unquenchable demand for health care services and related growth in new health care technology and health care costs; the sustainability of managed care rate increases; the slow erosion of employer-based health insurance; reductions in Medicaid eligibility and reimbursement; the growing burden of rising bad debt and charity care; the government's long-term ability to adequately fund Medicare without future reductions; and the availability of an adequate and affordable labor supply." The question for many providers, says S&P, is how well they can respond to "an environment that is expected to enter a period of more rapid change and mounting pressure." It added that the emerging pressure will be hardest on providers that are already struggling financially. If one of the most prominent credit rating agencies sees further financial difficulties on the horizon, then maybe hospitals should plan to aggressively campaign for new contributions.

CONSIDERATIONS FOR RELIGIOUS INSTITUTIONS

Although religious institutions may have larger portfolio balances then 40 or 50 years ago, they face several real challenges.

As an example, think of the typical Catholic religious order in the 1950s. There were an abundance of young men and woman choosing religious life as a vocation. Churches in the United States were well staffed by priests and nuns, and clergy were often sent overseas on foreign missions.

Rev. Michael Renninger, who oversees priest vocations for the Richmond Diocese, describes the abundance of priests years ago: "We were one of the countries sending surplus, mission priests to places like Africa, Central America and the Philippines."

Not anymore. In 1965, there were nearly 1,000 priests ordained in the United States. Today that number has fallen to less than 500. Other religious institutions have experienced similar declines. Several special challenges that religious non-profit organizations face today are identified below.

Doing More with Money . . . Less with People

Given the dramatic reduction in clergy, some catholic institutions now achieve more by writing checks instead of committing clergy to various missions. The shortage of nuns and priests also has a significant impact on Catholic schools and hospitals. Full-salary laypeople have essentially replaced clergy in most positions.

Aging Institutions

You simply need to read the popular press to appreciate how shaky our Social Security system is. The number of workers supporting each retiree has plummeted over the years. Once at 10 workers to every retiree, we have fallen to 3 to 1 now, and will be at 2 to 1 in a few years. However, compared with the precarious state of many religious orders, the social security picture appears almost rosy.

The decline in the number of young people choosing religion as a vocation places great strain on the institution. Some orders will choose to merge or even close. In any event, religious institutions are forced to think outside the box in the way they manage their money.

Lots of Real Estate . . . No Money

Some religious institutions own vast amounts of real estate yet lack sufficient return and liquidity from their investment portfolios. When an institution is "house rich" and cash poor, they must consider alternatives that might include:

- *Outright Property Sales.* With fewer clergy and/or a change in mission, certain properties may no longer serve a useful purpose. In this scenario, real estate can be liquidated and proceeds invested in a more traditional portfolio that generates sufficient liquidity, earnings, and cash flow.

- *Sale and Leaseback.* If the institution is cash strapped and the property continues to play an important role, a sale and leaseback can be considered. Here, real estate is sold—typically to an institutional investor—and a long-term lease is simultaneously put in place. The religious institution essentially shifts from being a landlord to a tenant. A large amount of cash is generated and the use of the property continues.

SUMMARY

Religious institutions must incorporate many factors into how they structure an investment portfolio. Demographics, time horizon, liquidity requirements, and other issues specific to the institution all play a role in developing an effective investment policy.

## CHAPTER 3

The Total Return Approach

Y our nonprofit organization has a mission. Whatever that mission, you will ultimately need to spend to achieve your goals. Spending policy is discussed in great detail in Chapter 5, but at this point we want to explore a basic fork in the road. Although most not-for-profit organizations have adopted a total return spending policy, a few still are structured to spend "income" (dividends and interest) and preserve "principal" (everything else). We would like to examine the ramifications of that distinction.

EARLY HISTORY

The Oxford English Dictionary states that the word "endowment" dates from the 15th or 16th century. In fact, as early as the 12th century, land was donated as a perpetual support for ecclesiastical organizations. According to Ennis and Williamson, this land-based funding source is important in explaining the traditional approach to spending policy. Land generates rental income for the endowed institution. But both land values and income tend to rise over time, enabling the institutions to "cope not only with rising costs but with expanded activities as well." In this context it made sense to spend "income" but preserve "principal." By the 1800s, the Church of England had accumulated so much endowed wealth that the British Parliament legislated spending restrictions on the church.[1]

However, by the late 19th century, most institutions were endowed not with land but with bonds and mortgages—"fixed return investments." The built-in

---

[1] Richard M. Ennis and J. Peter Williamson, *Spending Policy For Educational Endowments* (Westport, CT: The Common Fund, January 1976), 6.

inflation hedge of the land endowment had vanished. According to Ennis and Williamson, "preservation of capital meant preservation of 'book value', not preservation of purchasing power or real value."[2]

The first foray into equities had not gone well. In 1719, the British Parliament approved the purchase of shares in the South Sea Company by English trustees. Unfortunately, the company folded a year later, causing huge losses. Parliament responded by issuing a list of "safe" trust investments (mostly government bonds). Equities were not to be added again for 140 years.[3]

The above prejudice passed into American law in 1830. Judge Samuel Putman presided in the case of Harvard College v. Amory (see Chapter 18). To clarify what it meant to be prudent, courts and state legislators created lists of acceptable investments. On these "legal lists," bonds were deemed prudent and stocks were considered speculative. Other types of investments were classified according to the belief system of those doing the classifying. The point is that each investment was considered on its own merit. There was no attempt to integrate investments into a coherent portfolio.[4]

THE MODERN ERA

In 1952, a young graduate student named Harry Markowitz published his doctoral thesis on the diversification of portfolios. In his thesis and in his 1959 book *Portfolio Selection: Efficient Diversification of Investments*, he outlined what came to be known as Modern Portfolio Theory (MPT). Using the first computers to analyze daily transaction records going back to 1926, researchers had made a startling discovery. Market returns were normally distributed (actually log-normal distributions). This meant that robust statistical tools could be applied. This was a watershed event. Markowitz' mathematical model became the bedrock of financial management. In 1990 he shared the Nobel Prize in economics for that work.

MPT is based on several assumptions. First, that risk and return are linked; more volatile investments tend to produce higher return over time. Second, rational investors seek to maximize return at each given risk level. Third, the risk and return of a single investment are immaterial. What counts is the impact that each investment has on the total portfolio (its correlation coefficient). By combining investments with low correlation with each other, one could create a port-

---

[2]Ennis and Williamson, *Spending Policy For Educational Endowments*, 7.
[3]Kevin Coventon, "Prudent Investors, New Rules for Centuries-Old Problem," *Non Profit Times* (2001).
[4]Coventon, *Non Profit Times*.

folio that was less risky than any of its components. Finally, central to MPT is the idea that a dollar of income is equal to a dollar of growth—the total return concept. In fact, it is impossible to optimize for anything other than total return (see Chapter 7).

THE LEGAL CHALLENGE

By 1969 it had become widely recognized that traditional approaches to the management of endowed funds (e.g., spending "income" only) were less than optimal. However, trustees wouldn't veer from those suboptimal practices for fear of exposing themselves to litigation under existing trust law. So, in that year the Ford Foundation commissioned two reports. The first report, by law professor William L. Cary and Craig B. Bright, Esq., argued that trust law (the prudent man rule) did not apply to endowed funds.

Under traditional trust law there are typically two parties with conflicting interests: (1) the income recipient, who would prefer to maximize current income at the expense of future growth, and (2) the remainderman, who receives the proceeds of the trust upon the death of the income recipient. The remainderman's interest, of course, would be to maximize future growth rather than current income. Trust law existed to protect the interest of both parties: "Spend income, preserve principal."

However, in the case of a typical endowed fund there is only one party. The fund fiduciaries must balance the current spending needs with the requirement for future spending, taking into account the loss of purchasing power caused by inflation. Cary and Bright argued that the more applicable law was that which governs corporations. Under corporate law, realized gains are clearly part of the income of the corporation.[5]

THE BARKER REPORT

The second Ford Foundation report, Managing Educational Endowments, also known as the Barker Report (after the chairman of the committee, Robert R. Barker), was even more compelling. The advisory committee analyzed the investment results of 15 large educational endowments and compared their performance to that of 21 randomly selected balanced funds, 10 large growth funds, and

---

[5]William L. Cary, Craig B. Bright, *The Law and Lore of Endowment Funds*, (New York: The Ford Foundation, 1969).

EXHIBIT 3.1 **1959-1968 TOTAL RETURN**

	Cumulative	Annual Average
15 educational institutions—average	134%	8.7%
21 balanced funds—average	143%	9.2%
University of Rochester	283%	14.4%
10 large general growth funds—average	295%	14.6%

the endowment of the University of Rochester; the results were dismal. Exhibit 3.1 summarizes their findings.

The authors wrote,"What is the explanation for so striking a contrast? We believe the fundamental reason is that trustees of most educational institutions, because of their semi-public character, have applied a special standard of prudence to endowment management that places primary emphasis on avoiding losses and maximizing present income. Thus, the possibility that other goals might be reasonable—and perhaps even preferable—has hardly been considered. . ." The Barker report went on to recommend that educational endowments adopt the total return approach, that a "small portion of realized gains may be used to supplement interest and dividends for operating purposes. . ." Furthermore, the advisory board recommended that the management of those funds be delegated to professional money managers.[6] Following this report, most large university endowment began to adopt the total return approach.

UMIFA, ERISA, UPIA, AND THE PRUDENT INVESTOR STANDARD

In 1972 the National Conference of Commissioners on Uniform State Laws recommended the adoption of the Uniform Management of Institutional Funds Act (UMIFA). This act sought to codify the findings of the two Ford Foundation reports. Since then, the other important pieces of legislation listed above have all sought to bring uniform fiduciary practices in line with the discoveries of MPT (see Chapters 18 and 19).

Although most state laws have now been brought in line with MPT, some fund fiduciaries may still feel that spending "income" and preserving "principal" is more conservative. We think otherwise.

---

[6]Ford Foundation Advisory Committee on Endowment Management, *Managing Educational Endowments*, (New York: The Ford Foundation, 1969).

THE CASE FOR THE TOTAL RETURN APPROACH

There are several compelling reasons that the thrust of academic theory, federal law, and state law has been a movement toward a total return spending policy:

- A rational investor would choose to maximize return and minimize risk. The artificial distinction between income (dividends and interest) and principal forces an "income only" investor into inefficient portfolios (lower expected return at the same risk level). For example, the need to spend income forces one toward a larger and larger percentage of income-producing securities while the purchasing power of that income shrinks due to inflation (see Chapter 7).

- The artificial distinction further forces fiduciaries into short-term decisions that may be contrary to the long-term good. That is, maximizing current income is often antithetical to the real goal of creating an ever-increasing income stream and principal value. To accomplish that objective there must be sufficient growth in the portfolio—and a mechanism to harvest that growth.

- Asset allocation should drive spending, rather than the reverse. The "income only" approach often leads to reduced spending in real terms—exactly the opposite effect from that intended.

- Another unintended consequence of the "income only" approach is that it forces yield-hungry investors toward riskier investments. They'll invest in bonds with longer duration (which suffer worse declines in a rising interest rate environment), lower credit quality, or high prepayment risk (mortgage-backed securities).

- The total return approach can smooth spending during times when available yields in the marketplace become low. Such a policy avoids undue, and unnecessary, hardship for the beneficiaries of the trust. For example, a fund with an expected 8% return might adopt a policy of spending 4% of the three-year average year-end balance. Half the time, returns would likely be above the 8% target and half the time returns might be below the target. But over long periods of time the fund would be expected to grow 4% above the spending rate. In other words, over long periods of time spending would grow by 4%.

- Furthermore, the three-year averaging would smooth the effect of temporary market declines. Additionally, the fund could be more broadly diversified once it was freed from the constraints imposed by the pursuit of "income." Broader diversification generally has led to smoother total return experience, although, as the disclaimer reads, past performance is no guarantee of future results.

- The total return approach facilitates rebalancing efforts. Such an approach makes it possible to profit from inevitable cycles in the capital markets. Sometimes stocks outperform, sometimes bonds, sometimes small stocks, and so forth. If you can freely rebalance, you can harvest the gains from the winning asset class and rebalance to the underperformers (which turn into the winners in the next phase). By using such rebalancing methods, an investor not only keeps the risk profile of the portfolio constant, but also is able to add excess return.

POTENTIAL NEGATIVES

- Fund fiduciaries need to be cautious in the asset allocation process. The portfolio must be optimized to control risk, not merely to seek the highest expected return.

- During periods of strong market performance, trustees must avoid the temptation to spend the "extra" return. Markets are mean-reverting; above-target returns must be banked for the inevitable below-target period that will follow.

- Once the focus is shifted to total return, there is a natural human tendency to change strategy at inopportune times. That is, most people want to "sell out" at market bottoms and "buy in" at peaks (that is what creates peaks and bottoms). Therefore, you need to adopt a well-reasoned investment and spending policy and avoid reactive decisions.

SUMMARY

Based on academic research and current best practices, most large funds have adopted a total return approach to the prudent investment of trust assets. We concur. Exhibit 3.2 summarizes important landmarks leading to that recommendation.

EXHIBIT 3.2 LANDMARKS TO THE TOTAL RETURN APPROACH RECOMMENDATION

Year	Landmark Event	Spending Policy
Early history		
12th Century	First land endowments	Spend "income only"
1720	First "legal lists"—Great Britain	Spend "income only"
1830	Prudent Man Rule	Spend "income only"
Late 19th through early 20th centuries	"Legal lists" of acceptable investments	Spend "income only"
Modern era		
1952	First academic research Beginning of Modern Portfolio Theory	Total return
1969	First Ford Foundation Report challenges the legal basis for applicability of trust law to endowed funds	Total return
1969	The Barker Report analyzes performance and espouses a move toward a total return spending/investment policy	Total return
1972	The Uniform Management of Institutional Funds Act codified the Ford Foundation Reports and since has been adopted by most states	Total return
1974	The Employee Retirement Income Security Act (ERISA) was passed by Congress to establish a higher standard for retirement plan fiduciaries	Total return
1994	The Uniform Prudent Investor Act of 1994 shifted the focus from the "prudent man" to the "prudent investor"	Total return
1997	The Uniform Principal and Interest Act of 1997 was designed to permit trustees to make investment decisions on a total return basis	Total return

## CHAPTER 4

The Prudent Steward

In the 1990s, when stocks and bonds experienced tremendous performance, investment committee members had it relatively easy. Even if they lacked a well-conceived strategy, the bull market of the 1990s generated outsized returns and committee members often basked in their perceived success. Not anymore.

With the start of a new millennium, the stock market declined for three straight years for the first time in roughly 70 years! Various financial scandals and the jail sentences that followed made board and committee members very concerned about personal liability.

Suddenly, volunteering to oversee a nonprofit organization's investment program is no longer a simple thing. Committee members have to work hard to seek adequate returns and at the same time avoid personal liability. Prudent stewardship is being redefined.

BUILD A HOUSE . . . BUILD AN INVESTMENT PROGRAM

Just as there is a tried and true method to constructing a home, there is a systematic way to build an investment portfolio. Although some committees consider hiring investment managers to be the most important task, this is far from the truth. A successful construction project begins with a plan, and so too should the construction of your investment program.

SET GOALS: THE BLUEPRINT

Prior to hiring or even evaluating investment managers, committees should create their own version of a blueprint. The process begins with an effective *goal-setting* exercise. You need to raise and answer important questions:

- What is the purpose of this investment fund?
- Who should oversee the fund?
- What are our *spending goals* and limitations?
- What socially responsible investment screens should be used, if any?
- What is our time horizon?
- What asset classes or investment types are we willing to consider?

ALLOCATE ASSETS

The last question on asset classes is extremely important because it begins to address your most important decision, *asset allocation*. Virtually every academic study shows that asset allocation is the main contributor to investment returns. It is also the prime mechanism used to quantify and control risk.

Once your committee has a sense of its return targets, spending objectives, risk tolerance, and asset class preferences, you can begin to determine the most appropriate, or optimal, asset allocation for your nonprofit organization's unique needs. To get back to our construction analogy, the investment policy statement becomes your program. This investment policy should be reduced to writing and modified as circumstances merit.

MANAGER SELECTION: HIRE THE SUBCONTRACTORS

Armed with the investment policy, committee members are in a position to hire specialists for each of the areas of investment management called for in your asset allocation. Chapter 8 addresses this topic in great detail, but suffice it to say that beginning the hiring process without first establishing an investment policy is more than a waste of time. It can be detrimental to your investment performance.

REBALANCE

Even when performance on all fronts is good, market movements cause a portfolio's weightings to differ from target allocations. A systematic rebalancing program is absolutely necessary—otherwise your asset allocation strategy won't work. Chapter 9 presents a logical and effective way to answer the question of when to rebalance.

MONITOR PERFORMANCE

Creating a plan and hiring specialists to help implement it goes a long way toward achieving success, but a committee member's job is never done. Performance must be evaluated to ensure that individual managers as well as the entire fund are comparing favorably to established and meaningful benchmarks. When underperformance occurs, an effort must be made to determine if problems are likely to persist. At times, difficult decisions must be made.

In summary, volatile financial markets and increased fiduciary responsibilities make for greater challenges. The strategies described in this book can help you in your quest to act as a prudent steward.

## CHAPTER 5

Set Goals

INTRODUCTION

"The crew looked back to shore not knowing where the winds would push them. . ." This sounds like the start of a novel about a perilous voyage. Will the boat arrive safely? What is the destination? Will the crew encounter dangerous storms? How long will their supplies last? However, if the story begins, "The crew set sail for their four-day journey to the shores of Spain with maps in hand and . . ." the reader has a greater sense of certainty. There may be risks, but the crew appears more prepared for the task.

To chart a successful journey for your fund, you need to determine the destination and have the right tools. You need a clear vision of your time horizon and goals in order to create a sense of purpose for members, staff, and donors.

You will face several challenges in this important step. Can the committee reach a consensus? How will you balance short-term needs and long-term objectives? How will members, employees, and donors react? The following steps may provide a useful framework:

1. Define the mission.
2. Determine a spending policy.
3. Establish the required return.
4. Understand your risk tolerance.
5. Designate the time horizon.

DEFINE THE MISSION

As a first step, the board should compose a clear mission statement. Address the following questions:

- What is the organization's purpose?
- Who or what will benefit from the funds?
- What do members, staff, and donors need to understand?

An organization may have several objectives, but it's helpful if you can boil the mission down to a single well-defined statement. For example, the Society of Thoracic Surgeons' Web site clearly articulates their mission to "Help Cardio-thoracic Surgeons Serve Patients Better." The By-Laws of the Society list several objectives that support this mission.

DETERMINE A SPENDING POLICY

Once you articulate the mission and objectives for the funds, the next step is to formulate a spending policy. This critical step requires balancing short-term needs and long-term objectives. An effective spending policy facilitates current initiatives but also preserves principal for longer-term expenditures. A spending policy, however, does not exist in a vacuum. It must incorporate investment, funding, and cost expectations. There may also be legal requirements, notably the 5% spending requirement for private foundations.

In a perfect world, your fund's purchasing power would consistently grow through a combination of strong market returns, a high level of donor support, and low inflation. Such an environment existed during most of the 1980s and 1990s. In such boom times, organizations can spend without appearing to drain principal. In fact, it's easy to overspend. For example, in 1999 many funds found themselves with 2% inflation, a 5% spending policy, and 20% fund returns. The tendency was to regard some of the "excess" return as found money. The problem is that market returns are lumpy. That is, money made in good years must be preserved to tide your fund through the inevitable downturns. In short, there was no excess return.

So what should a nonprofit organization's board expect for returns? A review of long-term market results by decade may be helpful. Over the past 78 years (1926–2003), stocks have averaged returns of 10.4% and long-term government bonds 5.4%. A look at performance by decade paints a different picture.

Bonds

Over the full 78-year period, long-term bonds have averaged 1.2% above inflation. However, a majority of this return has come in the past few decades. Bond
yields rose steadily from the 1940s up until their peak in 1981. From there, yields
have fallen faster and farther than any time in history, creating the greatest bull
market the asset class has seen. (When interest rates go down, bond prices go up.)
Not only were absolute returns high, *real* returns (above inflation) in the 1980s,
1990s, and 2000s were enormous—7.5%, 5.9%, and 7.2% above inflation, respectively. This period accounts for almost the entire premium above inflation long
term. Real returns in the 1940s (–2.2%), 1950s (–2.3%), 1960s (–1.1%), and 1970s
(–1.9%) paint a much bleaker picture.

With bond yields below 5% by 200, there is little room for further declines.
The great tail wind of falling rates is gone. In fact, the current low interest rate
and low inflation environment looks more like the 1950s and 1960s. The likelihood of absolute returns above 5% (to meet the typical spending target) seems
small. More importantly, the likelihood of real returns above inflation seems even
more remote.

Stocks

Even with the recent negative experience, stocks' long-term average of 10.2% looks
much more attractive. However, a closer look at annual returns over the past 77 years
shows that only three years actually fell in the 10% to 11% range. Most of the return
for large-cap stocks came during four bull markets: the late 1920s, 1941–1961,
1982–1987, and 1991–1999. If the present, post-1990s environment is more like the
post-1950s, stock returns may be well below average. Returns in the 1960s were
7.8%, and the 1970s were worse at 5.9% (actually, a negative real return).[1]

Assuming 3% inflation and adding a 6.2% premium for stocks and 1.2% for
bonds produces targets of 9.2% and 4.2%, respectively. Assuming some reversion
to the mean suggests potentially lower average returns. Achieving a spending target of 5% above inflation may be quite difficult.

---

[1]Calculated by DiMeo Schneider & Associates, L.L.C. using data presented in *Stocks, Bonds, Bills, and
Inflation® 2004 Yearbook,* © 2004 Ibbotson Associates, Inc. Based on copyrighted works by Ibbotson and
Sinquefield. All rights reserved. Used with permission.

The Perfect Storm

The beginning of the 21st century ushered in a "perfect storm" for not-for-profit organizations. Shrinking government and donor support, an economic downturn, and a three-year bear market quickly turned excessive spending into reduced spending. Nonprofit organizations continue to struggle with rising costs, increased demand, and reduced ability to meet funding requirements. The golden decade of the 1990s is likely the exception rather than the rule.

Looking forward, it may be hard to generate double-digit returns on assets, resulting in continued pressure on spending policy. Exhibit 5.1 illustrates how various spending policies impact the ability to preserve real (inflation-adjusted) dollars. In this example, the portfolio's expected annual return is 7.3% with annual inflation of 2.5%. The 4% spending policy is the only approach that preserves principal in real terms. The other spending rates all result in decreased wealth. And note, this analysis shows median expected results. Half the time results might be worse and half the time they might be better. The possibility of higher inflation only exacerbates the problem.

Traditional Spending Methods

Many funds spend a percentage of assets. However, a variety of other approaches exist. One possibility is to designate a fixed dollar amount. When returns are high, this method will build principal; however, you may eat into principal when returns are low. Alternately, withdrawals may be based on a percentage of return,

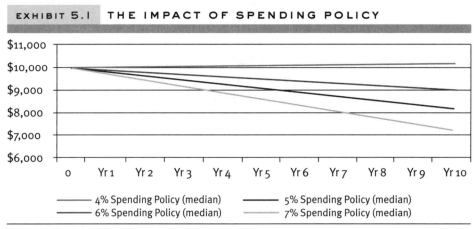

EXHIBIT 5.1   THE IMPACT OF SPENDING POLICY

———— 4% Spending Policy (median)   ———— 5% Spending Policy (median)
———— 6% Spending Policy (median)   ———— 7% Spending Policy (median)

Source: DiMeo Schneider & Associates, L.L.C.

for example, "75% of last year's gain." This method ensures that you will not invade principal, but will result in years in which there is no spending. This is an unacceptable outcome for most funds.

As we said, the most common method is a fixed percentage of assets, for example, "5% of three-year average year end balances." The three-year average provides a smoothing effect. Of course, you must set spending policy below the expected return on your assets.

The bear market of 2000–2002 revealed the flaw in all these approaches. Spending a fixed percentage of assets when fund balances declined resulted in fewer dollars to meet rising costs. The smoothing techniques resulted in rising *average* balances even though the *actual* fund balances had decreased. Conversely, during periods of high returns like the 1990s, these policies result in higher spending. Unfortunately, once you increase spending it is difficult to lower it again. People rapidly come to depend on those funds.

New Approaches

A number of institutions are exploring alternative spending policies. One such method is to choose a nominal dollar amount of spending and then adjust it upward by the inflation rate. For example, an initial dollar amount equal to 4% of current asset value is adjusted annually for inflation. The underlying principle is to tie spending to cost increases rather than investment returns. An inflation band, such as 3% to 6%, ensures a minimum and maximum annual expenditure (Exhibit 5.2). Research suggests that this approach helps smooth spending amounts, and increases the likelihood of principal growth over time. Some organizations take the inflation-based method a step further by using a more relevant price index than the consumer price index (CPI). For example, colleges might use the higher education price index (HEPI).

Another, very simple, approach is to use the current nominal level of spending as a fixed target. The finance committee can then readjust the target every few years based on the circumstances. If fund returns are generally positive, this simplistic spending approach should allow the pool to grow, although, in real terms, spending will actually decline.

Defining spending policy requires critical self-examination of short-term spending needs, long-term capital objectives, fund-raising initiatives, and investment strategy. Once the spending methodology is identified, an organization will undoubtedly face challenges and even resistance in adopting the new approach. However, today's spending decisions translate into tomorrow's financial health.

EXHIBIT 5.2 EXAMPLE OF AN INFLATION BAND

Inflation Indexed (No Contribution)
HEPI
4% Spending rate

Simulation Trials

Portfolio value	Year 1	Year 5	Year 10	Year 15	Year 20
10th Percentile:	$55,043,376	$75,914,312	$105,708,952	$142,932,624	$194,526,448
25th Percentile:	$51,651,464	$64,966,168	$83,476,904	$105,685,248	$132,894,904
50th Percentile:	$48,109,864	$54,487,764	$63,736,552	$73,554,080	$82,451,408
75th Percentile:	$44,810,616	$46,024,416	$48,240,160	$49,034,408	$47,107,100
90th Percentile:	$42,080,784	$39,206,932	$37,135,252	$32,760,294	$23,602,518

Spending bands (based on simulation trials)

Percentile	Band	Year 1	Year 5	Year 10	Year 15	Year 20
10th Percentile:	3.00%	($1,651,301)	($2,277,429)	($3,171,269)	($4,287,979)	($5,835,793)
Fixed flow		($1,859,000)	($2,175,000)	($2,646,000)	($3,219,000)	($3,917,000)
10th Percentile:	6.00%	($3,302,603)	($4,554,859)	($6,342,537)	($8,575,957)	($11,671,587)
25th Percentile:	3.00%	($1,549,544)	($1,948,985)	($2,504,307)	($3,170,557)	($3,986,847)
Fixed flow		($1,859,000)	($2,175,000)	($2,646,000)	($3,219,000)	($3,917,000)
25th Percentile:	6.00%	($3,099,088)	($3,897,970)	($5,008,614)	($6,341,115)	($7,973,694)
50th Percentile:	3.00%	($1,443,296)	($1,634,633)	($1,912,097)	($2,206,622)	($2,473,542)
Fixed flow		($1,859,000)	($2,175,000)	($2,646,000)	($3,219,000)	($3,917,000)
50th Percentile:	6.00%	($2,886,592)	($3,269,266)	($3,824,193)	($4,413,245)	($4,947,084)
75th Percentile:	3.00%	($1,344,318)	($1,380,732)	($1,447,205)	($1,471,032)	($1,413,213)
Fixed flow		($1,859,000)	($2,175,000)	($2,646,000)	($3,219,000)	($3,917,000)
75th Percentile:	6.00%	($2,688,637)	($2,761,465)	($2,894,410)	($2,942,064)	($2,826,426)
90th Percentile:	3.00%	($1,262,424)	($1,176,208)	($1,114,058)	($982,809)	($708,076)
Fixed flow		($1,859,000)	($2,175,000)	($2,646,000)	($3,219,000)	($3,917,000)
90th Percentile:	6.00%	($2,524,847)	($2,352,416)	($2,228,115)	($1,965,618)	($1,416,151)

Fixed flow and 90th percentile are the actual spending dollar amounts.
Highlighting represents those trials in which the spending bands are violated.

EXHIBIT 5.2 (CONTINUED)

Market Value (No Contribution)
CPI
4% Spending rate

Simulation Trials Portfolio value	Year 1	Year 5	Year 10	Year 15	Year 20
10th Percentile:	$54,444,524	$72,150,416	$95,372,760	$121,436,800	$153,240,000
25th Percentile:	$51,221,132	$63,032,772	$78,611,400	$95,848,992	$115,389,944
50th Percentile:	$47,988,536	$53,878,216	$62,861,432	$73,766,232	$84,882,688
75th Percentile:	$44,828,404	$46,295,600	$50,681,968	$56,538,108	$62,634,620
90th Percentile:	$42,035,216	$40,624,800	$41,887,968	$44,156,768	$47,546,516

Spending bands (based on simulation trials)

Percentile	Band	Year 1	Year 5	Year 10	Year 15	Year 20
10th Percentile:	3.00%	($1,633,336)	($2,164,512)	($2,861,183)	($3,643,104)	($4,597,200)
10th Percentile:	6.00%	($2,268,522)	($3,006,267)	($3,973,865)	($5,059,867)	($6,385,001)
10th Percentile:		($3,266,671)	($4,329,025)	($5,722,366)	($7,286,208)	($9,194,400)
25th Percentile:	3.00%	($1,536,634)	($1,890,983)	($2,358,342)	($2,875,470)	($3,461,698)
25th Percentile:	6.00%	($2,134,214)	($2,626,366)	($3,275,475)	($3,993,708)	($4,807,915)
25th Percentile:		($3,073,268)	($3,781,966)	($4,716,684)	($5,750,940)	($6,923,397)
50th Percentile:	3.00%	($1,439,656)	($1,616,346)	($1,885,843)	($2,212,987)	($2,546,481)
50th Percentile:	6.00%	($1,999,522)	($2,244,926)	($2,619,226)	($3,073,593)	($3,536,779)
50th Percentile:		($2,879,312)	($3,232,693)	($3,771,686)	($4,425,974)	($5,092,961)
75th Percentile:	3.00%	($1,344,852)	($1,388,868)	($1,520,459)	($1,696,143)	($1,879,039)
75th Percentile:	6.00%	($1,867,850)	($1,928,983)	($2,111,749)	($2,355,755)	($2,609,776)
75th Percentile:		($2,689,704)	($2,777,736)	($3,040,918)	($3,392,286)	($3,758,077)
90th Percentile:	3.00%	($1,261,056)	($1,218,744)	($1,256,639)	($1,324,703)	($1,426,395)
90th Percentile:	6.00%	($1,751,467)	($1,692,700)	($1,745,332)	($1,839,865)	($1,981,105)
90th Percentile:		($2,522,113)	($2,437,488)	($2,513,278)	($2,649,406)	($2,852,791)

ESTABLISH THE REQUIRED RETURN

The decades of the 1980s and 1990s were unprecedented in capital market history. Bond and stocks rallied as interest rates declined, inflation decreased, and productivity grew. Never before had there been back-to-back decades with annualized stock returns above 17%. Exhibit 5.3 compares long-term market returns to the abnormal gains during those decades. The market bust of the early 2000s erased some of those gains. Looking forward, uncertainties surround interest rates, inflation, terrorism, and global economic growth. Future return expectations may be dramatically lower.

Defining required return goes hand in hand with spending policy formulation. Is it possible to set a 5% spending rate if real return expectations are below that level? Should you pursue higher returns or ratchet down spending needs? Are you prepared to invest in riskier asset classes? Your required return is one that meets your short-term spending needs, preserves principal, and grows capital over time. The required return and assumed risk represent critical inputs in determining your investment approach.

Although stocks generated high double-digit returns in the 1980s and 1990s, historical evidence suggests more moderate returns in the future. Unreasonable return expectations are a precursor to failure. But lower return expectations make it more difficult to achieve your required return. Investment committees will be forced to revamp their asset allocations and incorporate new investments. Finance committees may have to lower the target spending rate. Fund-raising will become more important. Nonprofit organizations must face these challenges if they are to operate effectively or even survive. It goes without saying that not-for-profit

EXHIBIT 5.3   AVERAGE ANNUAL RETURNS OVER VARIOUS MARKET PERIODS

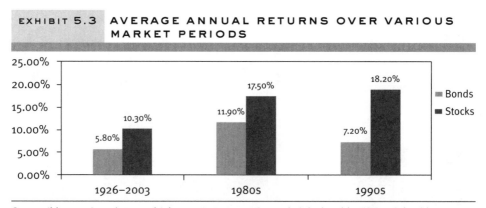

Source: Ibbotson Associates and Johnston Investment Counsel. Calculated by DiMeo Schneider & Associates, L.L.C. using data presented in *Stocks, Bonds, Bills, and Inflation®* 2004 Yearbook, © 2004 Ibbotson Associates, Inc. Based on copyrighted works by Ibbotson and Sinquefield. All rights reserved.

funds should adopt a total return approach. The combination of interest income and capital gains increases the likelihood of generating the required return and meeting spending needs.

Inflation and Goal Setting

Like a vampire, inflation sucks away the purchasing power of your dollars. In recent years, inflation has been relatively benign, but it has not gone away. In an environment where costs increased at barely 2% annually, even modest investment returns increased real purchasing power. Higher inflation rates diminish investment returns. You must factor in inflation expectations as you formulate your spending policy.

For example, imagine a university endowment with a 5% spending policy. Required real return for the next 20 years is 6% and inflation is expected to track its long-term average of 3.1%. This equates to a required target return of 9.1%. If actual long-term inflation rates fall below 3.1% and the fund achieves its target return, the university maintains purchasing power. It can continue to provide the same level of financial support 20 years from now as it does today. However, if inflation increases at a rate higher than 3.1%, more dollars will be needed (Exhibit 5.4).

UNDERSTAND YOUR RISK TOLERANCE

"No pain, no gain—no risk, no reward." Perceptions of risk vary greatly among individuals. Climbing a ladder may feel risky to one person while another wants

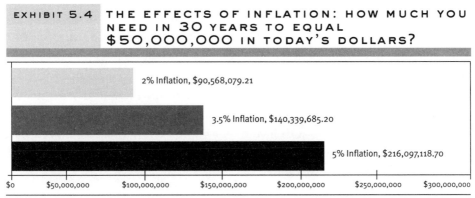

EXHIBIT 5.4 **THE EFFECTS OF INFLATION: HOW MUCH YOU NEED IN 30 YEARS TO EQUAL $50,000,000 IN TODAY'S DOLLARS?**

2% Inflation, $90,568,079.21

3.5% Inflation, $140,339,685.20

5% Inflation, $216,097,118.70

$0 $50,000,000 $100,000,000 $150,000,000 $200,000,000 $250,000,000 $300,000,000

Source: DiMeo Schneider & Associates. L.L.C.

to climb Mount Everest. How is this relevant to setting goals? Your required return inevitably requires you to assume some level of risk. The recent bear market reminded investors that risk is more than a theoretical construct. Today, "How much can I lose?" is often the first question posed by investors.

For example, in late 1998, a university investment committee hired us to provide investment consulting services. At the time, they had a single manager who allocated assets between domestic stocks and bonds. They sought our assistance for two primary reasons: to further diversify assets and to generate higher returns. Our first step with any client is to understand their goals, current perceptions, and risk tolerance. Exhibit 5.5 is a sample committee input questionnaire we use to gather information and start the dialogue. In this case the committee's responses were inconsistent. Their consensus return objective was over 10%, most committee members were comfortable with a 100% stock allocation, the majority felt they had a high risk tolerance, yet most agreed they would change strategies if they experienced a 5% loss on assets. Clearly they did not understand that a 100% equity allocation had the potential to fall significantly more than 5%. As you may recall, by the end of 1998, the S&P 500 index had generated four consecutive years of double-digit returns and last experienced a down year in 1990. "The risk is being out of stocks" was the mantra during the late 1990s. Nowadays, capital market risks are all too apparent. Volatility, or the risk of incurring negative returns, now concerns investors. However, there are other risks to consider, such as not beating inflation or not achieving long-term goals. The committee needs to set their goals in light of all these trade-offs.

DESIGNATE THE TIME HORIZON

Your time horizon plays a critical role in your investment decisions. Does your fund have a long- or short-term period for investing? Different funds have different time horizons. Many funds are expected to last into perpetuity; others exist to achieve a specific goal. Is there uncertainty about your time horizon? The answers to these questions dramatically impact asset allocation. An organization having uncertain or imminent spending demands might be forced to maintain a high cash or fixed-income position. Most organizations have a long-term, if not infinite, time horizon. They can take more short-term risk and seek greater returns from higher equity allocations. Sometimes it's necessary to segregate funds with varying time horizons into investment pools, each with a customized asset allocation. Whatever your circumstance, defining your time horizon is critical to the investment planning process.

EXHIBIT 5.5   SAMPLE COMMITTEE QUESTIONNAIRE

Introduction

This questionnaire will help us gain a better understanding of your thoughts regarding our fund's risk and re-turn objectives, time horizon and investment approach. The collective responses will help establish a start-ing point for our asset allocation analysis. We appreciate your responses.

I. General Thoughts

   1. What do you feel is the primary objective(s) for the funds?
- ☐ Capital preservation.
- ☐ Maximize current income.
- ☐ Maximize total return through income and capital growth.
- ☐ Maximize capital growth with little consideration for income.

   2. What do you feel are the most critical issues facing the fund in short-term (less than 3 years)?

   3. What do you feel are the most critical issues facing the fund longer-term (over 10 years)?

   4. Please specify any other issues, concerns or obstacles you feel may impact the fund's effectiveness?

II. Risk and Return Objectives

   1. I define investment risk as: (check one):
- ☐ Losing principal.
- ☐ Not matching inflation.
- ☐ Not having enough money to meet fund goals.

   2. Starting with $10,000,000, I would change strategies if the fund had a one-year loss of   (check one):
- ☐ −2% or $200,000
- ☐ −5% or $500,000
- ☐ −10% or $1,000,000
- ☐ −15% or $1,500,000
- ☐ −25% or $2,500,000

   Other: _____

   3. How concerned are you with fluctuations in market value?
- ☐ Very concerned with market value fluctuation.
- ☐ Somewhat concerned, but more focused with the long-term growth.
- ☐ Not concerned because funds are invested for the long-term.

   4. Circle the one portfolio (A–E) with which you are most comfortable:

Annual Return	A	B	C	D	E
Optimistic	17.2%	20.6%	24.8%	29.5%	34.4%
Expected	6.1%	6.7%	7.3%	7.9%	8.4%
Pessimistic	−5.0%	−7.2%	−10.3%	−13.8%	−17.5%

The pessimistic scenario represents the potential downside likely to occur in any given year. There is a small (2.5%) probability of achieving either the pessimistic or optimistic results. There is a high proba-bility (50%+) of achieving the expected results. There is a very high probability (95%) of falling between the optimistic and pessimistic scenarios.

III. Investment Structure

   1. Indicate which investment categories you feel should be excluded from your asset allocation (in gen-eral, the more asset classes included, the better the diversification effect):

_____ Money Market	_____ Small U.S. Stocks	_____ Inflation Linked Bonds
_____ International Stocks	_____ High Yield Bonds	_____ Emerging Markets Stocks
_____ Investment Grade Bonds	_____ Real Estate	_____ Large U.S. Stocks
_____ Hedge Funds	Other:_____	

   2. I am most comfortable with stock exposure of . . .
- ☐ 0 to 20%
- ☐ 20% to 40%
- ☐ 40% to 60%
- ☐ 60% to 80%
- ☐ 80% to 100%.

   3. Please outline any specific investment management restrictions you feel should apply

_____

_____

SUMMARY

"Those who fail to plan, plan to fail." Proper goal setting leads to a better investment process. The five steps outlined in this chapter should guide committee members in setting short- and long-term objectives. In Chapter 7, we describe in detail how these steps become inputs in the asset allocation process:

1. Define the mission.
2. Determine a spending policy.
3. Establish the required return.
4. Understand your risk tolerance.
5. Designate the time horizon.

By working through these steps you will build a solid foundation for the work that will come. Your committee can better respond to questions raised by donors, employees, or the public about the investment process. You'll avoid the panic that often clouds investor thinking during periods of market unrest. Most importantly, you'll demonstrate that you have a solid, well-conceived investment program focused on achieving your organization's goals.

The next chapter shows you how to formalize your process into a written investment policy statement. This important document is the "blueprint" to building success for your fund.

## CHAPTER 6

Investment Policy

OVERVIEW

An architect's blueprint provides direction to a builder, plumber, electrician, and other contractors. Most importantly, it gives the home owner a clear vision of the project and the ability to monitor its progress. The blueprint designates responsibilities and goals for the involved parties. Can you imagine building a home or even adding a deck without a blueprint?

How could anyone hope to oversee a multi-million dollar fund without written guidelines? It is imperative that you formalize your goals and investment strategy in writing. The written policy should be clear, concise, and specific. A well-written *investment policy statement* (IPS) outlines your investment philosophy and defines the investment management oversight and long-term objectives of your organization.

WHY IS IT IMPORTANT?

The IPS is critical to the ongoing oversight of your investment process. It memorializes your vision. It sets the parameters by which you will monitor responsibilities and track the progress of associated parties. It also outlines your procedures for fund oversight. A written IPS also provides for continuity in the supervision of your fund. It's not uncommon for members to serve limited terms, sometimes as short as one or two years. A constant rotation in members presents challenges.

New committee members may want to make their mark. Unfamiliar with the initial goal-setting process outlined in the previous chapter, they may question the existing investment approach and objectives. They may have preconceived notions about the use of certain asset classes or overall asset allocation. They may even have a basic misunderstanding of investing or diversification principles. A well-written investment policy educates new members. It acts as an "employee manual" to provide new and existing members with a clear, concise description of your fund's purpose, standards, and objectives.

Inevitably, your committee will face periods of market turmoil. Committee members may question existing strategy and consider reacting to short-term events. At such times, the IPS acts as an anchor to steady the ship in rough seas. It prevents knee-jerk reactions that may impede the fund's long-term objectives.

CONTENT

The policy consists of several sections addressing critical areas of oversight. Typically these should include:

- Purpose
- Spending policy
- Investment policy
- Liquidity needs
- Asset allocation
- Rebalancing
- Manager selection
- Performance evaluation
- Manager termination procedures
- Proxy voting
- Responsibilities of all parties

Organization is the key to drafting your policy. The IPS should provide a clear road map for committee members. Specifically, it must provide policy direction and procedural guidelines. An IPS checklist can be a good starting point (Exhibit 6.1).

SAMPLE INVESTMENT POLICY STATEMENT

A sample IPS may be helpful. However, it's important to customize the document to address your organization's specific needs. To get started, please see the sample policy provided in Appendix A.

EXHIBIT 6.1   INVESTMENT POLICY STATEMENT CHECKLIST

Investment Policy Statement Sections	√	Comments
I. Purpose		
Identifies the organization and fund.		
Outlines the mission of the organization and fund.		
Establishes the specific short-term and long-term objectives for the fund.		
II. Spending policy		
Sets the specific spending requirements for the funds.		
Designates who has authority in establishing spending policy.		
Establish liquidity needs.		
III. Investment policy		
Enumerates total return targets on a nominal and inflation-adjusted basis.		
Sets risk parameters for overall fund.		
IV. Asset allocation		
Establishes commitment to diversify across a broad range of asset classes.		
Defines specific asset classes and target asset allocation.		
Prescribes authority and process for reviewing and adjusting asset allocation.		
V. Cash flows/rebalancing		
Establishes process for handling contributions and disbursements.		
States purpose for rebalancing.		
Designates authority, process, and timing for portfolio rebalancing.		
VI. Investment manager selection		
Designates criteria for investment manager selection.		
VII. Performance monitoring		
Specifies timing for manager reviews.		
Outlines investment manager reporting responsibilities.		
VIII. Investment manager termination		
Designates performance expectations for investment managers.		
Outlines issues other than performance that may result in manager termination.		
IX. Proxy voting policy		
Designates responsibilities and procedures for voting proxies.		
X. Responsibilities of investment consultant		
Outlines role and responsibilities of investment consultant.		

IMPLEMENTATION AND MAINTENANCE

It's a good idea to have all committee members review a draft IPS. Once the IPS is amended, all committee members should acknowledge their review and acceptance of its terms. We recommend an annual redistribution and review of the IPS. Of course, any interim changes in investment managers, allocations, or spending policy may require revisions to the policy statement.

SPECIFIC INVESTMENT GUIDELINES

The degree of specificity in your investment guidelines depends on the type of investment vehicles you use. There are various procedures and considerations that are appropriate for different investment vehicles:

- *Mutual Funds.* A mutual fund pools assets of multiple investors. As a result, an individual investor cannot establish specific investment management guidelines. The mutual fund's prospectus informs investors about the fund's strategy, investment restrictions, risks, performance, expenses, and administrative guidelines. Your IPS language should therefore focus on the role of the mutual fund and your standards for fund review, not on guidelines for the fund manager (who won't take your direction anyway).

- *Commingled Funds.* A commingled fund pools together assets from multiple investors, but usually requires a higher minimum initial investment. Commingled accounts are usually sponsored by a bank or trust company. Unlike a mutual fund, commingled accounts are exempt from registration under the Investment Company Act and do not have a prospectus. However, an individual investor still cannot establish specific investment management guidelines. Commingled account investment guidelines are set forth by the investment management firm. Your IPS language for commingled funds should be similar to language used for mutual funds.

- *Separate Accounts.* A separate account portfolio is managed exclusively for one person or institution. This allows you to establish specific investment guidelines and restrictions. For example, you may wish to prohibit certain types of securities such as alcohol or tobacco stocks. Because it's a customized portfolio, an investor needs to establish specific investment guidelines for the manager. The investment management guidelines should provide specific direction on investment objectives, restrictions, risk parameters, performance measurement, and reporting responsibilities.

INVESTMENT BENCHMARKS

It's important that you establish specific investment benchmarks for mutual funds and investment managers. The investment benchmarks guide the committee's review of investment manager performance. We recommend a multidimensional approach. You should compare the returns of the fund as a whole and each manager to an appropriate *index*, and a style-specific *peer group* or universe. You should also designate a way to measure risk, and incorporate the fund or manager's risk-adjusted performance. See Appendix A for an example of designated benchmarks for fixed income, domestic equity, and international managers.

In Chapter 13, we discuss in greater detail performance evaluation, designating specific benchmarks, and instituting an effective oversight process.

SUMMARY

Your IPS is a summation of your goals, philosophy, and process. As such, it requires careful thought and execution. Our sample policy may provide a starting point, but an effective IPS should be customized to fit your goals and objectives. Once finalized and approved, it serves as a blueprint for your investment program. The IPS designates the procedures and guidelines critical to the ongoing oversight of your fund.

There is little doubt your investment committee will face questions and even criticism from time to time. The IPS can be an anchor to windward during turbulent times. The IPS can provide well-documented rationale to avoid the latest investment craze, short-term market events, or individual investment biases.

## CHAPTER 7

Asset Allocation

A sset allocation, the strategic diversification of your portfolio, is the most important determinant of return. Academic studies support the conclusion drawn by Brinson, Hood, and Beebower that asset allocation accounts for over 94% of investment return.[1] Security selection and market timing together contribute less than 4% to investment results. In other words, the key question is not in which stock or bond to invest, but rather "What percentage should I allocate to stocks, bonds, or other asset classes?" (Exhibit 7.1).

While individual security selection decisions are usually delegated to specialists, asset allocation is your responsibility. Once you have determined the asset mix there are literally hundreds of money managers who can handle the implementation. However, only you can decide how much volatility or risk the fund should assume.

THE EFFICIENT FRONTIER

In the 1950s, Dr. Harry Markowitz developed a theoretical framework to manage the asset allocation decision. In 1992 he was awarded the Nobel Prize for this work. Dr. Markowitz postulated an "efficient frontier," the line describing the highest expected return at each risk level. Today, commercial software programs called mean variance optimizers incorporate Markowitz's algorithm. If you plug in the appropriate input assumptions described below, the optimizer will generate an efficient frontier defining the "optimal" portfolio mix at each risk level. "Optimal" means having the highest return at that risk.

---

[1]Gary P. Brinson, L. Randolph Hood, and Gilbert L. Beebower, "Determinants of Portfolio Returns," *Financial Analysis Journal* (July/August 1986).

EXHIBIT 7.1   WHAT DETERMINES SUCCESS?

Components of Investment Return

Market Timing
2%

Security Selection
4%

Asset Allocation
94%

Source: Brinson Hood Beebower, 1986.

For example, if your portfolio consisted of Mix A in Exhibit 7.2, you would no doubt prefer either Mix B (equal risk but higher expected returns) or Mix C (equal expected return but lower risk). Mixes B and C are on the efficient frontier. Mix A is inefficient.

So, how should you go about determining the asset allocation for your not-for-profit organization's fund? Nowadays, there are numerous commercial software programs that incorporate Markowitz's algorithm. But be careful. The output of these programs is *heavily* input sensitive. The programmer's adage "Garbage in = garbage out" applies!

EXHIBIT 7.2   EFFICIENT FRONTIER

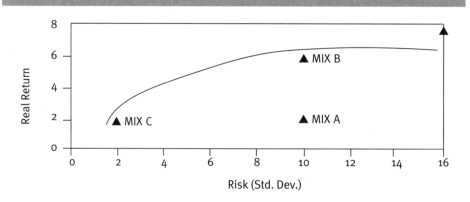

CAPITAL MARKET ASSUMPTIONS: THE BUILDING BLOCKS OF PORTFOLIO CONSTRUCTION

The first stage in the portfolio optimization process is to develop three key inputs:

- Expected return of each asset class
- Expected standard deviation of the returns
- Expected correlation among different asset class returns

The problem, of course, is that the inputs are forecasts, and as Yogi Berra is quoted, "Forecasting is tough, especially if it involves the future." Let's examine each of these inputs.

Expected Return

The expected return of any asset class should be viewed in a *probabilistic* rather than *deterministic* sense. In other words, not as an exact number but rather as the midpoint estimate of possible and likely future outcomes. Even those of us who fancy ourselves as esteemed forecasters need to admit that whatever forecast we make will likely be wrong. In a probabilistic sense, the litmus test for our assumption should be that we believe our return forecast has an equal chance of being too high or too low. We'll discuss estimation methods shortly.

Standard Deviation

Investment professionals use the *standard deviation* of returns as the most common measure of risk. It is a statistic that measures the variability of returns around the average. The higher the annual standard deviation, the more uncertain the outcome. In a normal distribution, about 68% of returns fall within (plus or minus) one standard deviation of the mean. For example, assume that your portfolio has an expected annual return of 10% and a 10% standard deviation. The annual return should fall between 0% and 20% two thirds of the time (10% plus or minus 10%). About 95% of annual returns fall within two standard deviations of the mean (in our example between −10% and +30%). About 99% of annual returns fall within three standard deviations from the mean (or −20% to +40%).

Correlation

The *correlation coefficient* measures the degree to which two asset classes move together. Statisticians use the Greek letter rho (ρ) to signify this statistic. The value of the correlation coefficient ranges from −1 to +1. Assets that have a ρ of −1 are perfectly *negatively* correlated. Every time one goes up in value, the other declines. Assets that have a correlation coefficient of +1 are perfectly *positively* correlated; values always move in the same direction at the same time. ρ = 0 indicates there is no relationship at all. In reality, most assets have some positive correlation, although it may be small.

DEVELOPING EXPECTED RETURN ASSUMPTIONS

The above three inputs are *forecast* numbers. And if the inputs are substantially wrong, the output will be wrong. Consultants jokingly call optimizers "error maximizers." So, how do you develop these crucial inputs?

Well, you could guess—probably not a great idea. Or you could take long-term historical averages as your input assumptions. For reasons we'll discuss shortly, using this method alone is also not a very good idea.

Following are various methods to generate the expected return for each asset class. Each method has strengths and weaknesses.

CASE STUDY   THE CAPITAL ASSET PRICING MODEL

Nobel Prize winner William Sharpe developed the *Capital Asset Pricing Model* (CAPM). The CAPM is a single factor economic model. You regress an asset's return against that of a *market portfolio* (the index) to calculate a *beta* (β) or *slope coefficient*. Beta measures the sensitivity of an asset's price to the market portfolio. Beta in combination with the *risk-free rate* (e.g., Treasury bills) and the expected market portfolio return determine the expected return of the investment. Sharpe's formula is:

$$E(R) = Rf + \beta(RM - Rf)$$

Where $E(R)$ = Expected return of the asset

   RM = Return of the market Index (broad market index containing all risky assets)

   Rf = Risk-free rate

Exhibit 7.3 shows a regression analysis to calculate the β of the Russell 2000 small-cap index compared with the Wilshire 5000 index as a proxy for the "market portfolio."

We can apply the β calculated by the regression analysis:

Expected return (small-cap) = risk-free rate + β × (expected return of market portfolio − risk-free rate)

β = 1.10

EXHIBIT 7.3 CAPM REGRESSION ANALYSIS (1979-2004)

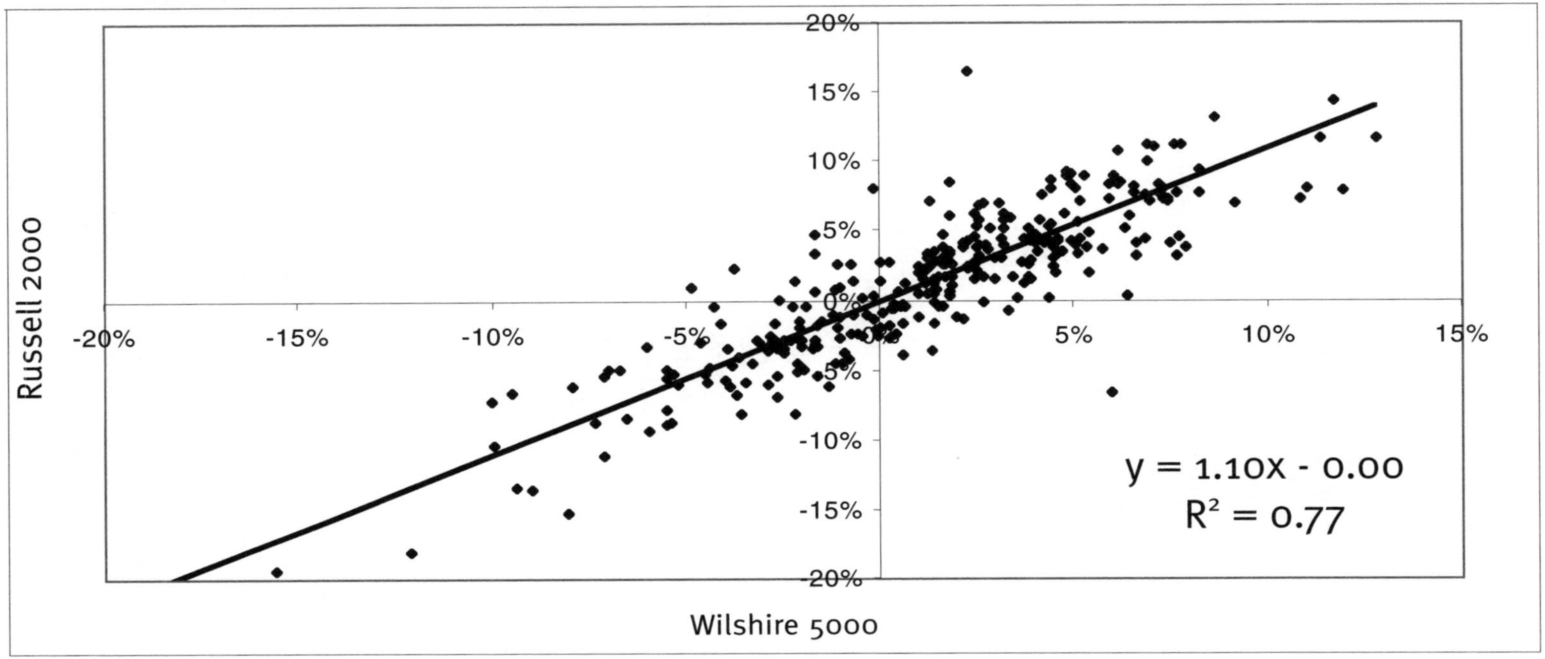

Russell 2000
Wilshire 5000
-20%
-15%
-10%
-5%
0%
5%
10%
15%
20%
y = 1.10X - 0.00
R² = 0.77

Expected return of market portfolio = 9.0%

Risk-free rate = 3.0%

Expected return (small-cap) = 3% + 1.10 × (9.0% – 3.0%) = 9.6%

Because the CAPM requires the use of regression analysis, it is inherently a historical measure. Also, it describes return in terms of a single factor: *systematic risk*, or risk sensitivity to the overall market portfolio. Another serious drawback to using the CAPM is that the market portfolio can be difficult to specify. Often a proxy for the market portfolio is used (e.g., Standard & Poor's [S&P] 500 index, Wilshire 5000 index, etc.). Of course you still have the problem of developing an estimate for the return of the market portfolio. But some of the methods described in the following sections can be helpful in coming up with that starting number.

Beta can be misleading when an asset class has low correlation with the proxy. A general rule of thumb is that when the correlation of an investment relative to the proxy market portfolio is less than 0.70 or the *R-squared* (another statistic that measures dispersion) is less than 0.49, the CAPM is *not* an effective forecasting tool for the asset class. For example, real estate investment trusts (REITs) and commodities have historically exhibited low correlation (and sensitivity) to the proxy market portfolio, giving the asset classes a low β measure. This low β leads to artificially low expected return numbers when applying the CAPM (Exhibits 7.4 and 7.5).

Arbitrage Pricing Theory

Unlike the CAPM, which is a single-factor model, the *Arbitrage Pricing Theory* (APT) is a multifactor model that describes investment return and risk as a combination of factors (e.g., gross domestic product [GDP], consumer price index [CPI], interest rate changes, etc.). However, the specifications of the APT are quite difficult to estimate (and are quite possibly limitless) and the independent variables (e.g., GDP, CPI, interest rate changes, etc.) are often at least as difficult to forecast as the dependent variable (the asset class's expected return) itself. The APT is an interesting academic exercise, but generally is not very practical for developing capital market assumptions. The APT formula is

$$E(R) = Rf + \beta_1 \times (GDP) - \beta_2 \times (CPI) - \beta_3 \times (INT) \ldots$$

Risk Premium

The *risk premium* method is a sort of "building block" method. The expected return of an asset equals the risk-free rate plus a risk premium (a return above the risk-free rate or other referenced asset). If markets are efficient, investors should demand a higher expected return for asset classes with higher risk. Theoretically, markets would be self-regulating. If investors don't expect the higher-risk asset to lead to higher returns, they would sell it. The price of the higher-risk asset would then decline until its future expected return became higher than that of the lower-risk asset class. The risk premium of an investment can be described in *absolute* terms (vs. the risk-free rate) or relative

EXHIBIT 7.4 CAPM REGRESSION ANALYSIS (1978-2004)

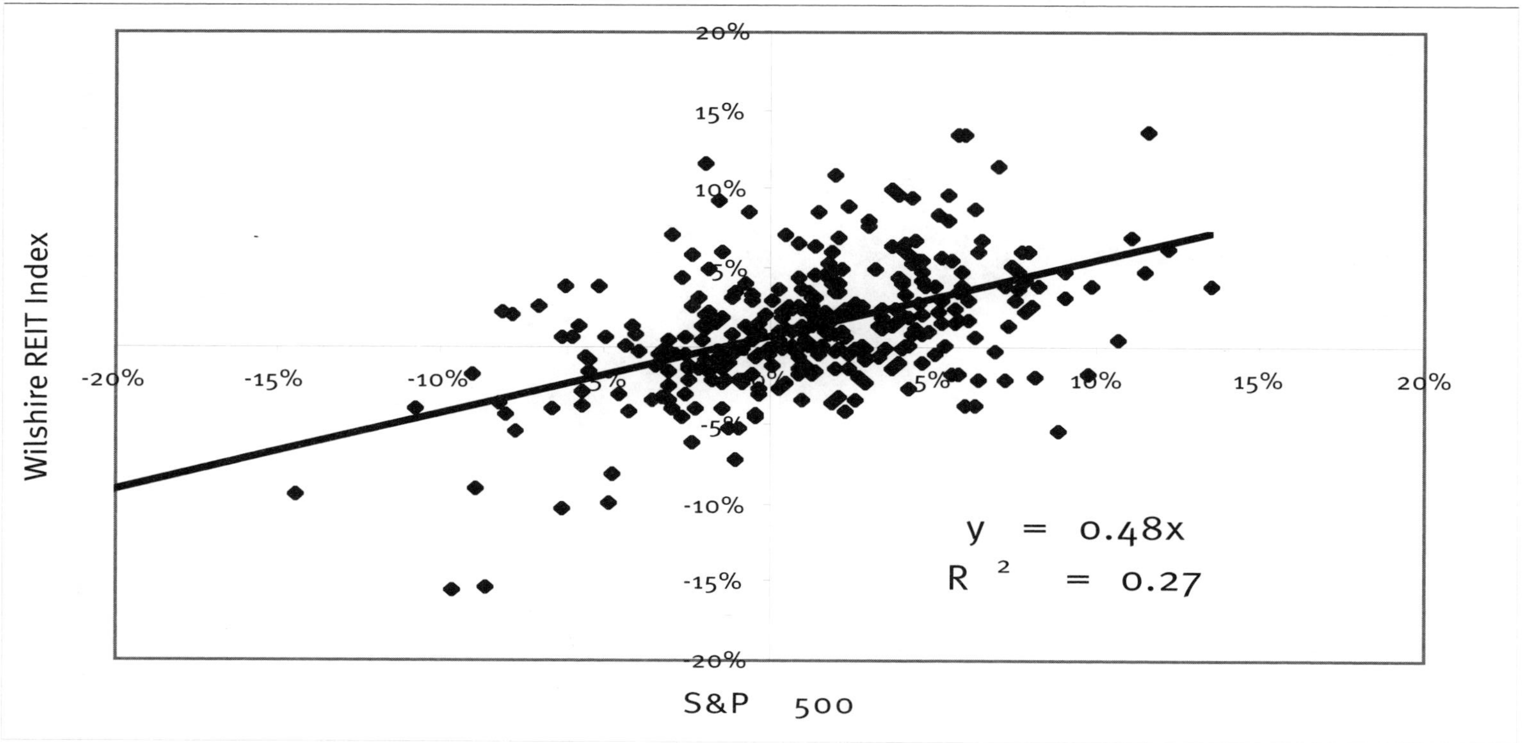

Wilshire REIT Index
20%
15%
10%
5%
-5%
-10%
-15%
-20%
-20%
-15%
-10%
-5%
5%
10%
15%
20%
y = 0.48x
R 2 = 0.27
S&P 500

EXHIBIT 7.5 CAPM REGRESSION ANALYSIS (1979-2004)

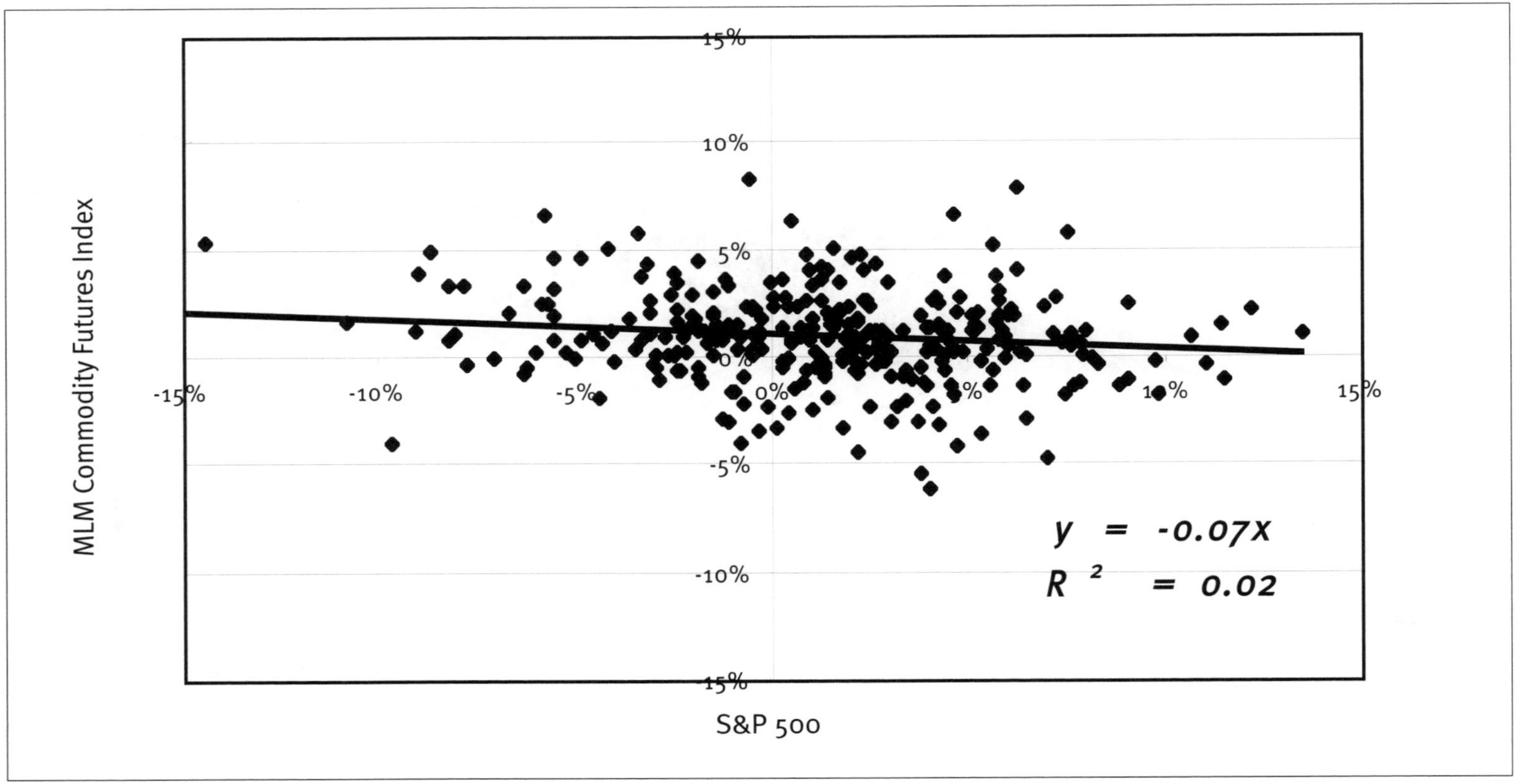
MLM Commodity Futures Index
S&P 500
15%
10%
5%
0%
-5%
-10%
-15%
y = -0.07X
R 2 = 0.02

terms (vs. a reference risky investment). The following equations are examples of absolute and *relative* risk premium calculations:

Absolute: Expected large-cap equity return = [10-year treasury yield] + [large-cap equity risk premium]

Relative: Expected small-cap equity return = [large-cap equity return] + [small-cap equity risk premium]

The *small-cap equity risk premium* is defined as the excess return investors demand from holding riskier small-cap stocks. The risk premium method is both practical and easy for most people to conceptualize, making it an effective method for developing capital market assumptions. We also have an abundance of data on historical risk premiums. This method is useful for assets like real estate that have low correlation and low betas to the proxy market portfolio.

Historical Analysis

History is not destiny, but it can provide valuable insights into the expected returns, risks, and correlations of assets. Historical analysis is particularly helpful for statistics like standard deviation and correlation coefficients because they tend to be less end point sensitive than return numbers.

An unbiased estimate of expected long-term returns should not vary too much from long-term historical data. What is too much? One way to answer that question is to calculate *a time horizon standard deviation*. That measure can be estimated by dividing the annual standard deviation by the square root of the time horizon. For example, if large-cap stocks have a 16% annual standard deviation, you can approximate the 10-year standard deviation by dividing 16% by the square root of 10 (3.162). The result is a 10-year standard deviation of about 5%. Thus, if your time horizon is 10 years and the long-term return is 10%, an unbiased estimate of a 10-year return should lie between 5% and 15% (10% plus or minus 5%).

However, beware of the human tendency to extrapolate the recent past. During the bull market of the late 1990s, many investors became overly optimistic and extrapolated 10 or 20 years of historical data to come up with far higher return estimates than were warranted. See Chapter 16 for a discussion of behavioral finance.

Returns Decomposition

The *returns decomposition* method requires the investor to break the total return down into its various components. For example, bond returns can be broken down into (1) the yield, (2) price changes caused by interest rate fluctuations, (3) yield spread changes, and (4) default losses. For investment-grade bonds, the default component is very small. It is extremely difficult to predict interest rate movements (and the accompanying effects of price changes) over a 5- or 10-year time horizon. Thus, the current yield should be the largest component of expected returns for investment grade bonds (interest rates can't increase or decrease forever).

On the other hand, equity returns are composed of (1) dividend yield, (2) return on reinvested earnings, (3) inflation, and (4) price-earnings (P/E) ratio expansion or contraction.

Long-term equity returns = [(1 + DIV) × (1 + P/E) × (1 + GDP × ERR) × (1 + CPI)] − 1

Where   DIV = dividend yield
          P/E = P/E ratio expansion or contraction
          GDP = GDP growth
          ERR = earnings retention ratio = (1 − dividend payout ratio)
          CPI = consumer price index (inflation)

The current dividend yield and earnings retention ratio figures can be used along with forecasts of GDP, CPI, and P/E expansion or contraction to arrive at our long-term expected equity return. The one drawback of the returns decomposition method is that GDP growth, future trends in CPI rates, and P/E multiple expansion or contraction can be difficult to estimate, although GDP and CPI inflation have historically moved in narrower ranges than returns.

MODERN PORTFOLIO THEORY

As mentioned, with his article "Portfolio Selection," which appeared in the 1952 *Journal of Finance,* Harry Markowitz introduced Modern Portfolio Theory (MPT). MPT provides a context for understanding the interactions of systematic risk and reward. Markowitz' model has profoundly shaped the management of institutional portfolios. Because asset class investment returns are (approximately) normally distributed, Markowitz was able to apply statistical techniques to optimize portfolios (i.e., maximize return at every risk level). Today, virtually all fiduciaries rely on MPT, to some extent, when overseeing the investment of institutional assets.

MPT and mean variance optimization (MVO) have been generally beneficial to the investment process. Over the past 50 years, there was a paradigm shift. Each investment was no longer judged solely on its individual merit, but rather by how it affected the portfolio as a whole. MPT allowed fiduciaries to understand that adding additional "risky" investments (with low correlation) to a portfolio could actually reduce the volatility of the entire portfolio. Exhibit 7.6 demonstrates how allocating 13% to a riskier asset class (e.g., stocks) in an all-bond portfolio can actually reduce the risk of the entire portfolio (and increase expected returns). The driver of its risk reduction is the relatively low correlation between stocks and bonds. One asset often "zigs" when the other "zags." The offsetting fluctuations decrease overall portfolio volatility. The expected return (geometric) of a two-

EXHIBIT 7.6 TWO-ASSET EFFICIENT FRONTIER

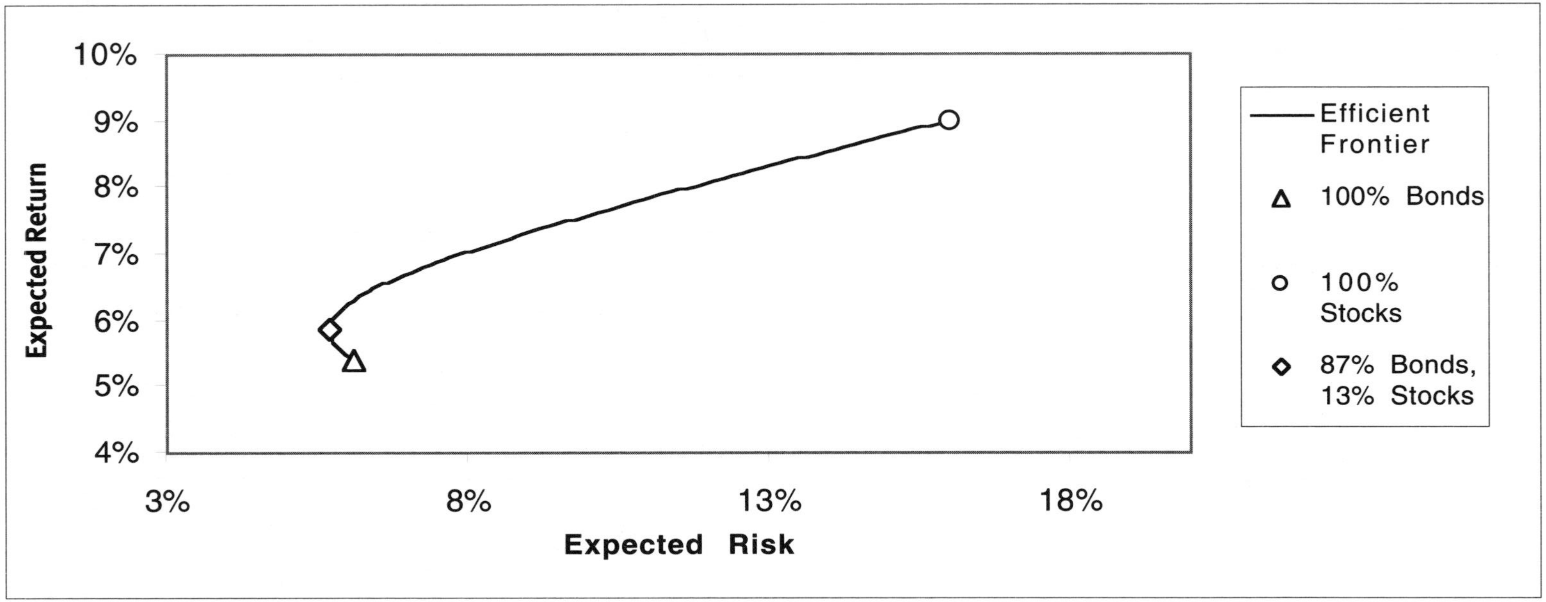

Legend:
- —— Efficient Frontier
- △ 100% Bonds
- ○ 100% Stocks
- ◇ 87% Bonds, 13% Stocks

Y-axis: Expected Return (4%, 5%, 6%, 7%, 8%, 9%, 10%)

X-axis: Expected Risk (3%, 8%, 13%, 18%)

asset portfolio is the weighted average expected return (arithmetic) of the two assets minus half the variance. When two assets are less than perfectly correlated, the standard deviation of the portfolio is less than the weighted average standard deviations of the asset classes. This diversification benefit is one of the few quantifiable free lunches offered by the financial markets!

SHORTCOMING OF TRADITIONAL MEAN VARIANCE OPTIMIZATION

The Markowitz algorithm (mean variance optimization, or MVO) is very elegant. It has precise mathematical calculations and draws unambiguous conclusions. This output gives fiduciaries a sense of security and confidence and is certainly better than other seat-of-the-pants asset allocation methodologies. However, humans tend to overestimate the precision and importance of information, including the Markowitz model. While the mathematical application of the model is "precise," the basic inputs (return, risk, and correlation assumptions) are difficult to forecast. As shown above, there are several methods to develop input assumptions, each of which provides different numbers. The only thing we can be certain of is that we are likely to be wrong on all three inputs. Even the smallest change in an expected return input can have a dramatic effect on output. For example, a 1% reduction in the expected return on large-cap stocks (from 9% to 8%) can make a tremendous difference in the construction of the "optimal" portfolio. In Exhibit 7.7, the large-cap allocation declines from 56% to 0%!

Statisticians make a distinction between accuracy and precision. *Precise* means sharply defined or measured, while the term *accurate* means truthful or correct. Data can be very precise, but inaccurate. It would be precise, but inaccurate, to say that a meter equals 29.49734 inches. It would be more accurate to say that a meter equals a little over one yard, although that may not sound as impressive. By overemphasizing the importance of "precise inputs" relative to "accurate inputs," traditional MVO forces the investor to forecast precise assumptions that cannot be accurate. For example, it may be accurate to say that small-cap stocks have higher expected return and risk relative to large-cap stocks. However, traditional MVO requires the practitioner to go beyond such a simple forecast and actually assign a precise number to the risk premium between the two assets. Should the expected return difference be 0.50% or should it be 1.5%? Such a small difference can lead to enormous differences in output.

Another problem with MVO is that it assumes that asset class returns fall into a normal distribution (the bell-shaped curve). This assumption is not completely accurate. For example, the four worst monthly returns for the S&P 500 index be-

EXHIBIT 7.7 LARGE-CAP ALLOCATION DECLINE

Scenario 1

Assets	Return	Risk
Large-cap	9.00%	16.00%
Small-cap	9.50%	20.00%
Intermediate bond	5.40%	6.10%

Correlation Matrix

	Large-cap	Small-cap	Intermediate bond
Large-cap	1		
Small-cap	0.83	1	
Intermediate bond	0.27	0.17	1

Most efficient allocation to achieve an 8% return

Large-cap	**56%**
Small-cap	14%
Intermediate bond	30%

Scenario 2

Assets	Return	Risk
Large-cap	8.00%	16.00%
Small-cap	9.50%	20.00%
Intermediate bond	5.40%	6.10%

Correlation Matrix

	Large-cap	Small-cap	Intermediate bond
Large-cap	1		
Small-cap	0.83	1	
Intermediate bond	0.27	0.17	1

Most efficient allocation to achieve an 8% return

Large-cap	**0%**
Small-cap	63%
Intermediate bond	37%

tween 1978 and 2004 were October 1987 (–21.5%), August 1998 (–14.5%), September 2002 (–10.9%), and March 1980 (–9.8%). Based on the observed monthly returns and standard deviation between 1978 and 2004, you would only expect a 21.5% loss (e.g., October 1987) to occur once every 441,322 years! One would also only expect a 14.5% loss to occur once every 353 years. The losses observed in September 2002 and March 1980 would only be expected to occur once every 24 and 11 years, respectively (Exhibit 7.8). On the other hand, the best monthly return, which occurred in January 1987 (+13.5%), would only be expected to occur about once every 28 years. Based on our 26-year sample, a 1 in 28-year event is not far off from what we would expect. The monthly returns of the S&P 500 index have exhibited both excess kurtosis (fat tails) and negative skewness (more observations on the left side of the distribution), just what you *don't* want. At least for the past 26 years, the normal distribution has not been a good predictor of downside risk.

The ultimate conclusion must be that traditional MVO is helpful as an exercise to demonstrate the value of diversification, but has little practical value in determining a specific optimal mix of assets in the portfolio construction process. In order for a portfolio optimization model to have value as a practical tool, it must account for the likelihood that an asset's short-term results may not match long-term expectations.

THE LONG RUN

Let's make the assumption that large-cap U.S. stocks are expected to achieve their long-run historical return and risk characteristics over a specified future horizon. What is "the long run"? There were 56 rolling 20-year periods between 1928 and 2002. The average annualized return (of the S&P 500) for these 56 twenty-year periods was 11.33%. The returns ranged from 2.4% to 17.7%. About two thirds of 20-year returns (or one standard deviation) ranged between 14.9% and 7.8%. In Exhibit 7.7 we saw how the efficient portfolio (generating an 8% return) went from a 56% allocation to large-cap stocks to 0% with just a 1% decline in the expected return for large-cap stocks; but large stocks have had a 7% spread over 20-year periods. To state the obvious, one standard deviation events are pretty common![2]

A nonprofit organization may have an infinite time horizon, but the members of your investment committee probably don't have infinite patience. Therefore,

---

[2]Calculated by DiMeo Schneider & Associates, L.L.C. using data presented in *Stocks, Bonds, Bills, and Inflation® 2004 Yearbook,* © 2004 Ibbotson Associates, Inc. Based on copyrighted works by Ibbotson and Sinquefield. All rights reserved. Used with permission.

EXHIBIT 7.8   S&P 500 HISTOGRAM OF MONTHLY RETURNS
(1978-2004)

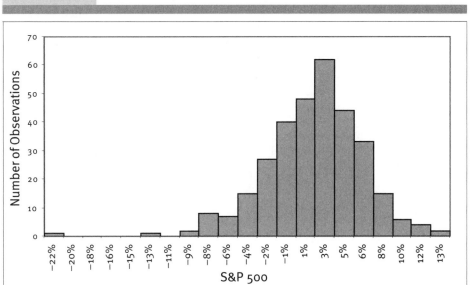

your investment horizon should not be defined as "infinite," but should be defined as the length of time that the committee will stick with a strategy that does not appear to be working. Much like casinos, human beings have hard-wired "table limits."

In Las Vegas, a $5 minimum bet table might have a $500 table limit. Why would a casino want to prevent anyone from betting over $500 at this table? For a gambler with infinite patience and resources (and no table limit), there is a perfect gambling strategy that will always win, eventually. If every time the gambler lost a hand at Black Jack he doubled the bet, the gambler would eventually make back everything that was lost plus the value of the initial bet. Exhibit 7.9 illustrates the theoretical payoff diagram for such an investor (assumes a 50% chance of victory).

Trustees of your fund may not be able or willing to wait 5, 10, or 20 years for mean reversion to bail out the investment or investment strategy. So what's the solution?

PROBABILISTIC OPTIMIZATION MODELS

The Frontier Engineer (a proprietary DiMeo Schneider & Associates, L.L.C. program) and other probabilistic optimization models are evolutionary improvements to the Markowitz portfolio optimization process. Ten tosses of a coin won't always yield five heads and five tails. Probabilistic models account for short-term uncertainty. Markowitz developed his optimization model in the first place be-

EXHIBIT 7.9   THEORETICAL PAYOFF DIAGRAM

Trial	Chance of Cumulative Losing	Bet to Make if Lost Last Hand	Total Accumulated Loss	Profit Generated upon Eventual Victory
1	50%	$5	($5)	$5
2	25%	$10	($15)	$5
3	13%	$20	($35)	$5
4	6%	$40	($75)	$5
5	3%	$80	($155)	$5
6	2%	$160	($315)	$5
7	1%	$320	($635)	$5
8	0.4%	$640	($1,275)	$5
9	0.2%	$1,280	($2,555)	$5
10	0.1%	$2,560	($5,115)	$5
11	0.05%	$5,120	($10,235)	$5
12	0.02%	$10,240	($20,475)	$5
13	0.01%	$20,480	($40,955)	$5
14	0.01%	$40,960	($81,915)	$5
15	0.003%	$81,920	($163,835)	$5
16	0.002%	$163,840	($327,675)	$5
17	0.001%	$327,680	($655,355)	$5
18	0.0004%	$655,360	($1,310,715)	$5
19	0.0002%	$1,310,720	($2,621,435)	$5
20	0.0001%	$2,621,440	($5,242,875)	$5
21	0.00005%	$5,242,880	($10,485,755)	$5
22	0.00002%	$10,485,760	($20,971,515)	$5
23	0.00001%	$20,971,520	($41,943,035)	$5
24	0.00001%	$41,943,040	($83,886,075)	$5
25	0.000003%	$83,886,080	($167,772,155)	$5

cause he realized an investment's expected return might not be realized over an investor's time horizon. Presumably, if the high-return/high-risk assets *always* outperformed low-return/low-risk assets over the investor's time horizon, we wouldn't need the model in the first place. We would just invest in the highest-returning asset class. Unfortunately, no such guarantee is available in the real world. Higher-risk assets have a nasty habit of achieving a much lower time horizon return than expected (Exhibit 7.10). Markowitz's model implies that a 1-year return is uncertain as defined by the one-year standard deviation measure as a dispersion of possible annual returns, but remains silent on the time horizon expected return. This silence leads the model to be applied (through no fault of Markowitz) so that the long-term expected performance of the asset equals the one-year forecast.

Probabilistic optimization models run Monte Carlo simulations to generate many possible outcomes. These multiple outcomes are generated by simulating

EXHIBIT 7.10 RETURNS ON HIGH-RISK ASSETS

Asset Class	Expected Return*	Annual Standard Deviation*	10-Year Standard Deviation	Pessimistic 10-Year Return	Optimistic 10-Year Return
Large-cap	8.1%	15.4%	4.9%	−3.2%	19.4%
Small-cap	8.3%	19.7%	6.2%	−6.2%	22.8%
Mid-cap	8.2%	17.6%	5.6%	−4.7%	21.1%
International Equity	8.1%	17.1%	5.4%	−4.5%	20.7%
REIT	7.6%	15.6%	4.9%	−3.9%	19.1%
High-yield Bond	5.8%	8.7%	2.8%	−0.6%	12.2%
Short Bond	3.2%	3.2%	1.0%	0.8%	5.6%
International Bond	5.6%	10.3%	3.3%	−2.0%	13.2%
Em. Mkt. Eq.	7.5%	28.8%	9.1%	−13.7%	28.7%
TIPS	4.6%	8.6%	2.7%	−1.7%	10.9%
Intermediate Bond	4.6%	6.3%	2.0%	0.0%	9.2%

Optimistic and pessimistic returns are defined as three standard deviation events.
*For illustrative purposes only.

numerous "what if" scenarios based on the annual expected return and standard deviation. For example, in one simulation large-cap stocks may be assumed to return 11%, in the next 4%, and so on. Then all the possible outcomes are sorted and somehow combined to produce an "all-weather" efficient frontier. There are various methodologies to accomplish this goal (see Appendix G for a list of vendors). The greater the expected precision of inputs (for longer time horizons), the more the probabilistic models look like the traditional Markowitz efficient frontier. The less confident you are about the inputs, the more broadly diversified the portfolios become.

The traditional model requires three inputs: expected risk, expected return, and expected correlation among asset classes. Probabilistic models add a fourth input, an uncertainty adjustment.

SUMMARY

Modern Portfolio Theory provides an academic rationale for the benefits of diversification, but unfortunately is less helpful in forecasting efficient portfolios. Traditional MVO requires the heavy use of constraint in order to generate portfolios that make intuitive sense. (The model is faulty, the inputs are faulty, or the intuition is faulty.)

Recently developed probabilistic-based optimization models produce output that is more useful for an investor with a finite time horizon. Even if your time horizon is 30 years, you will see very different output from that of the traditional model. Although it is impossible to make error-free input assumptions, probabilistic optimization models equip us to make asset allocation decisions that don't "bet the ranch" on the precision our forecasts. As a fiduciary overseeing your nonprofit organization's investment allocation, you might conclude that a probabilistic-based approach will help you to minimize your maximum regret. And that's a good thing!

## CHAPTER 8

New Asset Classes

We have explored the importance of asset allocation and some of the latest enhancements to the models. Perhaps we should mention a useful rule of thumb: in general, the more broadly diversified the portfolio, the better. If you hold several noncorrelated asset classes in your portfolio, it is likely that at least one or two may perform well even if everything else is declining. Nowadays most nonprofit funds hold large and small U.S. stocks, U.S. bonds, cash (Treasury bills), and even non-U.S. stocks. In this chapter we discuss additional asset classes that can enhance your portfolio diversification. We examine real estate investment trusts (REITs), high-yield bonds, non-U.S. bonds, and inflation-indexed bonds.

REAL ESTATE INVESTMENT TRUSTS

Real estate investment trusts are companies that buy, develop, manage, and sell real estate assets. REITs afford investors an opportunity to invest in professionally managed portfolios of properties. So long as at least 90% of income is paid out in the form of dividends to shareholders and at least 75% of the investments are in real estate, the cash flows of REITs can be distributed to investors without taxation at the corporate level. Tax-qualified investors escape direct and indirect income taxation altogether. As pass-through entities, REIT business activities are restricted to the generation of property rental income.

REITs offer a major advantage over direct ownership of real estate: liquidity. REIT shares are traded on the New York Stock Exchange and other major exchanges, making it easier to acquire and liquidate real estate than to buy and sell private properties.

REITs share some performance characteristics with small-cap stocks and fixed-income investments. The relatively low market capitalization of REITs puts them in the small-cap category. In fact, REITs make up a significant portion of the Russell 2000 small-cap index. But real estate, and therefore REITs, are truly a separate asset class. REITs have some advantages over stocks and bonds in terms of dividends. Between 1995 and 2002, the average dividend yield on REITs was over 7%, far greater than the dividend yield on traditional equity investments. Furthermore, *all* REITs pay dividends, whereas less than half of the Russell 2000 stocks pay dividends. REITs show a relatively low correlation with other equities, including small-cap stocks (Exhibit 8.1).

The long-term investment performance of REITs is determined by the cash flow yields generated by rents, the growth in the underlying nominal value of the real estate over time, and multiple expansion (or contraction) afforded REITs in the marketplace. One of the primary incentives for REIT investment is the low correlation with other financial assets. REITs have low correlation with other financial assets because (1) they are income-generating assets and (2) they provide some degree of inflation protection. REITs are some of the few financial assets that won't necessarily react adversely to unanticipated increases in inflation. A sudden increase in inflation (and interest rates) may cause the yield component of REITs to become less attractive, but it also increases the terminal value of the

EXHIBIT 8.1 RETURNS AND RISKS OF REITS

Historical Return and Risk*

Asset Class	Return	Risk
Large-cap	13.9%	15.5%
Small-cap	14.3%	19.6%
International equity	11.8%	17.0%
REIT	14.5%	14.5%
Intermediate bond	9.1%	6.3%

Correlation Matrix†

	Large-Cap	Small-Cap	International Equity	REIT	Intermediate Bond
Large-cap	1				
Small-cap	0.83	1			
International equity	0.57	0.51	1		
REIT	0.51	0.62	0.31	1	
Intermediate bond	0.25	0.15	0.16	0.22	1

*Period beginning 1/79–10/04 (risk is measured by standard deviation).
†Large-cap (Russell 1000), small-cap (Russell 2000), international equity (MSCI EAFE), REIT (Wilshire REIT), intermediate bond (Lehman Aggregate Bond).

underlying real estate. In one sense, a REIT may be viewed as a fixed-income instrument with an embedded call option on inflation.

However, as with other publicly traded equity vehicles, REITs can rapidly win and lose the favor of the investing public. This can lead to periods of over - or undervaluation. REITs have experienced painful market sell-offs when the luster fades and their prices fall to a discount to the value of the real estate held by the trust. In recent years, more and more investors have recognized the tremendous diversification benefit that REITs offer a portfolio. As of this writing, REITs are "in favor," trading at the high end of their normal valuation range (Exhibit 8.2).

An efficient portfolio (containing large-cap stocks, small-cap stocks, REITs, international stocks, and intermediate investment grade bonds) that generated a 14% annual return from January 1979 to October 2004 would have had about 62% allocated to REITs (Exhibit 8.3). Had you excluded REITs from the allocation, to achieve a 14% return you would have increased your portfolio's risk by about 3.6% (16% vs. 12.4%). Although history is not destiny (and few would suggest a 62% allocation to REITs), the diversification benefit seems obvious.

THE STATISTICAL PROPERTIES OF HISTORICAL REIT RETURNS

At the risk of getting too technical, REITs have historically exhibited excess *kurtosis* (fat tails) relative to what the normal distribution (the traditional bell-shaped curve) would predict. They have also shown a slight *negative skew* (more observations in the left, or negative, tail). Based on the assumption of a normal distribution and the observation of historical monthly returns and standard deviations, you would have expected an 8.3% monthly price decline in REITs three times

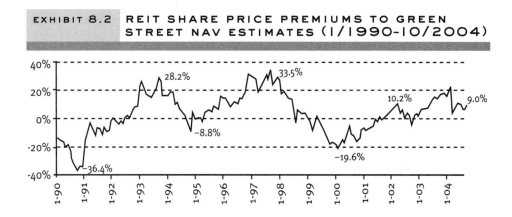

EXHIBIT 8.2   REIT SHARE PRICE PREMIUMS TO GREEN STREET NAV ESTIMATES (1/1990-10/2004)

EXHIBIT 8.3 EFFICIENT FRONTIER (1/1979–10/2004)

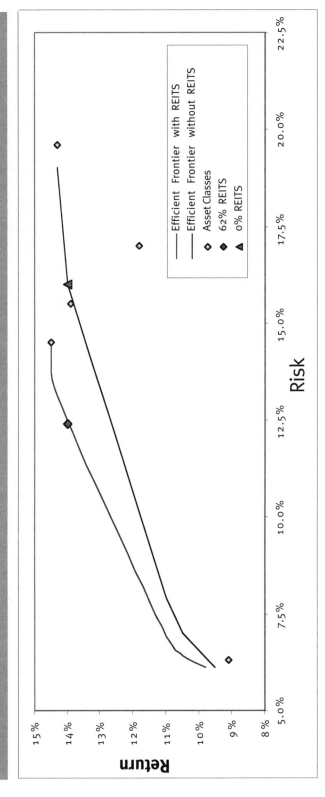

over the past 25 years. In reality, it occurred six times, or twice as frequently as expected. Conversely, you would have expected a 10.7% monthly increase three times over the last 25 years. It occurred six times, again twice as frequently as expected. REITs appear to exhibit more extreme values (or fat tails) than a normal distribution would predict (Exhibit 8.4).

So what does all of this mean for your not-for-profit fund? Simply this: not only does this asset class offer a diversification benefit, but *if you rebalance systematically,* the fat tails allow you to "engineer" excess return into the portfolio. (See Chapter 12 for more information on rebalancing.)

HIGH-YIELD BONDS

High-yield is a euphemism for bonds that are rated "below investment grade" by the major rating agencies, Moody's and Standard & Poor's (S&P). The highest-quality bonds get AAA ratings, while the lowest-quality bonds (not in default) get C ratings based on the creditworthiness of the issuer. Anything in default gets a D rating. Bonds considered to have an acceptable default risk are deemed "investment grade" and encompass BBB bonds and higher. Bonds BB and lower are called high-yield or "junk bonds" and have a higher risk for default. High-yield bonds offer greater yields to compensate investors for the significant increase in credit risk. Like any other fixed-payment bond, high-yield bonds are also subject to *interest rate risk.* Oftentimes, *liquidity risk* is also greater for high-yield bonds than for their investment-grade counterparts. In periods of stress when investors seek to unload their high-yield holdings en masse, bid-ask spreads can widen dramatically. So why would anyone want to own junk bonds?

History

Before the 1980s, most junk bonds resulted from a decline in credit quality of former investment-grade issuers. These issues are known as "fallen angels." Any given high-yield bond has a substantially greater default risk than an investment-grade bond. However, a *portfolio* of such bonds is another matter entirely. The tenets of Modern Portfolio Theory (MPT) led researchers to observe that the risk-adjusted returns for portfolios of junk bonds were quite high. The higher yields associated with a portfolio of such bonds more than compensated for the credit risk; the actual default losses were exceeded by the higher-interest payments.

In addition to having higher coupon payments, high-yield bonds offer investors potential capital appreciation (or increase in the bond's price). For exam-

EXHIBIT 8.4 WILSHIRE REIT MONTHLY RETURN DISTRIBUTION OF RETURNS (1/1979–2/2004)

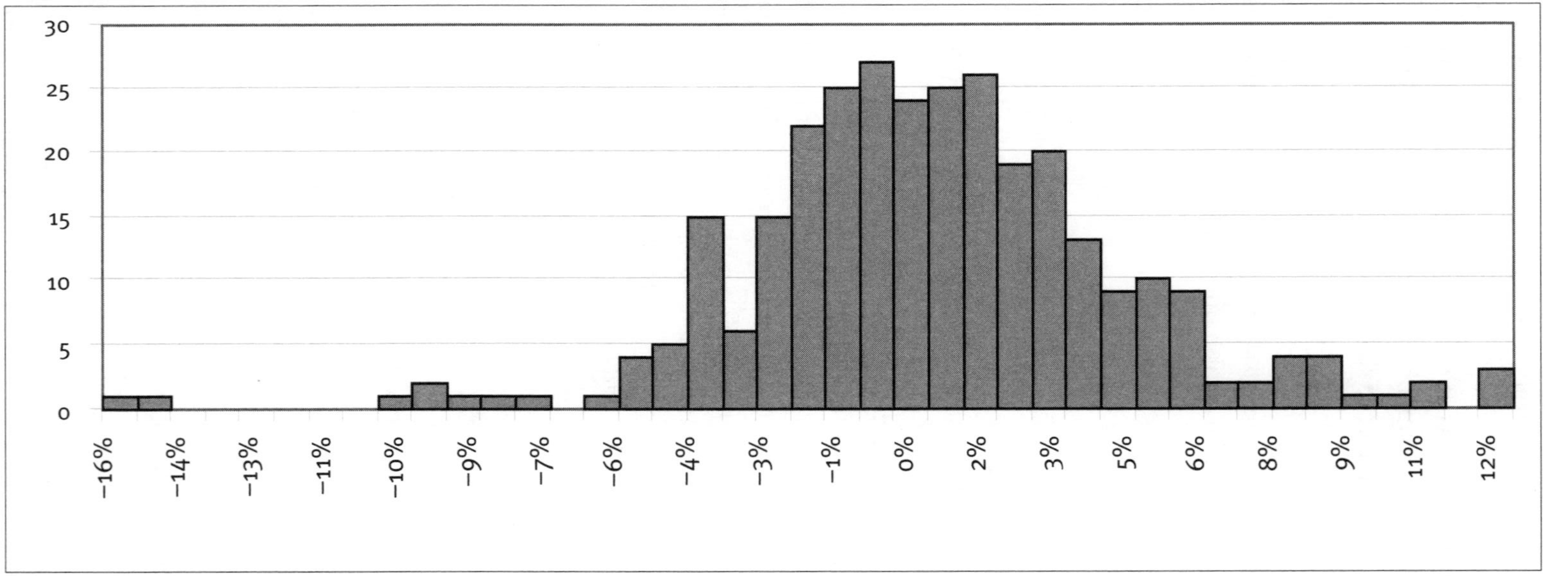

ple, if the borrower's debt rating is upgraded due to a merger, improved earnings, or positive industry developments, one would expect to see the yield spread between a high-yield bond and investment-grade corporate bond tighten significantly. In other words, the junk bond price would rise. Also, if investors become less risk-averse, credit spreads can tighten between the high-yield bond market and the investment-grade bond market as a whole.

Although risk for default is higher for high-yield bond holders, they do have senior claim over preferred and common stock holders in the event of liquidation. Of course, the greatest reason to include junk bonds in a portfolio is that they may zig when other investments are zagging. For example, in the latter stages of an economic recovery, interest rates may rise, causing a sell-off in investment-grade bonds. However, the strong economy may make high-yield bond investors more sanguine about default risk. So junk bonds may increase in value while the value of investment-grade bonds is falling. In fact, high-yield bonds have relatively low correlation with most of the major asset classes (Exhibit 8.5).

High-yield bond due diligence requires significant credit analysis. Credit analysis concentrates on fundamentals and a "bottom-up" process. The focus is

EXHIBIT 8.5 CORRELATION OF HIGH-YIELD BONDS TO ASSETS

Historical Return and Risk*

Asset Class	Return	Risk
Large-cap	13.3%	15.5%
Small-cap	12.3%	19.3%
International equity	12.2%	17.4%
High-yield bond	10.0%	6.2%
Intermediate bond	8.8%	4.5%

Correlation Matrix†

	Large-Cap	Small-Cap	International Equity	High-Yield Bond	Intermediate Bond
Large-cap	1				
Small-cap	0.83	1			
International equity	0.57	0.51	1		
High-yield bond	0.51	0.55	0.36	1	
Intermediate bond	0.25	0.15	0.16	0.32	1

*Period beginning 11/84–10/04 (risk is measured by standard deviation).
†Large-cap (Russell 1000), small-cap (Russell 2000), international equity (MSCI EAFE), high-yield bond (Merrill Lynch High Yield Master), intermediate bond (Lehman Aggregate Bond).

generally on the downside risk of default. First, you need to calculate the likelihood of default. Next, you need to gauge the consequence of a potential default. High-yield bond managers typically diversify by industry group and issue type. Due to the high minimum size of bond trades and the credit expertise required, most investors use high-yield mutual funds or commingled investment vehicles rather than separate accounts.

The Portfolio Construction Benefits of High-Yield Bonds

An historically optimal portfolio (containing large-cap stocks, small-cap stocks, high-yield bonds, international stocks, and intermediate investment-grade bonds) that generated an 11% annual return from November of 1984 to October 2004 would have had about 54% allocated to high-yield bonds. Had high-yield bonds been *excluded* from the allocation, you would have increased portfolio risk by 0.70% (8.3% vs. 7.6%) (Exhibit 8.6). As with REITs, it seems compelling to include high-yield bonds in a diversified portfolio.

All Junk Is Not the Same

It is important to differentiate among the various components of the high-yield bond market. For example, there is a big difference between the risk and correlation factors of BB- and C-rated securities. C-rated securities have the lowest correlation with both stocks and investment-grade bonds and possess the highest volatility. BB- and B-rated securities show higher correlations with investment-grade bonds and stocks, but lower risk than C-rated bonds. High-yield managers that focus on BB and B securities perform quite differently than do those managers that focus on B- and C-rated securities. Within an MPT context, BB and B securities have relatively attractive return/risk relationships, but C-rated securities may offer greater diversification potential. See Exhibit 8.7 for a more detailed analysis.

The Statistical Properties

Like REITs, high-yield bonds have historically exhibited excess kurtosis (fat tails) and negative skew (more observations in the left tail). In hindsight, extremely negative monthly return events (1/100 probability events) should have happened about two times over the past 16 years. For B-, BB-, and C-rated securities, these events actually occurred two to three times more often than ex-

EXHIBIT 8.6 EFFICIENT FRONTIER (11/1984–10/2004)

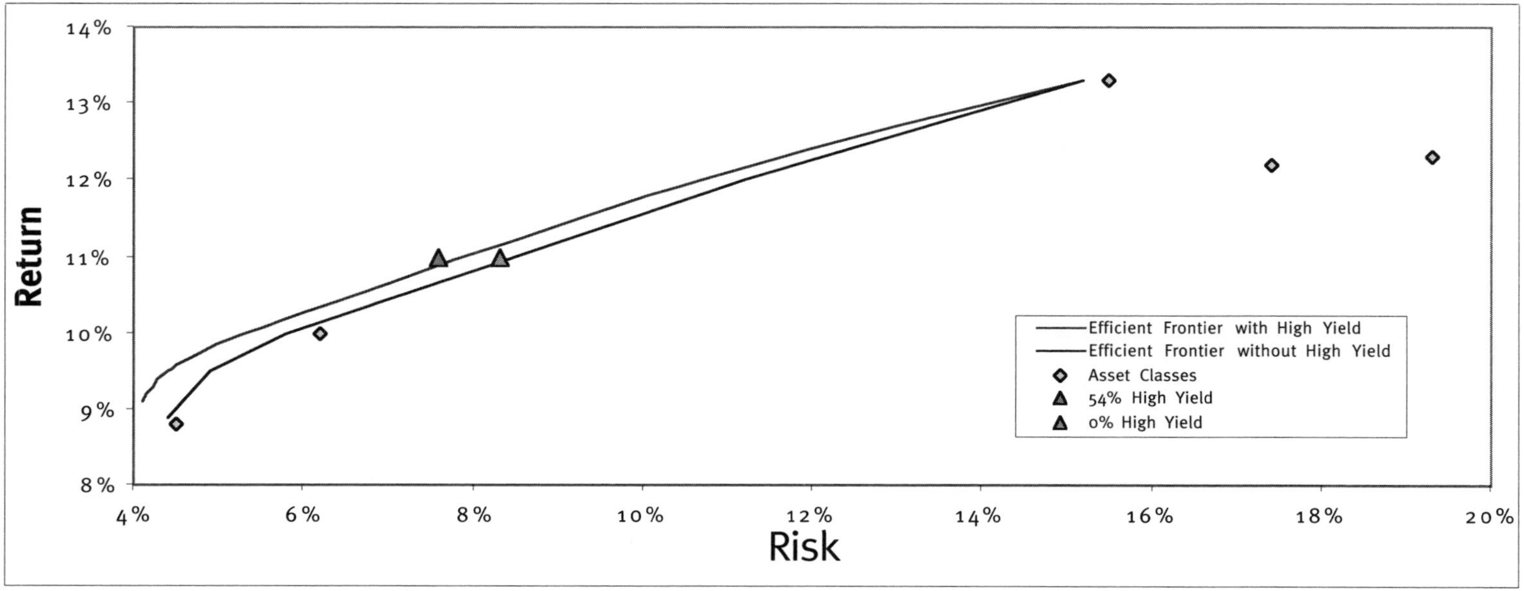

Legend:
— Efficient Frontier with High Yield
— Efficient Frontier without High Yield
◆ Asset Classes
▲ 54% High Yield
▲ 0% High Yield

Risk

Return

EXHIBIT 8.7   RETURN/RISK RELATIONSHIPS

Historical Return and Risk*

Asset Class	Return	Risk
Large-cap	12.4%	14.5%
High-yield bond	9.1%	6.4%
Intermediate bond	8.0%	4.0%
High-yield bond (BB)	9.2%	5.1%
High-yield bond (B)	8.9%	7.2%
High-yield bond (C)	7.7%	11.3%

Correlation Matrix†

	Large-Cap	High-Yield Bond	Intermediate Bond	High-Yield Bond (BB)	High-Yield Bond (B)	High-Yield Bond (C)
Large-cap	1					
High-yield bond	0.51	1				
Intermediate bond	0.25	0.32	1			
High-yield bond (BB)	0.46	0.9	0.45	1		
High-yield bond (B)	0.48	0.97	0.17	0.78	1	
High-yield bond (C)	0.36	0.86	0.01	0.66	0.84	1

*Period beginning 9/88–10/04 (risk is measured by standard deviation).
†Intermediate bond (Lehman Aggregate Bond), BB (ML high-yield BB), HY B (ML high-yield B), HY C (ML high-yield C), large-cap (Russell 1000).

pected! Investment-grade bonds saw two such events, matching predictions based on the normal distribution. While the highest-quality BB-rated bonds had twice as many extremely negative return events, they had no extremely positive return events (Exhibit 8.8). You couldn't ask for a worse combination—negative skewness coupled with excess kurtosis.

Particularly for this asset class, the unconstrained traditional (mean variance) optimization model allocates a higher percentage to high-yield bonds than may be warranted (see Chapter 7). This is partly why high-yield bonds are usually constrained in optimization models. Nonetheless, high-yield bonds still warrant shelf space in the portfolio construction process because of their relatively low correlation with other asset classes.

INTERNATIONAL BONDS

After nearly 20 years of declining interest rates, the prospect of rising rates looms on the horizon. Fund fiduciaries wonder what to do with their fixed income al-

EXHIBIT 8.8 NEGATIVE VERSUS POSITIVE RETURN EVENTS

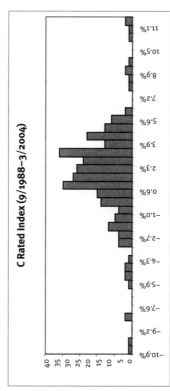

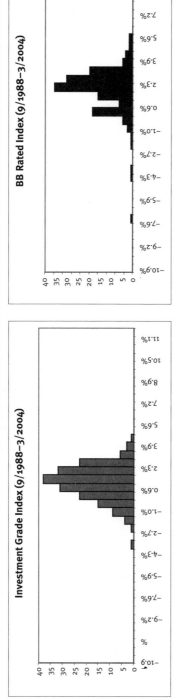

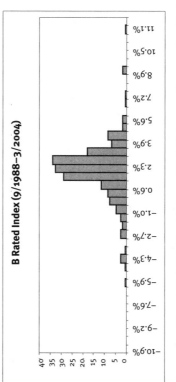

Source: Merrill Lynch High-Yield Bond Indexes (BB, B, C). Lehman Aggregate Bond index.

location. (Nearly every asset allocation strategy for all types of funds includes bonds.) The primary reason you include bonds is risk management. Low volatility and low correlation with stocks make bonds the "bedrock" of a portfolio. If the stock market goes down, hopefully the bond portion of a portfolio will hold its value, which will help prevent large losses. But what happens if the U.S. bond market goes down? What if the stock and bond markets both decline? While domestic bonds generally provide some of the diversification that a portfolio needs, foreign bonds can further diversify a portfolio's total risk.

Why do foreign bonds make sense? They offer a large opportunity set of securities in which to invest, provide access to alternative interest rate environments, and provide a strong tool for risk management. This section touches on all three of these reasons plus the impact of foreign currencies on U.S. investors. Available investment vehicles are also discussed.

Opportunity Set

Nearly 60% of all bonds are issued outside the United States. Nowadays, non-U.S. stocks are a part of most pension, foundation, and endowment funds' equity allocations. Foreign bonds offer similar diversification benefits for the fixed-income portion. Non-U.S. bonds offer access to some of the world's most financially sound governments and corporations. *Sovereign debt* (bonds issued by foreign governments) currently makes up the lion's share of the overseas bond market. Governments in developed markets such as the EuroZone, Scandinavia, Great Britain, Japan, Australia, and New Zealand all issue traditional fixed-income securities. In addition, a number of those countries also issue inflation-indexed bonds. These bonds offer the full faith and credit of their respective governments and behave, in their local markets, in a similar fashion to U.S. government bonds. Exhibit 8.9 shows the foreign bond market broken down by issuer.

Foreign Corporate Debt

The fastest growing sector in the non-U.S. fixed-income market is corporate-issued debt. Foreign corporations have historically used direct bank borrowing and the equity markets to finance growth but have started turning more toward the bond markets as a source of funds. Corporations have increased their debt issuance in most developed countries and in many emerging markets (Exhibits 8.10 and 8.11). As in the United States, purchasing nongovernment fixed-income securities carries added risk, but investors are rewarded for that additional risk with higher yields. Credit risk, or the risk that a company may default on its

EXHIBIT 8.9   FOREIGN BOND MARKET BY ISSUER

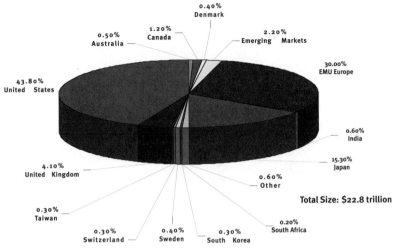

0.40%
Denmark

1.20%
Canada

2.20%
Emerging   Markets

0.50%
Australia

30.00%
EMU Europe

43.80%
United   States

0.60%
India

15.30%
Japan

4.10%
United   Kingdom

0.60%
Other

Total Size: $22.8 trillion

0.30%
Taiwan

0.20%
South Africa

0.30%
Switzerland

0.40%
Sweden

0.30%
South   Korea

Source: Bank for International Settlements.

debt obligations, is a primary risk associated with such securities. Credit rating agencies, such as S&P and Moody's, have increased their coverage of non-U.S. corporate debt, making it easier for a purchaser to identify investment-grade securities overseas.

As can be seen in Exhibits 8.10 and 8.11, the size of these markets offers a vastly increased opportunity set for U.S. investors.

An important subsector of the foreign bond market is *emerging market debt.* Emerging or developing markets are generally considered to be those outside the

EXHIBIT 8.10   GOVERNMENT SHARE OF GLOBAL BOND
               MARKET

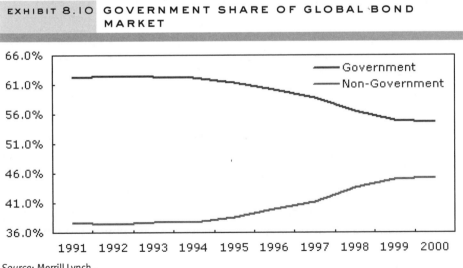

Government
Non-Government

Source: Merrill Lynch.

EXHIBIT 8.11   GLOBAL CORPORATE BOND ISSUANCE

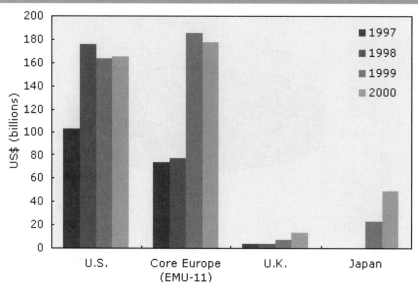

Source: Goldman Sachs.

Morgan Stanley Capital International Europe, Australia, and Far East (MSCI EAFE) index. Countries in Latin America, Eastern Europe, and Asia (excluding Japan) issue both sovereign and corporate debt to finance government spending and corporate growth. Emerging market bonds offer opportunities, although with an additional layer of risk. Increased government spending and lower interest rates have had a significant impact on the size of the bond markets in some of these developing countries. While accounting for less than 5% of the world bond markets, emerging countries are experiencing tremendous growth in terms of both gross domestic product (GDP) and the size of their capital markets.

Volatility in the local economies and political instability are the most significant factors effecting debt securities in these countries. The Russian debt crisis of 1998 is an example. In that year, Russia defaulted on its debt obligations and threw the entire emerging debt market into crisis. However, with higher risks come higher yields. Government debt issued by emerging market countries often carries significantly higher yields than bonds issued in the United States, United Kingdom, or EuroZone countries. Moreover, credit quality seems to be slowly improving in these markets. Nearly 49% of the securities in the J.P. Morgan Emerging Markets index are now rated as investment grade. Improving credit quality may provide price appreciation if economic conditions around the world improve.

A second, equally important, benefit of these securities is their low correlation with other asset classes. Correlation is the degree to which two investments move together. As we have mentioned earlier, the prospect of rising interest rates may dim investors' enthusiasm for domestic bonds. Why should international bonds be any different? Why do we think they can help an overall asset allocation structure? Take a look at Exhibit 8.12, which details how both hedged and unhedged foreign bonds correlate with other major asset classes.

A correlation coefficient of 1.00 is perfect positive correlation. In other words, every time one asset class moves a certain direction, the asset class being compared moves in exactly the same direction. A correlation coefficient of -1.00 means that every time one asset moves one direction, the other asset moves in exactly the opposite direction. The correlation of unhedged international bonds to domestic bonds is 0.36. This means that the returns of these two asset classes move in exactly the same direction only 36% of the time! That is, over 60% of the time, when U.S. bonds decline in price, foreign bonds may stay flat or even appreciate.

Interest Rate Environments

Regardless of where a bond is issued, it responds similarly to changes in local interest rates. Foreign central banks (European Central Bank, Bank of England, Bank of Japan, etc.) control the interest rate environment in their economies in much the same way as the Federal Reserve dictates rates domestically. Why is this important?

As each region's economy strengthens or weakens, the central banks raise or

EXHIBIT 8.12 ASSET CLASS CORRELATION DATA (1/1985–10/2004)

	Large-Cap Equity	International Equity	Domestic Bonds	Hedged International Bonds	Unhedged International Bonds
Large-cap equity	1.00				
International equity	0.57	1.00			
Domestic bonds	0.25	0.16	1.00		
Hedged international bonds*	0.10	0.21	0.60	1.00	
Unhedged international bonds†	−0.05	0.44	0.36	0.48	1.00

*Hedged international bonds: Citigroup Currency-Hedged Non-U.S. World Government Bond Ten-Market.
†Unhedged international bonds: Citigroup Non-U.S. Dollar World Government Bond.
Large-cap = Russell 1000, international equity = MSCI EAFE, domestic bonds = Lehman U.S. Aggregate Bond.

lower rates in order to effect economic growth. Their actions shape the interest rate environment in each market. Foreign economies are seldom on exactly the same path as that of the United States. Exhibit 8.13 details average annual interest rates for several major countries.

The manager of a foreign bond fund has more interest rate environments from which to choose than does a domestic bond manager. When rates are low in the United States, they may be higher in Europe and the United Kingdom. Belief that the European Central Bank may lower rates to encourage economic growth may stimulate the European bond markets at a time when the U.S. bond markets are looking at rate increases and the prospect of falling bond prices.

Currency Risk and Hedging

Why does it matter to a U.S. investor if the dollar gains or loses value against the euro, pound, or yen? Currency movement can, at times, have the single greatest impact on a portfolio's return! Here is an easy way to think about the impact of currency. Assume that the U.S. dollar and the euro trade at about the same level, $1 for €1. You buy a German government bond that is issued with a par value of €1,000. At this exchange level it costs $1000 to buy the bond. Over time, the value of each currency changes. Assume that now €1 can be exchanged for $1.15 (a loss of 15% in the value of the U.S. dollar). After selling the bond, the €1,000 is exchanged for U.S. dollars. Because the U. S. dollar weakened against the Euro, the 1,000 Euros is converted into $1,150. This represents a 15% gain on a bond that has not really appreciated in value!

But currency movements work both ways. If, instead of rising in value against the U.S. dollar the euro declines, U.S. investors can suffer substantial losses. For example, if €1 can only be exchanged for $0.85, your $1,000 investment is now worth $850, a loss of 15% from currency movement alone!

But, there is a solution: hedge away the impact of currency. Derivative instruments can remove the impact of currency swings (both positive and negative). Futures contracts, primarily in the major currencies (euro, yen, and British pound), and currency swaps can be used to remove currency risk while not effecting the value of the underlying bonds. This hedging directly impacts the return that a U.S.-based investor can earn from foreign securities. While it's almost impossible to predict the direction of a particular currency, about half the time U.S. investors gain from currency exposure and half the time they lose. Some investors prefer to avoid the risk and adopt a hedged strategy.

One of the primary decisions the investment committee must make is whether or not to allow currency exposure. International bond managers generally fall

EXHIBIT 8.13 AVERAGE ANNUAL INTEREST RATES BY COUNTRY

Long-Term Interest Rates Percentage per Annum

	1990	1991	1992	1993	1994	1995	1996	1997	1998	1999	2000	2001	2002	2003
Australia	13.2	10.7	9.2	7.3	9	9.2	8.2	6.9	5.5	6.1	6.3	5.6	5.8	5.4
Canada	10.7	9.5	8.1	7.2	8.4	8.2	7.2	6.1	5.3	5.5	5.9	5.5	5.3	4.8
Denmark	10.6	9.3	9	7.3	7.8	8.3	7.2	6.3	5	4.9	5.7	5.1	5.1	4.3
Finland	13.2	11.7	12	8.8	9	8.8	7.1	6	4.8	4.7	5.5	5	5	4.1
France	9.9	9	8.6	6.8	7.2	7.5	6.3	5.6	4.6	4.6	5.4	4.9	4.9	4.1
Germany	8.7	8.5	7.9	6.5	6.9	6.9	6.2	5.7	4.6	4.5	5.3	4.8	4.8	4.1
Ireland	10.3	9.4	9.3	7.6	8	8.2	7.2	6.3	4.7	4.8	5.5	5	5	4.1
Italy	13.5	13.3	13.3	11.2	10.5	12.2	9.4	6.9	4.9	4.7	5.6	5.2	5	4.3
Japan	7	6.3	5.3	4.3	4.4	3.4	3.1	2.4	1.5	1.7	1.7	1.3	1.3	1.1
Korea	15.1	16.5	15.1	12.1	12.3	12.4	10.9	11.7	12.8	8.7	8.5	6.7	6.5	5
Mexico	34.9	19.7	16.1	15.6	13.8	39.9	34.4	22.4	24.8	24.1	16.9	13.8	8.5	7.4
Netherlands	8.9	8.7	8.1	6.4	6.9	6.9	6.2	5.6	4.6	4.6	5.4	5	4.9	4.1
New Zealand	12.4	10.1	8.4	6.9	7.6	7.8	7.9	7.2	6.3	6.4	6.9	6.4	6.5	5.9
Norway	10.7	10	9.6	6.9	7.4	7.4	6.8	5.9	5.4	5.5	6.2	6.2	6.4	5
Spain	14.6	12.8	11.7	10.2	10	11.3	8.7	6.4	4.8	4.7	5.5	5.1	5	4.1
Sweden	13.2	10.7	10	8.5	9.5	10.2	8	6.6	5	5	5.4	5.1	5.3	4.6
Switzerland	6.4	6.2	6.4	4.6	5	4.5	4	3.4	3	3	3.9	3.4	3.2	2.7
United Kingdom	11.8	10.1	9.1	7.5	8.2	8.2	7.8	7.1	5.5	5.1	5.3	4.9	4.9	4.5
United States	8.6	7.9	7	5.9	7.1	6.6	6.4	6.4	5.3	5.6	6	5	4.6	4
Euro area	10.9	10.3	9.8	7.9	8	8.4	7.1	5.9	4.7	4.6	5.4	5	4.9	4.1

Note: Ten-year benchmark government bond yields where available or yield on proximately similar financial instruments (for Korea a five-year bond is used).

Source: Organization for Economic Cooperation and Development.

into two categories: currency hedged and unhedged. How large are the potential return differences between hedged and unhedged managers? Exhibit 8.14 details annual returns and annualized standard deviations for 5- and 10-year periods for both the Citigroup Currency-Hedged Non-U.S. Dollar and the Citigroup Non-U.S. Dollar World Government Bond indexes.

Investors face a dilemma when looking at currency risk. An unhedged portfolio provides the opportunity for equity-like returns but also exposes the investor to equity-like downside. The period 1999 through 2001 represents three consecutive years of losses. Could your fund afford to take nearly four times the risk in order to achieve high returns in years like 2002 and 2003? Or, is it more appropriate to hedge away most of the currency risk in order to achieve a smoother ride? These are questions for your investment committee and consultant. One option is to split the foreign bond allocation between these two strategies. As mentioned earlier, there is about a 50/50 chance of coming out on the right side of a currency bet. By using both the hedged and unhedged strategies and *rebalancing* (see Chapter 12), the fund may get the best of both worlds: higher returns than expected from the hedged approach alone and less potential downside than is typical for an unhedged portfolio.

MUTUAL FUND OR SEPARATE ACCOUNT?

This decision may be an easy one. Most non-U.S. bond managers have requirements of $100 million or more to open a separate account. For investment allocations smaller than that, mutual funds are the only possibility. Even if an investor could find a manager who accepts smaller mandates, increased trading and custody costs may be prohibitive. Custody costs for a foreign bond portfolio are significantly higher than for a comparable domestic bond portfolio. Custody costs include asset-based fees, transaction-based fees, foreign exchange fees, and

EXHIBIT 8.14   CALENDAR YEAR RETURNS AND STANDARD DEVIATION

Index	2003	2002	2001	2000	1999	1998
Hedged	1.88%	6.85%	6.12%	9.64%	2.88%	11.53%
Nonhedged	18.52%	21.99%	−3.54%	−2.63%	−5.07%	17.79%

Index	1997	1996	1995	Standard Deviation		
Hedged	11.07%	11.85%	17.92%	2.56%	3.01%	
Nonhedged	−4.26%	4.08%	19.55%	8.91%	8.45%	

the cost of hedging (if applicable). Large investment funds can offset these fees with reduced management expenses, but the only viable alternative for smaller endowments or foundations is often to use an institutional mutual fund. Such funds carry expense ratios that are lower than those of "retail" funds. The expense ratio includes most of the above-mentioned costs as well as the investment management fees. Trading costs are not included in the expense ratio but are netted against returns.

Don't ignore liquidity. Most foreign bonds are fairly liquid, and sovereign debt is very liquid, but if your nonprofit organization needs regular cash distributions, it is important to have a clear understanding of true liquidity.

EXPERIENCE COUNTS!

The world is a big place. More than half of all fixed-income securities are issued outside the United States. This is not an asset class for rookie managers. It is extremely important (as it is with virtually any asset class) to hire an investment manager with experience, depth of staff, knowledge, and understanding of foreign fixed-income markets. Performing credit research on a company in Brazil is very different from performing credit research on a company headquartered in Boston. Accounting standards differ, and there are cultural and managerial differences. Only a dedicated team of professionals can adequately perform the task. Leave implementing a currency futures overlay to the experts.

SUMMARY

Although the thought of using foreign bonds may raise the blood pressure of some investment committee members, such bonds can be a good tool for portfolio diversification. Considering the huge pool of fixed-income instruments outside the United States and the different interest rate environments, it is an asset class worth considering.

INFLATION INDEXED BONDS

Inflation indexed bonds are also known as *TIPS* (an acronym for their original name, *Treasury inflation protection securities*). TIPS and other types of inflation protection bonds (IPBs) represent a new asset class. These bonds have special applications for not-for-profit funds.

TIPS are relatively new instruments in the United States. However, other governments have used them for years. In addition, several corporations have issued such bonds. The advantage to the issuer is lower interest expense. The advantage to the purchaser is a positive rate of return even in periods of rising inflation. The purchaser should also enjoy less volatility.

TIPS are issued with a stated *real* rate of return. Every six months the bond's principal amount is adjusted based on changes in the consumer price index (CPI). The semi-annual interest payment is calculated by multiplying the new principal amount by one half the stated rate.

TIPS and Not-for-Profit Funds

Your fund shares many characteristics with other institutional pools of money (defined benefit pension plans, defined contribution retirement plans, insurance company reserves, etc.). However, there are some crucial differences.

First of all, you generally have a spending requirement. Second, your investment committee is probably a volunteer group. The members are usually intelligent people, often highly respected in their particular field. But their financial understanding may be uneven. There is often a tendency toward an overly conservative investment posture. (It's human nature to regret a loss more than a missed opportunity for an equal gain.)

One particularly problematic tendency is that of categorizing return into *income* and *capital gains*. The idea that "we can only spend income" is inherently flawed. In times of low interest rates, this posture forces the fund into a large percentage of debt instruments, virtually assuring that there won't be enough growth to stay ahead of inflation.

A more savvy approach is the *total return* concept (see Chapter 3). Return is return regardless of the source. This brings us to the question of why bonds should be part of a diversified portfolio at all. Since 1926, intermediate U.S. Government bonds have produced an anemic 2.4% per year over inflation. That includes the 1980s, when those bonds produced 6.49% per year above inflation! In fact, in many of the decades since the 1920s, bonds have produced negative real returns! So why would a rational investor include such securities in a portfolio?

The answer is that the bonds are included because of their diversification effect. Their relatively low correlation with stocks dampens the inherent volatility of an all-stock portfolio. If you could find another asset class with even lower correlation with stocks and that also happened to produce positive returns above inflation, you could shift the entire efficient frontier upward. That's exactly what TIPS do.

Nominal Bonds

Traditional, or *nominal*, bonds pay a stated rate of interest and promise to repay the lender's principal at maturity. When a bond's yield is initially set, that rate is made up of several components. You can think of the basic component as the current inflation rate. The second building block is a real return above the current inflation rate. But since inflation rates can change over time, there is also a third component of the nominal rate, an *inflation risk premium*. This component compensates the investor for the uncertainty of future inflation. Exhibit 8.15 depicts those components.

When interest rates rise in the marketplace, the value of existing bonds falls. Think of opposite ends of a teeter-totter.

Inflation Indexed Bonds

TIPS and other inflation protection securities, however, promise to pay a stated rate of return above inflation. Every six months the principal value of such bonds is adjusted upward based on changes in the CPI. The stated interest rate or coupon is paid on the new principal value; so both principal and interest rise. There is no inflation risk component built into the bond's yield (Exhibit 8.15). If

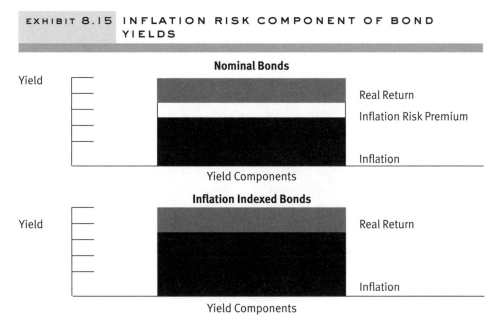

EXHIBIT 8.15 INFLATION RISK COMPONENT OF BOND YIELDS

Source: DiMeo Schneider & Associates, L.L.C.

EXHIBIT 8.16   HISTORICAL RETURN AND RISK*

Asset Class	Return	Risk
Large-cap	7.8%	17.1%
Small-cap	10.0%	21.7%
International	5.4%	16.2%
TIPS	7.7%	5.1%
Intermediate bonds	7.0%	3.7%

Correlation Matrix[†]

	Large-Cap	Small-Cap	International	TIPS	Intermediate Bonds
Large-cap	1				
Small-cap	0.83	1			
International	0.57	0.51	1		
TIPS	−0.18	−0.14	−0.16	1	
Intermediate bonds	0.25	0.15	0.16	0.75	1

*Period beginning 3/97–10/04 (risk is measured by standard deviation).
†Large-cap (Russell 1000), small-cap (Russell 2000), international equity (MSCI EAFE), TIPS (Citigroup Inflation Linked Securities), intermediate bond (Lehman Aggregate Bond).

real yields rise in the marketplace, existing TIPS will fall in price. However, *nominal* interest rates often rise because of increasing inflation or inflationary expectations. Real yields have been relatively stable. In periods of rising inflation, TIPS and other IPBs may experience little price fluctuation.

Diversification

To illustrate an after-inflation optimization using TIPS as an asset class, we used historical returns, standard deviations, and correlation coefficients for large-cap stocks, small-cap stocks, foreign stocks, nominal bonds, and TIPS from March 1997 through October 2004 (period of existence for TIPS) (Exhibit 8.16).

Exhibit 8.17 shows the comparison between an optimized portfolio using nominal bonds and a portfolio including TIPS. We've summarized a comparison in Exhibit 8.18. By using TIPS instead of nominal bonds, volatility was cut from 7.9% to 4.9%. In other words, you had significantly lower risk at the same return level.

EXHIBIT 8.17 EFFICIENT FRONTIER (1997–10/2004)

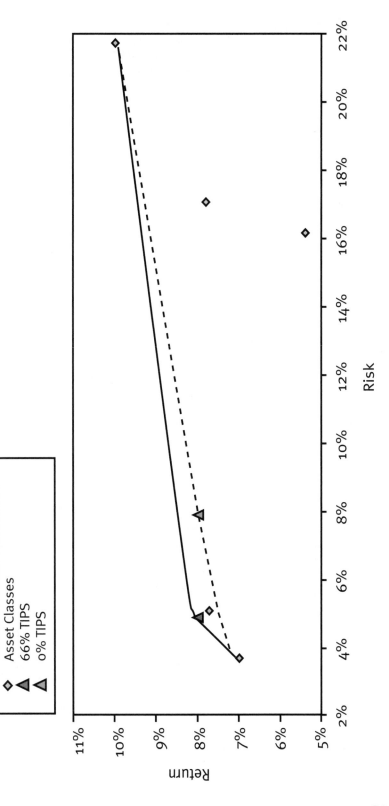

EXHIBIT 8.18 ASSET ALLOCATION ANALYSIS

Asset Allocation Table
Percentage of Portfolio

	Current Portfolio	TIPS Portfolio
Return	8%	8%
Standard deviation	7.9%	4.9%
Intermediate bonds	67%	0%
TIPS	0%	66%
Large stocks	0%	0%
Small stocks	12%	33%

RISK FACTORS

Of course, a major risk in the analysis discussed in the preceding section is that the estimates for TIPS are in error. Because these are relatively new securities, we can't rely on a wealth of historic data (currently less than 8 years). If such bonds turn out to have greater correlation to other asset classes than they exhibited during their short history, the relative advantage may be less. If *real* yields rise, TIPS will fall in price. Since their stated interest rate is low, these bonds will have great sensitivity to real interest rate changes.

CONCLUSION

Not-for-profit funds face a variety of challenges. Typically there is a spending requirement. That is an ongoing *real* liability; over time, the fund must increase nominal spending in order to stay even with inflation. In addition, most nonprofit funds tend toward a conservative investment posture. TIPS may prove to be a valuable tool to help your trustees face these challenges.

## CHAPTER 9

Investment Style

T here are two broad categories of equity style. *Growth* managers seek to identify companies with above-average earnings growth rates. *Value* managers attempt
to buy a dollar's worth of company for 50 cents. Both styles work, but they work
at different times. In other words, they go in and out of favor.

Exhibit 9.1 examines U.S. stock returns from 1989 through 2003. It is worth
noting that not only do the winning and losing styles change from year to year,
but also that the spread between them is frequently in double digits! It would be
wonderful if we could predict which style was going to be in favor over the next
year, but that type of forecasting is as hard as predicting whether the market is
going to go up or down (i.e., it's impossible). In fact, the best policy is to have a
style-neutral portfolio; that way, not only is some part of the fund always in favor,
but you have the opportunity to increase return through strategic rebalancing
(see Chapter 12).

ACADEMIC RESEARCH

William Sharpe, Stanford's Nobel Prize winner, and other researchers have found
that style is the most important determinant of return at the manager level. He
found that over 90% of a manager's return is attributable to style and less than
10% to skill or luck.[1]

In late 1996, Yale Professor Roger Ibbotson published the first research showing any predictive value whatsoever for performance numbers.[2] His research indicates that managers who rank well within a style category over one period are

---

[1] William Sharpe, "Determining a Fund's Effective Asset Mix," *Investment Management Review*
(November/December 1988), 56–59.
[2] Roger Ibbotson, *TMA Journal* (November/December 1996).

EXHIBIT 9.1   SPREAD BETWEEN MINIMUM AND MAXIMUM RETURNS BY U.S. EQUITY STYLE

	Large Growth	Large Value	Small Growth	Small Value	Hi–Lo Spread
1989	36%	25%	20%	12%	24%
1990	0%	−8%	−17%	−22%	22%
1991	41%	25%	51%	42%	26%
1992	5%	14%	8%	29%	24%
1993	3%	18%	13%	24%	21%
1994	2%	−2%	−2%	−2%	4%
1995	37%	38%	31%	26%	12%
1996	23%	22%	11%	21%	12%
1997	30%	35%	13%	32%	22%
1998	39%	16%	1%	−6%	45%
1999	33%	7%	43%	−2%	45%
2000	−22%	7%	−22%	23%	45%
2001	−20%	−6%	−9%	14%	34%
2002	−28%	−16%	−30%	−11%	19%
2003	30%	30%	49%	46%	19%

Source: DiMeo Schneider & Associates, L.L.C.

more likely to score high within that category over succeeding periods (although the entire style category may go in or out of favor with the market).

It is crucial to identify a manager's style. But how do we do that? Well, we could ask the manager, or look at his or her marketing materials. But managers don't always tell the truth. Their glossy brochure might talk about their adherence to a disciplined value approach. It might go into great detail about screening for companies that trade below their break-up value or at a discount to market multiples. However, when you examine their portfolio you discover that their largest holding is Cisco Systems. In fact, many managers exhibit some *style drift*.

So, you need to independently ascertain the manager's style. There are two basic approaches: *holdings-based* style analysis and *returns-based* style analysis. Each has its pluses and minuses.

Holdings-Based Style Analysis

Holdings-based style analysis is the traditional method. An analyst examines the securities in a manager's portfolio and sorts them by style and capitalization. For example, the analyst might categorize Intel as a large-cap growth stock and GM as a large-cap value stock. The securities are usually sorted on the basis of some metrics such as price-earnings (P/E) ratio, price-book value (P/B), or forecast earnings growth.

Although very thorough, this method has some significant drawbacks. First, it is extremely labor intensive. Every security must be categorized. And knowledgeable analysts are high-priced talent. Furthermore, because of the labor involved, it is impossible to screen a large number of managers at a single pass. Second, managers know how to "game" things. Since holdings are generally reported as of some cut-off date, like the end of a quarter, it's common for managers to change the portfolio with a large number of buys and sells on the last day. In fact, Wall Street calls such quarter-end trading activity "window dressing." Third, there's the problem of categorizing certain securities. For example, is GE a growth or value stock?

Returns-Based Style Analysis

Based on William Sharpe's research, returns-based style analysis doesn't tell you what securities a manager *holds*. It tells you how the portfolio *behaves*. The returns-based method solves many of the problems listed above.

Using quadratic analysis, the manager's quarterly or monthly returns are regressed against those of four indexes (e.g., the Russell 1000 Growth, the Russell 1000 Value, the Russell 2000 Growth, and the Russell 2000 Value indexes). One can then calculate an exact blend of the four indexes that replicates the manager's return pattern. Using the four style indexes as corners of a *style map,* it's easy to plot the manager's relative position (Exhibit 9.2).

You can also perform the analysis over rolling periods, for example, rolling 12 quarter windows. This gives you an idea of how the manager's style may have changed or *drifted* over time (Exhibit 9.3). The smaller symbols represent earlier periods; the larger symbols represent more recent performance.

One additional benefit of this approach is that instead of comparing the manager's performance to some generic benchmark like the Standard & Poor's 500 index, you can compare him to his true *style benchmark.* A manager that appears skillful when compared with the generic benchmark may turn out to underperform the more accurate style benchmark (Exhibit 9.4).

The development of returns-based style analysis was a great advance. There are now several commercial programs to perform such analyses. Although the software is expensive, it allows rapid screening of literally hundreds of managers at a time. Now style analysis can be the start of a screening process rather than occurring somewhere near the end. And you are no longer dependent on analyzing security holdings that may be out of date. (Mutual funds are only required to report holdings every six months.)

However, there are flaws with this method. Although the software is accurate

EXHIBIT 9.2 MANAGER STYLE MAP

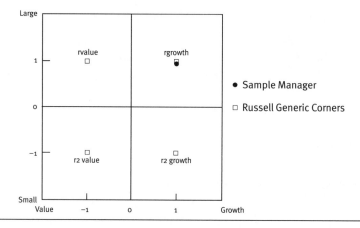

EXHIBIT 9.3 MANAGER STYLE MAP REFLECTING CHANGE

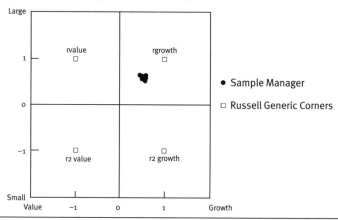

EXHIBIT 9.4   STYLE BENCHMARK

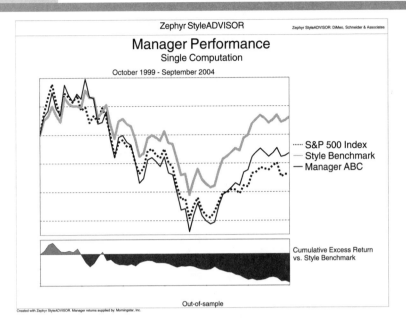

Zephyr StyleADVISOR
Zephyr StyleADVISOR: DiMeo, Schneider & Associates

Manager Performance
Single Computation
October 1999 - September 2004

····· S&P 500 Index
— Style Benchmark
— Manager ABC

Cumulative Excess Return
vs. Style Benchmark

Out-of-sample

Created with Zephyr StyleADVISOR. Manager returns supplied by: Morningstar, Inc.

the vast majority of the time, sometimes there are false readings. For example, imagine that we are in a period when value stocks are very much in favor (and growth is out of favor). If you analyze a growth manager who turns in large numbers, the software may think that the manager holds value stocks (since he or she is winning at the moment). Sometimes managers who hold a large number of utility stocks show up as having a weighting in fixed income. Like bonds, utilities are interest-rate sensitive. It is usually best to corroborate returns-based analysis with a look at the holdings.

ANCILLARY USES

The returns-based technology allows you be very specific in your manager search as well. Imagine that you have an excellent value style manager with whom you've worked for many years. If the goal is to have a style-neutral portfolio, you will need to add a growth manager. However, you need to add a manager who is an exact opposite match for your current manager. By first plotting your current manager on the style map, you can determine the exact style point that will make the portfolio style neutral. The name for this counterbalancing manager is a *completeness fund*. Exhibit 9.5 shows such an analysis.

EXHIBIT 9.5   COMPLETENESS FUND ANALYSIS

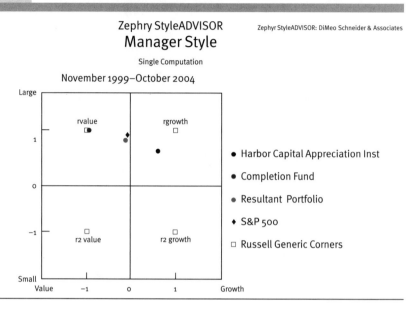

Zephry StyleADVISOR
Manager Style
Zephyr StyleADVISOR: DiMeo Schneider & Associates

Single Computation

November 1999–October 2004

- Harbor Capital Appreciation Inst
- Completion Fund
- Resultant Portfolio
- S&P 500
- Russell Generic Corners

THE CURRENT STATE

Over the past decades, institutional funds have adopted the practice of hiring style-specific managers. In fact one well-known consulting firm has staked out an "iconoclastic" position advocating indexing the bulk of a portfolio and then hiring non-style-specific managers to add alpha by pursuing whatever style is in favor. (This is a flawed premise. Who are these managers that are equally skilled in selecting small-cap growth stocks and large-cap value stocks and know exactly when to switch?)

SUMMARY

Style is the key determinant of manager performance. And only within a style category is past performance at all predictive. In the next chapter we'll examine how returns-based style analysis can help you select appropriate managers to implement your asset allocation.

## CHAPTER 10

Manager Selection

Once you have formulated an asset allocation strategy, the next step is to find appropriate investment managers to implement it. This is the second most important decision. Unfortunately, many nonprofit organizations have done a poor job of selecting managers. Despite your committee's good intentions, certain factors may overwhelm the process and lead to poor decisions. Corporate retirement plans must operate within the Employee Retirement Income Security Act (*ERISA*) and Financial Accounting Standards Board (*FASB*) rules. Fiduciaries for most nonprofit funds have greater freedom. Unfortunately, this can result in a less systematic and effective process.

Too often, money is given to a local bank or investment adviser. Sometimes these managers are simply not qualified or appropriate for the fund. This can lead to subpar results. Nonprofit boards tend to include some bright, successful, type A personalities. They often preempt the kind of procedural prudence used in corporate plans. There is a tendency to short-circuit detailed manager due diligence in favor of selecting the familiar—a bank, a retail stock broker, or a reference from a friend. The two primary reasons why you should be prudent and thorough in the selection process are:

1. It's your fiduciary responsibility. A fiduciary has an obligation to act prudently in all regards—including the selection of investment managers. Decisions should be informed and carefully executed. Fiduciaries are well-advised to generate full written documentation concerning all aspects of fund oversight. Your investment decisions are more defensible if you document the decision process. See Chapter 18 for more details.

2. Enormous sums of money are at stake. With billions of dollars in nonprofit assets, generating incremental return is extremely important. Exhibit 10.1 illustrates the impact of an additional 1% annual return.

EXHIBIT 10.1   IMPACT OF ADDITIONAL ANNUAL RETURN

$10 Million Initial Investment Value

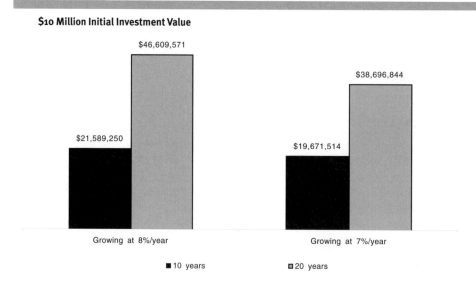

OVERVIEW

Manager selection is not easy. First, there are thousands of available money managers (and more daily). Second, there are no easy measures to identify investment managers who will perform well in the future. The required disclaimer "past performance is no guarantee of future results" is actually true. Finally, Wall Street has not helped investors to understand financial markets. In fact, most financial "information" is actually misinformation, "factoids" that are either untrue or irrelevant. Predictions about future market movements fall into the first category. If the seer could actually forecast market directions, he or she would not be working for a salary.

HERD MENTALITY

For eons mothers have chided their peer-pressured adolescents with "would you jump off the bridge because your friends did?" Adults are also subject to the herd mentality. Humans are not always logical. We have emotions and the ability to rationalize based on incomplete information. Many investors become fixated on the money managers with the best absolute performance records. Unfortunately, most investors focus on recent performance with no regard for risk. Why is this flawed? Styles of investing come in and out of favor, and often the manager with the best recent performance is hired merely because its style was in favor. All too often managers are hired just as the pendulum swings away from that particular style.

Investors seek the easy answer. They rely on the "top picks" from various non-professional publications. For example, a trustee may demand the inclusion of a fund that was ranked among the "10 best funds for next year" by a favorite business periodical. This trustee doesn't understand that such recommendations are generic, usually given by journalism majors, and don't address the nonprofit organization's specific policies in any way. Furthermore, magazines have no accountability. If today's recommended manager flops, so be it. Next year there will be a new list. Readers never seem to ask why there are so few repeats. Unfortunately, most mass-market publications ignore the prime determinant of a manager's performance: *style.* See Chapter 9 for additional details.

AVOIDING THE STAR SYSTEM

Morningstar, Inc. is a well-respected provider of financial information. They produce extensive financial analysis of mutual funds. This analysis includes *risk, return, style, expenses,* and *portfolio data.* They also rank funds according to their highly recognized star system. Ratings incorporate return and risk measures, and funds receive from one to five stars, with five being the best.

Mutual fund marketers love the stars. They splash a fund's Morningstar star rating across full-page ads. As we said, many investors seek an easy solution. They don't understand what is behind the star rating. This can lead to poor investment decisions.

What is the star system? The *Morningstar rating* (the star system) for funds is a measure of a fund's risk-adjusted return, relative to its peers. The funds are scored over three time periods: 3, 5, and 10 years, and these ratings are combined to produce an overall rating. Funds are graded on the curve. Ratings range from one to five stars. The top 10% of the funds in each category receive the highest rating of five stars. The next 22.5% receive four stars, the next 35% receive three stars, the next 22.5% receive two stars, and the final 10% receive one star. To its credit, Morningstar regularly cautions readers that the star ratings are a tool for identifying funds for further research, but shouldn't be considered buy or sell recommendations.

But shouldn't a five star–rated fund be superior? First, the star rating relies entirely on past performance, which academic research shows to be a poor predictor of future results. The star ratings will likely result in the choice of a fund with strong recent performance since all the above periods include the most recent one year.

Second, the system relies on the ability of Morningstar to accurately categorize the funds. Until June 2002, Morningstar lumped all stock funds into two groups: domestic equity and international equity. This meant that large-cap growth funds were ranked alongside small-cap value funds, and international equity funds were ranked against emerging markets funds. In response to significant criticism, Morningstar changed its methodology. Now categories are based on the underlying holdings of each fund. Morningstar places funds in a given category based on portfolio statistics and composition over the past three years. However, misclassification can still be a problem.

Frequently the fund's holdings are stale (currently mutual funds are required to report complete holdings only twice a year), and funds do not always stick to their stated investment styles. For example, small-cap funds often migrate into the mid-cap category. This reduces the reliability of a fund's history. Morningstar also has difficulty classifying sector funds. Although they have a separate category for sector funds, because the classification uses holdings, sector funds can find their way into other categories. For example, as of this writing, Fidelity Select Automotive is classified as a mid-cap value fund.

We are not knocking Morningstar. They provide a great deal of useful information that can help investors. However, no rating system can replace the considerable amount of research and due diligence one should perform, especially when the organization's decision makers are held to fiduciary standards.

WHERE TO BEGIN

Assume that your nonprofit fund has already developed an appropriate asset allocation strategy. This allocation was well thought out and takes into account the risk tolerance and spending policy. You selected multiple asset classes. The committee decided to retain the current large-cap value manager. Therefore, to maintain a style-neutral posture, the fund needs to add a large-cap growth manager.

The following example shows a mutual fund search; however, you would follow virtually identical steps when conducting a separate account manager search.

Top on the to-do list is to seek input from the committee members and other key decision makers. Trustees are usually well connected and have some level of investment experience. It's best to solicit this input up front to keep the process flowing. Otherwise, you run the risk that spurious managers will be inserted late in the process, delaying a decision. Exhibit 10.2 is an example of a form to gather such input.

Let's define *money managers*. It may be helpful to say what professional money management is *not*. Stock brokers, consultants, and financial planners are not considered professional money managers.

A broker is a salesperson who recommends investments for a commission. Large brokerage firms understand the negative connotation of "stock broker," so

EXHIBIT 10.2 COMMITTEE MEMBER QUESTIONNAIRE

I. **Investment Categories.**   Research will be performed to produce appropriate candidates for each investment category with a check mark.

_____ Money market funds   _____ Large company U.S. stocks
_____ Emerging market stocks   _____ Small company U.S. stocks
_____ Bonds (investment grade)   _____ International funds (foreign only)
_____ TIPS bonds   _____ Real estate funds
_____ High-yield bonds

Please indicate any additional investment categories which you strongly feel should receive consideration:

_____

_____

II. **General Screens.**   Dozens of screens will be used in each category. The following applies to most searches:
- Portfolio manager tenure of at least three years
- Below average fund expenses
- Adequate infrastructure
- Organization's depth and resources
- Administrative compatibility
- Reasonable growth in asset base
- Well-defined investment process
- Consistency of style
- Appropriate average market capitalization
- Risk-adjusted return
- Absolute return
- Returns in up markets
- Returns in down markets
- Information ratio
- Sharpe ratio
- Alpha
- Tracking error

Please provide any specific criteria you would like incorporated into the screening process:

_____

_____

III. **Specific Funds/Investment Organizations.**   Please indicate specific funds or organizations which you strongly feel should receive consideration. (Please provide as much detail as possible.)

_____

_____

Completed by:

_____

_____

they now call their registered representatives "financial counselors" or "financial advisers." However, their job description remains the same.

Most of the large firms have also created managed money products. These are often called *wrap fee products* because the money manager's fee, the trading costs, and the broker's commission are "wrapped" into one fee. Such programs typically involve a certain measure of manager due diligence on the part of the brokerage firm and are certainly an improvement over the traditional transaction-oriented mind-set of most brokers. Critics of such programs point out that often clients only have a handful of managers from which to choose. There may be only 40 or 50 in the entire program. The due diligence has also come in for criticism. In deciding which managers to include in their programs, the brokerage firms weigh two variables most highly:

1. Which managers will cut their fees significantly in order to be in the program?

2. Which managers will create a large marketing staff to support individual brokers in their sales efforts?

Critics also point out that the individual brokers who are the actual point of delivery to the client exhibit widely varying levels of knowledge. Some understand and espouse the diversification principles outlined in this book. Unfortunately, many sell the product as if it were another mutual fund. That is, they recommend the managers with the best recent performance—usually those whose styles have been in favor.

The brother in-law who works for a consulting firm is not an investment manager either. A consultant should be an expert in the design, implementation, and oversight of investment strategies for nonprofit organizations. Consultants do not buy and sell individual securities for a client's account. Instead, they assist in the selection and ongoing monitoring of managers.

Professional investment managers are, first of all, investment advisers registered with the Securities and Exchange Commission (SEC). They are paid a fee for one thing, and one thing only: to select securities for purchase and sale on a discretionary basis. They are not paid commissions. They should have a Federal form ADV and a track record of performance results that is *AIMR-PPS* compliant, preferably audited by a third party.

MANAGER SELECTION

Effective manager selection can be broken into 4 steps:

1. Quantitative screens

2. Minimum criteria

3. Qualitative analysis

4. The interview

The first three steps of the process are designed to produce a manageable number of candidates for face-to-face due diligence. The final step is geared toward the actual selection of managers for inclusion in the portfolio. Unfortunately, no single proven objective test can identify managers who will perform well in the future. Past performance alone is a poor predictor of future results. Although quantitative data such as risk measures, style, and other portfolio statistics are important, qualitative factors are even more important. These include the firm's decision-making process, and the experience and breadth of the firm's personnel.

One should begin with as broad a universe of potential candidates as possible. As of this writing, Morningstar identified 1,370 large-cap growth mutual funds. Obviously, this number is too large for the investment committee to consider. The screens shown in Exhibit 10.3 help narrow the field.

Step 1. Quantitative Screens

Armed with a list of criteria, you can begin to narrow the list of candidates to a more manageable number. A convenient way to begin is to use a computerized database screen. Computers are great tools—they just can't make the truly crucial decisions. Quantitative screens provide a rear-mirror view of past success or failure. The model only shows results, not how they were achieved. A manager that ranks number one may have taken considerable risk to achieve that ranking. Quantitative screens are useful when used in conjunction with other crucial analysis, particularly investment style.

Style screening is the first pass. Style can be analyzed using a returns-based regression methodology. There are several commercially available pieces of software that use William Sharpe's quadratic algorithm to analyze a manager's return relative to pure style indices. This analysis precisely identifies the manager's position on a style map (see Chapter 9). You should pay particular attention to style drift because this is a key measure of management's adherence to the stated investment process. *Returns-based analysis,* as this type of analysis is called, may be complemented by *holdings-based analysis.* Returns-based analysis tells how the manager behaved; holdings-based analysis looks at the actual positions he or she held. The holdings at various points in time reveal the portfolio's fundamental characteristics and sector exposure relative to the benchmark. Although using both methods paints the most accurate picture, a returns-based analysis is easier and cheaper. The data (historical returns) are readily available for analysis.

Garbage in equals garbage out. Data can be manipulated to produce the de-

EXHIBIT 10.3   POTENTIAL CANDIDATE ANALYSIS

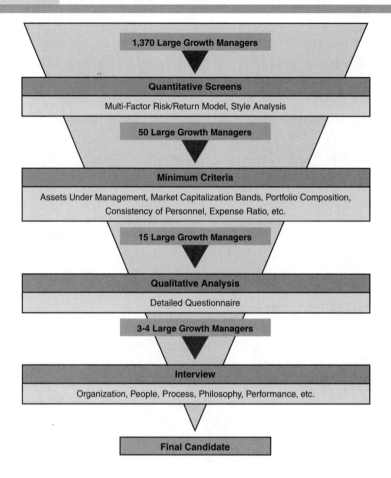

1,370 Large Growth Managers

Quantitative Screens

Multi-Factor Risk/Return Model, Style Analysis

50 Large Growth Managers

Minimum Criteria

Assets Under Management, Market Capitalization Bands, Portfolio Composition, Consistency of Personnel, Expense Ratio, etc.

15 Large Growth Managers

Qualitative Analysis

Detailed Questionnaire

3-4 Large Growth Managers

Interview

Organization, People, Process, Philosophy, Performance, etc.

Final Candidate

sired results. You need to think carefully about the risk/return profile of the desired manager and adjust the screens' weighting accordingly. In other words, if protection during down markets is foremost, a higher weight should be given to that criterion. Be certain that "independent" variables are not proxies for one another. For example, a high *Sharpe ratio* (see Glossary) often correlates highly with strong historical returns. Therefore, you should not overweight both these factors. Exhibit 10.4 is an example of a multifactor risk/return model that can be used as a first pass to identify attractive managers.

Step 2. Minimum Criteria

In the next step you should analyze the surviving managers from a qualitative perspective. Past performance is just that. The key is future performance, which

EXHIBIT 10.4 MULTIFACTOR RISK/RETURN MODEL

	5-Year Annualized Returns	5-Year Standard Deviation	5-Year Sharpe Ratio	5-Year Annualized Alpha	5-Year Information Ratio	5-Year Up Market Capture Ratio	5-Year Down Market Capture Ratio
Weighting	10%	10%	10%	20%	30%	10%	10%

can only be *estimated* through qualitative judgments. Exhibit 10.5 is an example of minimum screening criteria for a large growth mandate. The following are explanations of the *minimum* set of qualitative standards that managers should meet:

- *Assets Under Management.* The size of the product is very important. We consider the minimum acceptable size of a product to be $50 million. The primary risk to a product with fewer assets is viability. A small fund can quickly disappear if it does not attract enough assets to become profitable. Larger asset bases can allow expenses to be dispersed over a wider base. However, too large of an asset base can hinder a manager's ability to effectively maneuver among the markets. This is especially true for small-cap products. There is some evidence that alpha, or value-added, tends to vanish

EXHIBIT 10.5 LARGE COMPANY GROWTH SEARCH

The Screening Process

- Assets of greater than or equal to $50 million
- Median market capitalization of $10 billion or greater
- Foreign stock of less than 15%
- Cash holdings of less than 15%
- Bond holdings of less than 5%
- Manager tenure greater than or equal to three years
- Fund inception date of three years (preferably earlier but will consider funds with shorter history under special circumstances)
- Expense ratio less than equal to or less than peers

Intermediate Fixed-Income Search: The Screening Process

- Assets of greater than or equal to $50 million
- Average credit quality of at least A
- Average maturity between four and twelve years
- Average duration between three and six years
- Cash holdings of less than 20%
- Foreign holdings of less than 10%
- Manager tenure greater than or equal to three years
- Fund inception date of three years (preferably earlier but will consider funds with shorter history under special circumstances)
- Expense ratio less than or equal to peers

as a small-cap product's assets climb above $1.5 billion. Make sure that you aggregate all share classes and separate accounts when reviewing asset balances.

- *Market Capitalization* of a stock is the number of shares outstanding times the company's share price. The market capitalization of a portfolio is usually described as its median market cap (the capitalization of the middle stock in a portfolio arranged from lowest to highest). Definitions change over time; however, generally accepted guidelines are:
  - Large-cap stocks—$10 billion and above
  - Mid-cap stocks—$1.5 to $10 billion
  - Small-cap stocks—$1.5 billion and below

- *Portfolio Composition.* Review the portfolio's allocation to equity, fixed-income cash, and other asset classes. The cash component of an equity portfolio should be less than 10%. After all, you do not pay large fees to manage cash. Also, for domestic equity products, foreign exposure should be minimal (under 15%). Fixed-income portfolios may hold preferred stocks, convertibles, and other nontraditional bonds. Occasionally these securities are used as a tactical play but should not be the majority of assets, unless allowed in the investment policy. In fixed-income portfolios, the use of cash may actually be strategic. The manager may use cash to shorten portfolio duration or create a barbell structure—legitimate uses.

- *Consistency of Personnel.* Look for a stable organization with minimal turnover among investment professionals. A manager should be in place for *at least* three years, preferably five years. Otherwise the track record is meaningless.

- *Expense Ratio.* Expenses eat into total return. The higher the expense ratio, the less return on the investment. For example, a manager who charges an annual fee of 1.0% and has an additional 1.0% in trading costs needs to add 2% per year of value just to break even. A good rule of thumb is to exclude managers with expense ratios above the group average.

- *Fixed Income* investors face several types of risk.
  - *Interest Rate Risk.* As interest rates rise, bond prices fall. A bond's coupon and maturity are wrapped together in a single measure called *duration*. Duration is the measure of the sensitivity of a bond's price to changes in interest rates. Longer-duration bonds are more sensitive to changes in interest rates than shorter ones. For example, a bond with a duration of 2.0 will increase/decrease in price approximately 2% for a 100 *basis point* (1.0%) fall/rise in interest rates. Duration is often expressed in years. In the aforementioned example, the bond's duration is two years.

- *Credit Spread and Downgrade Risk.* An unanticipated downgrading of an issuer increases the *credit spread* on yields above treasuries. This results in a decline in price.
- *Default Risk* is the risk that the bond issuer will be unable to repay the loan. Standard & Poor's, Moody's Investors Service, and Fitch are the major credit rating agencies that evaluate the creditworthiness of various issuers.
- *Convexity* is a measure of the curvature of the price/yield relationship. Positive convexity indicates prices rise at an increasing rate as yields fall, and decline at a decreasing rate as yields rise. The opposite is true for negative convexity. Most bonds exhibit positive convexity. However, certain bonds with *embedded optionality* show negative convexity. For example, mortgage-backed bonds have negative convexity. Mortgage holders have the *option* of prepaying their mortgages. If interest rates rise, they generally stop prepaying, giving the bond a longer effective maturity (exactly what the bond holder does *not* want in a rising rate environment).

Step 3. Qualitative Analysis

Steps 1 and 2 should result in a manageable list of managers who screen well on a risk/return basis and meet the minimum requirements. The next step requires additional fundamental research on the remaining candidates. This analysis helps determine if all the factors that contributed to the past performance are still in place. You need to contact the management firms to solicit their responses to specific questions.

In this step you focus on issues such as the stability of an organization and the investment team, consistency of the investment strategy, compliance, operations, and compensation structure. An example of a detailed questionnaire to be completed by an equity manager can be found in Appendix B. Make sure that you review a copy of the firm's most recently filed Form ADV Parts I and II.

As part of the qualitative analysis, pay particular attention to the following:

- *Organization.* Consider the history and stability of the organization. Review its ownership structure, tenure of personnel, and goals for growth of assets. Can the firm grow substantially without corrupting the investment process? Has the firm been subject to any litigation or censured by a regulatory body? What compliance systems are in place?
- *People.* How many members are on the investment team and what is their tenure? Review their credentials to determine investment acumen. Are they knowledgeable in their strategy? How are they compensated? Does the

compensation package include incentive bonuses? Are they performance based or asset based? How much personal money is invested in their product? What is the succession plan if a key member of the team departs?

- *Investment Philosophy, Process, and Portfolio Construction.* Does the product have a well-defined investment process? Is management able to clearly articulate the buy and sell process? Is this process driven by an individual or an investment committee? Do the managers and the analysts articulate a consistent message? What are the normal minimum and maximum percentages of a total portfolio that would be invested in any one sector, industry, or stock (both absolute and relative to a benchmark)? Can management override these guidelines? Are checks and balances in place to ensure that the investment process is implemented uniformly across all accounts?

- *Performance.* During this phase of the process it is important to take a detailed look at the product's performance. This step only adds value in the context of a thorough understanding of the investment process. Chapter 13 provides greater detail on analyzing a manager's returns. In general, you want to see consistency of performance over rolling time periods. A positive ratio of quarters in which the manager outperforms to the quarters in which it underperforms is good. Examine performance over various market cycles, including up and down markets. How does a manager perform when its style is in favor compared to when it is out of favor? Don't forget risk. Modern Portfolio Theory statistics such as *alpha, Sharpe ratio, information ratio,* and *tracking error* measure how much performance is generated per unit of risk (see Glossary). To get the most complete picture, compare the manager's performance to both an index and peer group.

Step 4. The Interview

This is the crucial step. The goal should be to make the final manager selection. The earlier steps exist only to narrow the list of qualified managers. At this point, it's time to use the discrimination skills that humans have developed over millennia. You can discriminate between a good ballerina and a poor one, between a good basketball player and a poor one, between a good author and a hack. Human brains don't turn off just because they're evaluating money managers. Proper homework minimizes mistakes. Look beyond slick marketing materials and recent performance; assess the investment process. If your committee understands and appreciates the investment procedures and people, it is capable of making an informed decision.

It is easy to arrange the interviews for a private manager search. If the resources are available, make an on-site visit to the manager's office. You can glean a lot of valuable information just by seeing their place of business. However, a presentation in the nonprofit organization's office will work as well. Provided that your fund meets the minimum account size, a manager will be glad to attend the presentation. It's more difficult to get mutual fund managers to come in. However, you should be able to arrange a conference call with the portfolio manager or another member of the investment team. Presentations by a marketing person are the least helpful. If you can't arrange a conference call, they are telling you that they don't want your business.

Trustees for not-for-profit funds are generally very busy individuals. To optimize their time, limit the number of manager candidates to three or four. Also, prior to the presentations, give the trustees reference data in an easy-to-follow format. An example of such a comparative format can be found in Appendix C.

Arrange the candidates to present back to back. Provide strict time limits and adhere to them. For example, you may tell managers to limit their presentation to 30 minutes and plan for an additional 15 minutes of Q&A. Be sensitive to the time commitment. Don't be afraid to tell the presenter, "You've got about 5 minutes left, do you have any final comments?"

Although the marketer may put a slick spin on the presentation, the actual portfolio decision maker will provide the most useful insight. Be consistent—ask all the candidates the same questions. Take notes so that you can compare managers question by question. A sample interview questionnaire is located in Appendix E.

PASSIVE VERSUS ACTIVE MANAGEMENT

The previous steps make sense when selecting active managers. Passive management is an investment approach that seeks to merely replicate the performance of a specified index. This is the least expensive approach and is often used for asset classes that are *efficient*. Highly liquid, well-researched market segments like large-cap domestic stocks are deemed to be efficient. It is difficult for a large-cap core manager to know something about a stock that is not already widely understood and factored into the price. Academic research indicates that in such segments most active managers underperform the benchmark. Therefore, why not settle for the performance of the index and enjoy much lower fees?

On the flip side, the markets for small company stocks and foreign stocks are less efficient. Informational value can be added by money managers who are able to exploit the inefficiencies of these markets. Foreign equity managers have multiple opportunities to add value by making the right call on country, currency, or regional economies as well as through individual security research.

Everything goes in cycles. During certain environments, it is difficult for active managers to beat the indexes, while at other times they fare best. Trustees may want to hedge against these cycles by using both passive and active managers in your fund. For example, you might want to index the allocation to large-company core and use active managers for large-company value and growth. Remember, index funds capture the full return of the market but also the full risk. If the goal is to preserve capital in down markets, consider active managers who have a consistent history of performing well in down markets.

DATABASES

There are several databases and computer programs that provide the necessary information to begin a manager search. See Appendix G for a list of resources for this information.

A mutual fund is one large pool of assets with numerous investors. Its performance is reported according to strict guidelines. It's easy to obtain and verify fund results with various data vendors. Separate account managers' performance results are more suspect. The managers provide monthly and quarterly results to the databases. When firms present performance, they use *composite* figures. A composite is a mathematical calculation of the combined performance of a group of several accounts that the firm manages. The performance presented is a synthetic number.

This is an appropriate format for a manager to present performance. However, fiduciaries should not take these returns at face value. It is important to have a good feel for the data and understand how the composite was constructed. Following are some helpful questions to ask the manager:

- Are the returns compliant with the standards of the AIMR-PPS? Is this verified by a third-party source?
- How many accounts are in the composite?
- Which accounts are included in the composite?
- Which are excluded?
- Do the returns represent any simulated results?
- Are accounts size weighted or equally weighted?
- Are returns gross or net-of-fees?

Appendix D is an example of a comprehensive report on a separate account manager provided by eVestmentAlliance (www.evestmentalliance.com). The eASE Database is an excellent source for investment manager information. Many consulting firms use this database as a tool for identifying, sourcing, and monitoring managers.

ADMINISTRATIVE COMPATIBILITY

It is important to consider managers or mutual funds that are easily accessed. Make certain that the products are still available for new investors and that your nonprofit fund meets their minimum size requirements. Also, some mutual funds or commingled trusts can only be purchased by retirement plans. Although the major mutual fund families are readily available on most trading platforms, be sure to confirm that a selling agreement is established with the organization's custodian so they can execute your trades. If one is not established, work with the fund family and the custodian to put one in place.

TRADE EXECUTION

You need to understand separate account managers' policies on trading. Review trading costs and pay particular attention to both commissions and trade executions. Commissions on stock transactions are fairly easy to determine. They are usually expressed as a "cents-per-share" rate. An appropriate range is 1.5 to 5 cents per share, depending on the size of the trade. It's a bit more difficult to evaluate commissions charged on a bond transaction. Most bond trades are *principal transactions*; that is, the broker/dealer buys or sells the bond to you from its own inventory rather than acting as an agent. In such cases, the purchase or sale is usually quoted as a net price. Ask the investment manager to describe its approach to trading bonds. Most get quotes from two or three brokers and strive for a competitive price.

Although commissions are important, trade executions can have an even greater impact on performance. How well does the manager buy that new stock added to the portfolio? Does the manager take it on the chin when selling a security? Poor execution on stock transactions can have a hidden cost of one eighth or one fourth per share ($12^1/2$ or 25 cents), which comes straight out of performance. Fortunately, most managers seek good execution because poor execution hurts their performance. And ultimately, they must live or die by their performance.

SOCIAL INVESTING

Some nonprofit organizations have policies that restrict the types of companies in which they may invest (e.g., no gambling or tobacco stocks). If the fund imposes restrictions, be sure to incorporate them into your screening process.

Traditionally, social investing meant that the trustees identified restricted industries and found managers who would avoid purchases in those industries. Today, many managers offer a more proactive approach using various strategies.

They can actively screen for socially responsible companies for inclusion in a portfolio. See Chapter 14 for more information.

THE COMMONFUND

Plenty of investment firms want to manage your assets. However, many don't understand the specific needs of nonprofit institutions. One that does is the *Commonfund*.

In the late 1960s, college endowments struggled to earn enough to match the rate of growth in operating budgets. Historically, they had managed funds internally. Their goals were income and capital preservation—not to maximize *total return*. In 1969 the Ford Foundation published a study, *The Law and the Lore of Endowment Funds*. It challenged the long-held belief that endowment trustees faced restrictive legal constraints in managing their funds. A second Ford Foundation study, *Managing Educational Endowments*, attacked the income-oriented investment approach used by most institutions. It emphasized the need to achieve better returns over the long term. Together, the studies sparked a new way of thinking for trustees and brought their investment process into the modern age.

The Ford Foundation granted $2.8 million to establish *The Common Fund for Nonprofit Organizations* (Commonfund) in 1969. The Commonfund was officially founded in 1971. A total of 63 endowments invested $72 million on the first day of operations.

Eligible Commonfund clients include educational institutions, foundations, health-care organizations, and other mission-based and public benefit nonprofit organizations and their pension plans. Certain investment vehicles, known as the Educational Endowment Funds, are open to qualifying educational institutions only.

Commonfund uses a "manager of managers" approach. The objective is to hire high-quality managers with diversified and complementary investment approaches. Multiple managers are combined in a single fund. Multimanager funds are offered in each asset class. For example, *Commonfund International* allocates its dollars among several international investment firms, each specializing in *growth, value, large-cap,* or *small-cap* international stocks. Through this approach, Commonfund seeks consistent results, enhanced returns, and low volatility. The Commonfund process includes rigorous market analysis, in-depth manager research, active portfolio construction, and disciplined portfolio monitoring.

The Commonfund offers several benefits. It provides access to well-regarded managers at reasonable cost. Nonprofit organizations that lack the internal resources to research and monitor individual managers may benefit from

Commonfund's investment process. Commonfund portfolios also include asset classes or strategies that small to mid-sized organizations can't access. For example, *Commonfund Multi-Strategy Bond* allocates a portion of assets to private debt. A small college endowment would have trouble meeting the minimums for most private debt managers. Clients also benefit from Commonfund's continuing research and education.

The Commonfund approach does have some drawbacks. The Commonfund organization is, in essence, a money management shop. Although Commonfund employs nonproprietary managers and is willing to give advice, it is not a substitute for an independent consultant. Additionally, not all nonprofit organizations are eligible to invest in Commonfund or all of its investment offerings. As is the case with any investment firm, some of Commonfund's offerings are better than others. Any money manager, including Commonfund, should be thoroughly analyzed and evaluated prior to selection. Although Commonfund does a lot of work selecting underlying managers, ultimately your investment results will be determined by the total portfolio. It's critical to examine qualitative characteristics and quantitative performance prior to investing.

PROXY VOTING

Corporations regularly ask their shareholders to vote on a variety of issues affecting the company. One can vote in person at an annual meeting, or the shareholder can appoint a *proxy* to vote in his or her place. Most investors appoint a proxy. Trustees often delegate the responsibility of voting proxies to investment managers. If you choose this route, be sure the managers acknowledge their responsibility in writing. Carefully review their voting procedures, which should include documentation of their actions. ERISA plans are required to document proxy voting procedures, and it's a good idea for nonprofit organizations as well.

ACCOUNT TYPES

In today's environment, you can choose from among several investment vehicles. Factors that influence your decision include the type and size of the fund, the size of the initial investment, and your liquidity requirements. Below is a list of different vehicles available today:

- *Mutual Funds* are registered investment products. They are open-end funds operated by an investment company. The company raises money from shareholders and invests in a portfolio of stocks or bonds. Mutual funds offer diversification, professional management, and daily liquidity. Federal regulations and SEC reporting requirements add a layer of cost and complexity to this vehicle, partially offsetting the cost efficiencies gained by pooling funds.

- *Separate Accounts* are individually managed accounts for high-net-worth persons or institutions. They act in many ways like a private mutual fund, holding a portfolio of individual stocks or bonds. These accounts are each specific to one individual or holder. They are designed for long-term investors, as are mutual funds, but may not offer the same liquidity as mutual funds where shares can be sold and settled in one day. Separate accounts are not subject to the same reporting rules as mutual funds and have greater flexibility for taxable investors.

- *Commingled Funds* are unregistered investment products that combine some of the benefits of mutual funds with the cost efficiencies of separate accounts. Similar to a mutual fund, investors in a commingled trust pool their assets with other investors, and the holdings are "unitized" into individual shares. They lack the overhead of mutual funds, which keeps costs down. They are designed for long-term investors, and liquidity provisions vary per product.

NEGOTIATE FEES

Mutual funds are closely regulated, and fees are specified in the prospectus. Retail mutual fund shares often have a relatively high price tag. After all, funds provide a wide range of services to shareholders, including such add-ons as toll-free phone numbers and printed educational materials. These all add to the total cost of the fund. However, if the initial investment is large, you should seek cost advantages as an institutional investor. Certain funds are available only to institutional investors through either an institutional share class or via a commingled trust. Such funds are generally managed by the same portfolio managers as their retail counterparts but have higher minimum investment requirements and significantly lower expenses. If you must use retail shares of mutual funds, avoid paying any front-end load or back-end loads. By prospectus, virtually all mutual funds allow such fees to be waived for institutional investors.

It is generally easier to negotiate fees with private managers. One should approach the management of the not-for-profit fund as if it were a business. This means maximizing top line growth (investment returns) while minimizing costs (investment expenses) in an effort to enhance the bottom line earnings (net return). Carefully scrutinize the fees proposed by the investment manager. Determine whether fees being proposed are in line with fees charged by other comparable managers. If your committee has done its homework and can demonstrate to an investment manager that the fees are out of line with what the fund would pay elsewhere, you should be able to negotiate the fees downward. Often, costs can be dramatically reduced through effective negotiation and economies of scale.

Fees can be assessed on a fixed or performance basis (or a combination of both). Fixed fees are much simpler to monitor. Performance-based fees provide additional incentive for results. Performance-based fees can sometimes act as a double-edged sword by tempting the manager to expose the fund to additional risk in order to obtain higher returns. Furthermore, in periods of down markets, the fund can experience a loss but still pay the incentive fee if the manager loses less than the market.

When it comes to fees, you can seek a "most favored nation" clause in the contract. That is, the manager acknowledges, in writing, that your organization's fees will be at least as low as those of any similar clients of the manager. Also inquire if special fee discounts apply to nonprofit organizations; it never hurts to ask.

## CHAPTER 11

Alternative Investments

Over the past two decades, not-for-profit organizations have shown an increasing interest in alternative investments. These are investments beyond the plain vanilla world of stocks, bonds, and cash instruments. They include absolute return strategies (hedge funds), real estate, timberland, private equity, structured products, and commodity funds. Why the interest? First of all, several of the most prominent universities have used alternative investments for years, with very strong results. Harvard, Yale, the University of Chicago, Notre Dame University, and others allocate 30% to 50% of their endowments to alternative investments. So there is a bit of a "follow the leader" mentality.

The bear market of 2000–2002 was also a trigger. Lower return expectations for both stocks and bonds have forced most nonprofit organizations to at least consider alternative investments. Alternative managers tend to find niches where their skills can capitalize on market inefficiencies.

In theory, these investments can enhance the risk-adjusted return of a portfolio. Most alternative investments exhibit low correlation with stocks and bonds. Their addition to a traditional asset allocation pushes the efficient frontier upward, creating higher expected returns at each risk level.

However, there are a number of reasons to approach alternatives with some measure of caution:

- Most of these investments are illiquid.

- Fees tend to be high.

- There is often a limited ability to price the investments on an ongoing basis.

- There is limited transparency into the underlying strategies and positions.

- Short track records and survivorship bias make manager selection challenging, and manager selection is very important in the alternative space. The spread between top quartile and bottom quartile alternative managers is much larger than among traditional stock and bond managers.

- The explosion in popularity of alternative investments, particularly of hedge funds, may be the kiss of death. Normally, it is not a good sign when Wall Street brokerage firms begin to tout a particular strategy.

- For most of these strategies there is no passive index, which makes modeling almost impossible. Attempting to shoehorn alternatives into a mean variance optimization creates output that is highly suspect. (A more prudent approach is to come to agreement on the percentage of portfolio to be allocated, say 5%–20%, as a "carve-out.")

Following is a brief overview of the various alternative investment types.

HEDGE FUNDS (ABSOLUTE RETURN STRATEGIES)

There are no definitions of exactly what constitutes a hedge fund. However, there are certain common characteristics: They are usually private investment pools that fall outside of the rules of the Investment Company Act. As such, they are limited to a small group of *accredited investors,* institutions with at least $5 million in liquid assets. 3(c)1 funds are limited to no more than 99 accredited investors. 3(c)7 funds are limited to 499 *qualified purchasers,* institutions that have a minimum of $25 million in investment assets. The hedge fund managers have broad discretion to buy securities, sell securities short, employ leverage, and buy and sell options and other types of derivatives.

Hedge funds are also called *absolute return strategies* because their goal is to produce positive return regardless of market direction. Although hedge funds have been around since the late 1940s, their popularity has exploded in recent years. Over the past decade, assets have grown eightfold. By 2003, there were more hedge funds than the number of stocks on the New York Stock Exchange. Over 6,300 hedge funds manage over $800 billion.

Hedge funds usually target an absolute return objective such as "Treasury bills plus 800 basis points" (a basis point is 1/100 of 1%). Hedge funds use a wide variety of strategies. Many seek to exploit valuation disparities across several markets (Exhibit 11.1). Some strategies are *directional* (net long or short). A *multistrategy fund* may use a combination of several of these strategies to maintain a more market-neutral stance.

EXHIBIT 11.1   TYPES OF HEDGE FUND STRATEGIES

Strategies	Description
Nondirectional strategies (market neutral)	
Convertible arbitrage	Typically involves being long a convertible bond and short the underlying stock. The goal is to exploit the inefficiency in pricing by profiting on the long position and protecting downside with the short.
Equity market neutral	Involves being long and short matched positions. An example might be long GM, short Ford. Net equity exposure and market beta are designed to be very low. This relies on the manager's ability to pick stocks. The goal is that longs go up and shorts go down.
Event driven	Attempts to capture mispricing of corporate events such as mergers, reorganizations, and takeovers. Merger arbitrage involves going short the acquirer and long the acquiree. The risk is that the event does not materialize.
Fixed-income arbitrage	Arbitrage between interest rate securities through several techniques. The goal is steady, lower volatility returns. The risk is that high leverage used to exploit the small inefficiencies can amplify losses if spreads between cheap and expensive continue to widen.
Distressed securities	Investment in a company in financial distress or bankruptcy, with the goal of the company returning to financial health.
Directional strategies	
Long/short	Different from market neutral. Manager may be net long or short, and shift between style, market capitalization, sector, or country.
Global macro	Managers carry long and short positions in world capital markets, including stocks, bonds, currencies, commodities, and derivatives. These positions reflect news on overall market and/or economic trends.
Futures trading	Typically use technical analysis in the trading of commodities and futures.
Short bias	A profitable strategy during the 2000–2002 period. The manager maintains a net short position in equities and derivatives.

FUNDS OF FUNDS

Extremely large nonprofit funds may use several single-strategy managers. However, if you do not have at least $50 million to allocate to hedge funds, you will probably work with multistrategy managers. There are single managers that use a multistrategy approach. But more commonly you will need to invest through a *hedge fund of funds* (Hfof). There are a number of private partnerships that invest in portfolios of hedge funds. The managers research, select, and monitor the underlying hedge funds. The benefits of Hfofs include diversification, professional management, and access to funds that may have a very large minimum. The Hfof can provide an easy way to "stick your toe in the water."

Hfofs are clearly the fastest growing areas of alternatives. However, they have drawbacks as well. Of course, the managers charge for their professional oversight. This represents an added layer of fees; the Hfof manager may charge a management fee of up to 1.5% and may take a percentage of profits as well. These fees are on top of the underlying hedge fund managers' fees, which are also usually 1% to 1.5% plus a percentage of the profits (Exhibit 11.2). See Appendix G for a listing of sources of information on Hfofs.

RISKS

Risks that apply to other alternative investments include:

- *Lack of Transparency.* Most funds are unregistered, so they have no obligation to report positions on a regular basis. They may report net asset value (NAV) daily or weekly. However, audited review of actual positions may be available only quarterly or annually. In any case, hedge funds may report risk exposures but generally will not report actual positions. You may think you understand a manager's strategy, but the reality is that these portfolios are quite dynamic. Managers may make large global macro bets, carrying substantial risk. They may also use high leverage. From a marketing standpoint, a manager may present a strong case for not reporting positions or strategies to keep his competitive advantage at finding inefficiencies. Although this may be partially accurate, it shouldn't hinder appropriate transparency for investors. The ability to have at least limited transparency should be one of the primary objectives in initial screening of managers.

- *Lack of Liquidity.* Most funds have an annual lockup. After the first year you may have quarterly liquidity with a 45- to 90-day notice. In addition, there are also liquidity concerns at the security level. Many trading positions may be in very thin markets. Mispricing and extreme illiquidity have played a role in several fraud or blow-up situations. The manager's goal of a positive return with low monthly volatility can be in direct conflict with the pricing of these illiquid issues. Even though a fund may be audited, some funds have carried positions at inflated values (such as purchase price). Another problem is a highly volatile position. Managers have been known to smooth volatility by gradually adjusting prices. In adverse conditions, the price of a thinly traded security may change dramatically. The bid–ask spread is the difference between the price a dealer will bid to buy a security and the price at which the dealer will sell that same security. Spreads can widen sharply during times of crisis. Managers who have sold short borrowed securities can be *squeezed*. That is, they can be forced to buy back the borrowed securities at much higher prices.

• *Leverage.* Hedge funds often use leverage, sometimes in large amounts. Their goal is to generate greater returns than the cost of borrowing funds. With approximately $150 billion a year projected to flow into hedge funds, many arbitrage opportunities have become more efficient; the hedge fund managers have responded by increasing leverage. This substantially increases the risk for a potential blow-up. The downside of leverage can be a catastrophic event like the Long Term Capital debacle. *High Fees.* It's no secret that hedge fund fees are high. That's why so many traditional money managers are tripping over themselves to start hedge funds. You need to understand what you are paying for and the potential hurdle rate to generate alpha in your portfolio (Exhibit 11.2).

Exhibit 11.2 shows a typical fee structure for Hfofs. Hedge fund managers typically charge a 1% to 1.5% fee with an incentive of 20% of profits. Some managers establish a low hurdle rate of return that a manager must beat before taking an incentive. Variation may be a *high water mark*. A manager cannot take incentive fees after down periods until asset value use is back up to the old high. If a manager falls too far below, he may close the fund and reopen an identical fund to reestablish the ability to receive incentive fees.

• *Data Collection.* With so many institutional investors adding hedge funds or Hfofs to their portfolios, a number of data collection firms now track performance. Their goal is to measure risk and returns of these managers. Since there is no passive index, some firms simply track a large group of active managers and establish the aggregate return as an index. A look at the results of these indexes (Exhibit 11.3) shows huge dispersion. Each firm uses a different group of managers with different weightings. Some indexes, such

EXHIBIT 11.2 HEDGE FUND-OF-FUNDS FEES

Gross return	12.0%
Base fee 1%	−1.0%
Net before incentive	11.0%
Incentive fee @ 20% of profit	−2.2%
Net return	8.8%
Fund-of-funds base fee @ 1%	−1.0%
Net after fund-of-funds fee	7.8%
Fund-of-funds incentive fee 10% of profit	−7.8%
Net fund-of-funds return	7.02%

EXHIBIT 11.3 HEDGE FUND INDEXES ANNUAL RETURNS

Index	2002	2001	2000	1999	1998
Fund of funds					
HRFI FOF Diversified	1.2%	2.8%	2.5%	28.5%	−5.5%
MAR Hedge FOF Diversified	0.7	5.0	7.4	22.4	1.8
VAN Fund of Funds	1.3	4.2	8.7	24.9	4.4
Market neutral					
CSFB/Tremont	7.4	9.3	15.0	15.3	13.3
MAR Hedge Market Neutral	2.0	7.3	13.9	9.9	11.2
Van Market Neutral Arbitrage	8.5	10.0	11.5	20.9	9.1
Global Macro					
CSFB/Tremont	14.7	18.4	11.7	5.8	−3.6
HRFI macro	7.4	6.9	2.0	17.6	6.2
MAR Hedge Global Macro	2.8	5.6	10.0	8.5	8.1
Distressed					
CSFB/Tremont	−0.7	20.0	1.9	22.2	−1.7
HFRI Distressed	5.3	13.3	2.8	16.9	−4.2
MAR Hedge	6.9	9.2	5.9	17.9	−4.8

as the CSFB/Tremont index, are asset base weighted, while others are equally weighted across funds. Weighting itself has a big impact. For example, in a study by Bernstein Wealth Management in 2000, one index reported an average long/short manager return of 17%. Removing the top 3 of 94 managers dropped the average to 10.3%.

There are other data collection problems. First, performance reporting is on the honor system. Managers often only report good numbers. Some managers fund several small portfolios, or incubator funds. The top performers stay open and are marketed. The poor performers are simply closed. It's estimated that 15% to 20% of funds close each year through natural attrition.

Discrepancies in data, huge dispersion, and survivorship bias may overstate index performance dramatically. It has been estimated that index returns may be overstated by as much as 200 to 400 basis points per year. The addition of Hfof expenses might push that number over 500 basis points.

BENEFITS

Hfofs clearly offer certain benefits:

- *Diversification.* The ability of an Hfof to invest in several substrategies gives smaller investors the diversification without making large dollar commitments to each individual fund. An Hfof may have 10 to 100 managers in its portfolio.

- *Due Diligence.* It takes time, resources, and expertise to identify good managers. This research capability doesn't come cheaply. Hedge fund due diligence is not a do-it-yourself project for the amateur.

- *Access to Top Managers.* Often top performing hedge funds have limited or no access. A good Hfof can secure capacity to closed or limited access funds.

- *Risk Management.* Ongoing oversight of each manager can add substantial value. Often the Hfof also has a robust portfolio construction process for both allocating and rebalancing among the underlying funds. A good Hfof manager should keep a close watch on risk and leverage parameters, both on the manager and fund level.

FUND-OF-FUNDS SEARCH

Although similar to traditional manager searches, the Hfof search process tends to be somewhat more subjective. In the initial screening, less emphasis should be placed on performance numbers and more on qualitative issues. This is not to say that performance is not important, it's that process and risk control are crucial to creating that performance.

Initial screening should focus on defining objectives and parameters. You may have a specific target on expected return potential, maximum loss, maximum leverage, liquidity, reporting, and transparency. Your initial screens might produce a smaller list to focus on. An example of initial screens might include:

Projected return Treasury bills	+4%	Maximum drawdown	<6%
Actual 3 year annualized return	8%+	Maximum no. of managers	<40
Correlation with Standard & Poor's 500	<0.4	Maximum leverage	2.5 to 1
Minimum track record	10 years		

From this short list of managers, you now want to focus on more qualitative issues. Sending a detailed request for proposal can be extremely helpful in identifying managers with solid risk control measures as well as a diligent process. A sample request for proposal can be found in Appendix E.

Again, while numbers are important, you'll need to put a lot more art into your judgment of qualitative issues. You should be looking for positive responses in the following areas:

- People
  - Proven experience. Little turnover

- High integrity; check references
- Depth of team, diverse talent with specialists
- Any intangibles

- Analysis of investment process
  - Disciplined process
  - Identify competitive advantage over competitors
  - Understandable and well-quantified risk measures
  - Low emphasis on global macro
  - Appropriate use of leverage
  - Appropriate infrastructure
  - Sufficient diversification

- Business of firm
  - Focused business model
  - Lack of conflicts
  - Equal terms among investors
  - Satisfactory liquidity and transparency
  - Solid auditing and administrative procedures

- Performance
  - Past performance in several markets; monthly data for review of appropriate risk characteristics
  - Evaluation of poor performing periods and what changes were made

- Fees
  - Reasonable fee structure with well aligned incentives

The goal is to find funds with a consistent, well-defined, and repeatable approach. The request for proposal responses can help weed out managers that pass initial screens but may have inconsistencies in responses or potential conflicts.

Meeting with no more than four finalists can help you make your final decision.

REAL ESTATE

Many nonprofit organizations use publicly held real estate investment trusts (REITs; see Chapter 8), but privately owned real estate also plays a role in many portfolios. Real estate provides protection against unexpected inflation. A well-diversified real estate portfolio provides cash flow from leases. With inflation, income flows can rise as leases mature, or roll over. Inflation can also cause appreciation of the underlying properties.

The lack of liquidity in the private sector presents opportunities for the astute manager. Although REITs provide similar benefits, their daily liquidity and use of some leverage have resulted in more apparent short-term volatility than exhibited by private real estate. Of course, private real estate values are *appraised* rather than *transaction based*, so you are less certain about the value of each property until it is sold.

As with hedge funds, unless you have several hundred million dollars to allocate to private real estate, you are relegated to investing in a limited partnership or other commingled vehicle. The primary disadvantage of these vehicles is the lack of liquidity. The term is usually 10 to 15 years, and there is generally not a good secondary market for partnership units.

TIMBERLAND

Large institutional investors have added timberland to their investment portfolios for over 20 years. The recent bear market in equities has accelerated the trend. Prior to 1980, most timberland properties were owned by forest product companies. Although these assets were profitable, they were often carried on the balance sheet at substantially discounted values. Changes in tax laws and fears of hostile takeovers caused many companies to sell properties to monetize their investments and generate cash flows. This created an opportunity for institutional investors; the trend continues. Globally, timberland holdings by institutions now total over $12 billion.

Benefits of Timberland

Timberland provides competitive returns, low volatility, and low correlation with other financial assets.

Competitive Returns Timberland, as represented by the National Council of Real Estate Investment Fiduciaries (NCREIF) Timberland index, has historically produced returns 7% to 10% above inflation, or between 10% and 15% nominally. The return comes from four sources:

- *Appreciation in the Value of Trees and Lumber.* Historical price appreciation has been approximately 2%. Analysis of data suggests that increases in population and increases in living standards drive these price increases. Global population growth and improving standards of living may well continue to support price appreciation.
- *Cash Flows.* Income is generated throughout the life of an investment as trees are harvested and sold. Typically, income has been approximately one third of the annual total returns generated.

- *Growth of Trees.* Depending on the type of tree and location, annual growth ranges from 4% to 8%. Additionally, as trees get older and larger, they can be used for more valuable products. Trees less than 15 inches in diameter are only suitable for pulp wood used in paper production. Trees greater than 15 inches in diameter are more valuable. They are converted to *saw timber*, used for lumber. The largest hardwoods are most valuable for their use in furniture products.

- *Increase in Land Value.* Timberland often contains valuable mineral resources such as ore and coal. Timberland in some cases may be converted to higher uses, including commercial development. At the very least, land prices tend to increase with inflation.

Low Volatility   Exhibit 11.4 illustrates the historical risk/return pattern of timberland relative to other major asset classes. Not only has timberland offered competitive returns, but its volatility has actually decreased over the past few decades. Over this period, timberland has posted returns in line with domestic equities but volatility closer to long-term corporate bonds. Buying pressure from large institutional investors and a reduction in supply caused by environmental concerns have enhanced the stability of timberland returns. Continued capital inflow should enhance liquidity and help reduce demand shocks.

Diversification   From a portfolio theory standpoint, the most desirable attribute of timberland is its low correlation with most other assets (Exhibit 11.5). In fact, timberland has shown zero to negative correlation with all major asset classes—a portfolio manager's "Holy Grail." Timberland has the potential to reduce overall volatility when added to a portfolio of stocks, bonds, and commercial real estate.

Risks of Timberland

As with any financial asset, higher returns come with corresponding risk. The primary risks are as follows:

- *Lack of Liquidity.* Typical cash commitments can be from 8 to 10 years. Some investments may take up to 20 years to realize the return potential. Most timberland investments are structured as limited partnerships. Although there may be periodic cash flow, there is little opportunity to free up principal prior to the final sale of the underlying properties. Therefore, nonprofit fiduciaries should carefully consider their cash flow requirements before investing. The lack of liquidity also effects portfolio rebalancing. The

EXHIBIT 11.4 LONG-TERM TIMBERLAND RETURNS AND VOLATILITY

Asset Class	1960–2000	
	Return	SD
Timberland	13.30%	13.12%
Commercial real estate*	9.43%	5.55%
S&P 500	11.64%	15.65%
Small-cap equities	13.99%	24.55%
International equities*	12.00%	21.33%
Long-term corporate bonds	7.38%	10.79%
U.S. Treasury bills	5.98%	2.61%
CPI	4.44%	3.09%

*Data for commercial real estate and International equities are from 1969 to 2000.
Source: Hancock Timber Resource Group.

limited partnership structure makes it difficult for your nonprofit fund to rebalance to a specific overall target allocation.

- *Natural Disasters.* Natural disasters include fire, storms, insect infestation, and disease. One can easily recall television images of wildfires blazing out of control and destroying thousands of acres of timberland. Surprisingly, these natural risks are actually rare. Total loss for industrial managed forests in the United States is less than one half of 1% per year. Those dramatic television images are actually of *public* as opposed to privately owned forest land. However, it is still important to diversify a portfolio regionally to further mitigate this risk.

- *Price Fluctuations.* Pulp and lumber prices are subject to the laws of supply and demand. Harvesting timber during a period of falling prices would ob-

EXHIBIT 11.5 TIMBERLAND HAS LOW CORRELATION WITH STOCKS AND BONDS

Historical Correlation with Timberland	1960–2000
Timberland	1.00
Commercial real estate*	−0.11
S&P 500	−0.29
Small-cap equities	−0.12
International equities*	−0.22
Long-term corporate bonds	−0.30
U.S. Treasury bills	−0.02
CPI	0.37

*Based on annual returns from 1980 to 1999.
Source: Hancock Timber Resource Group.

viously impair the return on investment. However, unlike other agricultural commodities, timber is less subject to this risk. There are virtually no costs to "store trees on the stump" and wait until prices rise. In fact, every year that harvest is delayed, the timber grows and becomes more valuable. Longer term, there is some concern about the supply part of the equation. There are substantial timber resources in Asia and Russia. At this time, they don't have the infrastructure to readily harvest those forests, but that situation may change.

- *Government Intervention.* Supply shocks can occur if the government crafts legislation to protect threatened or endangered species. The spotted owl crisis of the early 1990s is a prime example. The most impact has been on public rather than private timberland.

Other Considerations

Geographic Diversification   Return and volatility vary substantially by region and species of tree. Due to soil and climate conditions, certain areas favor certain types of trees. The United States is typically divided into three regions: the Northwest, Northeast, and South. The Northwest and Northeast typically produce superior hardwoods (cherry, oak, maple, and ash), while southern timberland properties generally produce softwoods (pine, fir, and spruce). Additionally, areas such as New Zealand (similar to the southern United States) and British Columbia (similar to the northwestern United States) offer further opportunities to diversify a portfolio.

Monitoring   It is not as easy to track the performance of timberland as it is to monitor equity or bond managers. There are currently two timberland indexes, each with some limitations. The *Timberland Performance Index* (TPI) primarily consists of southern U.S. properties. The NCREIF Timberland index is a broader index of all three U.S. regions. It consists of approximately 250 properties. Although this index is more diversified, it contains no global properties and may not be in line with your investment's portfolio mix. Although performance is calculated quarterly, most appraisals are performed annually. This gives the appearance of a seasonal effect (most of the return appears to be in the fourth quarter). Appraisal data skew the apparent volatility as well. Either index should be taken with a large grain of salt.

Active Management   Most institutions invest via pooled vehicles because of the cost and time horizon involved in owning timberland. Pooled funds are managed by *timberland investment management organizations* (TIMOs). The typical investment structure is a limited partnership investing in a portfolio of properties diversified by location, timber market, tree age, species, and end product. As is the case with other alternative investments, fees are on the high side (generally a management fee of 1% to 2% and a portion of the profits above a hurdle rate, for example, "15% above a hurdle of 6%"). The length of investment is usually 7 to 15 years.

A manager can potentially add value in several ways:

- *Due Diligence in Negotiating Purchases and Sales.* One of the bigger risks is overpaying for timber properties. Paying too much for a property or paying for trees that are not there can substantially reduce return potential. Having experienced foresters on the ground is crucial.

- *Diversification.* Investing in multiple, diverse properties can enhance the risk-adjusted return.

- *Ongoing Forest Management to Maximize Timber Output per Field.* Manager research should focus heavily on the quality and depth of the management team. You need to have a strong understanding of the people, process, and philosophy of the management team as well as the structure of any limited partnership.

Conclusion

Despite the potential risks, timberland offers returns competitive with those of equities and lower volatility. Timberland also offers significant diversification potential. These benefits may somewhat offset the illiquidity and nonsystematic risks of the timberland portfolio. Timberland should be particularly attractive if your nonprofit fund has a long time horizon.

PRIVATE EQUITY

Since the 1980s, institutional allocations to *private equity* have increased steadily. Several billion dollars are committed annually. Private equity refers to ownership positions in securities that are not publicly traded or listed on an exchange. Private equity investment takes several forms:

- *Venture Capital*—financing of new businesses
- *Buyout Funds*—refinancing of existing or more mature businesses
- *Mezzanine Financing*—high yield debt, senior to equity financing
- *Special Situations*—investments in distressed debt or turnaround situations

Each of these market segments is characterized by limited available information flow and few able or willing investors. In short, there can be large inefficiencies. Knowledgeable investors can generate excess return. Many institutions view these types of investments as "alpha generators." Although these strategies are categorically different from traditional equity management, they do have some similar characteristics and can be highly correlated with the listed markets.

Private equity funds are generally structured as limited partnerships. Outside investors are the limited partners. The sponsoring private equity firm acts as the general partner. There are usually 10 to 30 underlying investments per fund. Investments committed to the partnership are typically *called* over a period of several years. For example, a foundation might agree to invest a total of $10 million dollars. But the money will actually be called by the private equity fund over the next 2 to 5 years as needed. The fund managers make capital calls as they find acceptable opportunities. The not-for-profit organization controls the capital until it is drawn down by the manager. The investor may put up only $1 to 2 million initially, but will need to keep the rest of the funds available for future calls. There are rather severe penalties if an investor fails to honor capital commitments when called. The life of the fund is usually 7 to 12 years. It is not unusual for a private equity sponsor to be raising money for a second fund even though all of the commitments from a first fund have not yet been called.

Fees

The fee structure for private equity is similar to that of hedge funds—in other words, rich. Annual management fees range from 1% to 3%. The general partner is also typically entitled to a share of any profits (the *carry* or carried interest). The split usually is 80% to the limited partners and 20% to the general partner. As with hedge funds, a not-for-profit organization could invest directly with a single fund manager focusing on one stage or industry, such as "early-round venture capital." Alternately, the investor might choose a more diversified manager or a fund-of-funds approach. In a fund-of-funds, the general partner invests in a number of other private equity funds. Although this approach provides diversification, it adds an extra layer of management fees.

Calculating Returns

The investor in a fund may actually start receiving back capital from early investments prior to the original commitment being fully drawn down. For this reason, returns are calculated only on the capital that has been drawn down. Often, managers target a return of 300 to 500 basis points (3% to 5%) above traditional equity. A look at long-term returns on over 1,750 funds in the Venture Economics U.S. Private Equity Performance index provides a good comparison with traditional markets (Exhibit 11.6). Venture Capital, which typically carries more risk, has significantly outperformed the Standard & Poor's (S&P) 500 index. However, overall private equity returns are slightly above those of the S&P 500 index over a 20-year period (13.6% vs. 12.9%).

Risks

Private equity seems to offer higher performance than traditional equities. The general partners have hands-on involvement in the management of each of the companies in their portfolio. The theory is that without Securities and Exchange Commission regulations or public scrutiny, the general partner can focus on adding real value over the life cycle of a company. He can identify unique situations that can be home runs for the portfolio. However, you must consider several potential risks:

- *Liquidity.* Because investments in each portfolio company are usually three to five years, returns in the first few years are often negative. Length of commitment is usually 10 years after the last funds are called.

- *Leverage.* The use of leverage, often two to three times the original capital, magnifies risk and reward. There is no simple way to quantify the additional

EXHIBIT 11.6 VENTURE ECONOMICS' U.S. PRIVATE EQUITY PERFORMANCE INDEX: INVESTMENT HORIZON PERFORMANCE THROUGH 12/31/2003

Fund Type	1 Yr	3 Yr	5 Yr	10 Yr	20 Yr
Early/Seed VC*	−7.0	−23.3	54.9	37.0	19.1
Balanced VC	11.0	−13.9	19.4	20.4	13.3
Later-stage VC	25.4	−18.8	3.5	17.0	13.8
All venture	8.10	−18.9	22.8	25.4	15.5
All buyouts	24.1	−2.1	2.2	7.8	12.4
Mezzanine	5.7	1.1	5.6	7.3	9.6
All private equity	18.3	−7.0	6.8	12.7	13.6
Nasdaq	50.0	−6.7	−1.8	9.9	12.4
S&P 500	26.4	−5.6	−2.0	9.1	12.9

*VC, venture capital.

risk assumed since positions are not priced regularly. Although clearly there is much more risk. Private equity looks much less compelling when compared with traditional markets adjusted for leverage.

- *Reporting Issues.* As is the case with hedge funds, private equity reporting is positively skewed. That is, results are only shown for deals completed. This eliminates poor-performing funds that do not report returns and funds where managers are simply prolonging the life of the partnership. There is an even larger dispersion of manager returns than in hedge funds. Results collected by Plan Sponsor Network show that, for the decade ending December 31, 2000, the difference in performance between top quartile managers and median managers was over 20% per year. This compares with an approximate 2% spread between top quartile and median managers in the domestic equity universe.

In summary, private equity is potentially an alpha generator rather than a risk reducer. Although top quartile managers can clearly add excess return, most managers have not produced a substantial increase in returns over traditional markets. There are additional risks, including liquidity, leverage, and high fees. The due diligence process should again focus highly on qualitative issues. You should try to identify strong management teams who can impose discipline on the companies in which they invest.

STRUCTURED EQUITY

An accepted strategy in Europe for years, *structured equity* has become more popular with U.S. institutions in the past few years. These products are *derivative instruments* linked to a popular index such as the S&P 500 or Nasdaq 100. They are derivatives because their risk and return characteristics are *derived* from the behavior of some other financial instrument. In design, the product is a forward contract, a customized agreement between two parties to deliver a specified amount of money based on the agreed price of an underlying financial instrument. Your nonprofit organization might be one party, putting up cash currently to be paid by a counterparty (typically a large money center bank or investment bank) upon maturity of the contract. The products are called equity-linked notes.

The bank profits from effectively designing a product that appeals to the particular needs and risk parameters of its customers. The counterparty uses a series of derivatives, such as put and call options, to manage the risk of the underlying index. The major risk is the financial strength of the counterparty.

Although structured notes may seem very straightforward, it is not easy for the average investor to understand the underlying mechanics. The term *derivative* has received a lot of bad press. However, structured investments range from very low risk to very high risk. The key is the amount of leverage used. Many nonprofit organizations' investment policy statements prohibit the use of derivatives.

The structured product uses a stated formula based on the movement of the underlying index to come up with an end value. Here are two examples:

1. Example A. (Limited downside)

    Structure: The note has an 18-month maturity. It is linked to the performance of the S&P 500 index. The investor receives any price increase in the index up to a cap of 30% over the period of the contract. However, if the index declines in price over that period, the first 10% of decline is protected. The investor participates in losses greater than 10%.

2. Example B. (Leveraged upside)

    Structure: The investor receives three times the upside of the S&P 500 index to a cap of 18% over 15 months. However if the index declines, the investor participates in all of the downside.

Often, the investor is distracted by the participation rate or protection feature. These products can have very complex triggers to dynamically manage the risk of the note over the life of the contract. It is important to have a good understanding of the following risks:

- How is money invested? Specifically, what derivatives are being used and how are they managed?

- Are there any circumstances where the investment can be terminated prior to maturity by the counterparty?

- What is the credit rating of the underlying counterparty? Does the counterparty have the ability to pay?

- Is there any secondary market for the note?

- How are end values calculated—at a specific date or some rolling average?

- How much leverage is being used?

If you have a clear understanding of the risk and return characteristics, these products may be useful in meeting a unique need. For example, one client with specific spending requirements used the aforementioned leveraged product to reduce the overall equity exposure by two thirds without giving up the upside return expectation of 6%. (Note: the trade-off was that this client was willing to give up upside *above* the return expectation.)

MANAGED FUTURES

The term *managed futures* refers to professional money managers known as *commodity trading advisers* (CTAs), who manage client assets on a discretionary basis using forward contracts, futures, and options. For the investor, managed futures provide exposure to many financial and nonfinancial asset sectors beyond stocks and bonds. These include financial, currency, and commodity futures and options. Managed futures are touted as improving the risk/return characteristics of a portfolio, especially in difficult environments for traditional investments. This potential benefit did not go unnoticed by investors during the recent bear market for stocks. Assets in managed futures grew from under $40 billion in 2000 to over $415 billion by mid-2004.

AN INVESTMENT STRATEGY

Because the industry is made up of money managers, it's important to note that managed futures are a skill-based strategy, not an asset class. Managers have the ability to go long or short (sell short) these markets in an effort to generate return. The manager's skill plays an important role in overall performance. More recent studies suggest a portion of return comes from basic trading strategies behind most CTAs. These strategies may be one of two approaches:

- *Systematic.* This approach is common where trading is mostly automated. Using technical analysis, a manager evaluates the price and volume movement of markets. He develops a model to go long or short a market based on its trend.

- *Discretionary.* Far fewer managers will take a total discretionary approach. Personal experience and judgment define their trading decisions.

Futures markets are a "zero sum game." If CTAs were only trading against other CTAs, returns would be based solely on manager skill. Someone has to lose a dollar for somebody else to make a dollar. However, some investors are hedging other positions, so they may expect to lose. For example, an airline might buy oil futures to hedge its fuel costs. If oil prices fall, the airline loses money on the futures contract but saves money on their fuel costs; they are indifferent. Managed futures traders provide liquidity to commercial hedgers and, in return, capture a profit. There seems to be a high correlation of performance among similar trend-following approaches.

BENEFITS OF DIVERSIFICATION

A review of performance of the largest 39 CTAs in existence from 1990 through 2003, tracked by the Center for International Securities and Derivatives Markets, shows returns in line with the S&P 500 index and a standard deviation that is slightly less. Compared with other alternatives such as Hfofs, however, the risk-adjusted performance has been substantially lower (Exhibit 11.7). The greatest benefit comes from the low to negative correlation with equity and bond markets.

Times of economic uncertainty or turmoil, which are typically bad for stocks and bonds, are exactly when CTAs have had their best performance. Exhibit 11.8 shows that the correlation of CTAs with the S&P 500 index, while virtually zero, has become negative in down markets. By contrast, the hedge fund index actually increased slightly.

RISKS

Leverage

The use of options and futures allows managers to have large national exposure to markets with small capital commitments. Studies have shown that the higher the leverage, the more volatile the manager's performance. Leverage for CTAs is often 10 to 1 and sometimes higher.

In a trend-following strategy, managers attempt to control this risk by diversifying across several markets or several positions. The use of *stops* seeks to control downside risk of any position to 1% to 2% of the portfolio. A stop or "stop loss" order is placed below the current price. It is triggered and becomes a market

EXHIBIT 11.7 PERFORMANCE FROM JANUARY 1990 TO DECEMBER 2003

	CISDM CTAs	Composite Hedge Fund Index	S&P 500	Lehman Government/ Corporate
Annualized return	11.34%	13.87%	10.94%	8.03%
Annualized SD	10.05%	5.82%	15.05%	4.45%
Minimum monthly return	−6.00%	−6.92%	−14.46%	−4.19%

Source: Center for International Securities and Derivatives Markets (CISDM).

EXHIBIT 11.8   CORRELATIONS IN BEST AND WORST 48 S&P
500 RANKED MONTHS (1/1990-12/2003)

	All S&P Months	Worst 48 S&P 500 Months	Best 48 S&P 500 Months
Managed futures			
CISDM CTA$	−0.12	−0.30	0.09
CISDM CTAEQ	−0.18	−0.41	0.12
CISDM Currency	0.05	0.22	0.37
CISDM Discretionary	−0.06	−0.18	−0.05
CISDM Diversified	−0.16	−0.44	0.04
CISDM Financial	−0.10	−0.32	0.15
CISDM Trendfollowing	−0.18	−0.40	0.13
Hedge funds			
Composite Event Drive	0.58	0.69	−0.18
CISDM Fund of Funds	0.51	0.53	0.00
Composite Equity Hedge	0.64	0.54	0.02
Composite Market Neutral	0.07	0.02	0.14
Traditional assets			
Lehman Government/Corporate Bond	0.14	−0.26	0.04

*CISDM, Center for International Securities and Derivatives Markets.

order if the security falls to that price. A manager often incurs several small losses that are offset by a few very large gains in the positions that have run.

Survivorship Bias

A 2003 study by Liang of 1,510 CTAs from 1994 through 2001 shows that survivorship bias is even higher than in hedge funds. The study found an average annual attrition rate of over 20%. Returns were overstated by survivorship bias to the tune of more than 5.89% annually. This figure was higher than in previous studies, and clearly shows the risk of looking simply at returns of surviving managers.

Fees

As with other alternatives, manager fees are performance based. Average manager fees are high at 2%. Incentive fees take another 20% of profits.

EXHIBIT 11.9 MLM INDEX FUND: CONTRACT

Financials
    Ten-year notes
    Treasury bonds
    Five-year notes

Energy
    Crude oil
    Heating oil
    Unleaded gas
    Natural gas

Currencies
    British pounds
    Canadian dollar
    Australian dollar
    Euro currency
    Japanese yen
    Swiss francs

Grains
    Soybean oil
    Corn
    Soybeans
    Soybean meal
    Wheat

Metals
    Copper
    Gold
    Silver

Softs
    Coffee
    Cotton
    Sugar

Meats
    Live cattle

Passive Approach

There is a passive investable index that is quite similar to many trend-following CTAs. The MLM index consists of the 25 most liquid futures contracts (Exhibit 11.9). They are equally weighted and rebalanced monthly based on a trend-following algorithm. The algorithm looks at the 12-month moving average of each futures market to determine a long or short position on the first day of each month. Long term, the index has shown similar benefits to that of active CTAs.

CONCLUSION

Although the risk-adjusted return of managed futures does not seem as attractive as other alternative investments, the strategy does offer the ability to lower standard deviation. An institutional investor needs to recognize both the potential risks and the fact that the performance may be subpar in most economic environments. It is periods of rising inflation or economic uncertainty that show the benefit of a hedged position.

## CHAPTER 12

Portfolio Rebalancing

As mentioned in Chapter 7, asset allocation is the single most important determinant of investment performance. Appropriately, investment committees dedicate substantial time and effort to determine their risk tolerance and optimal asset allocation. Then capital market fluctuations change everything. Stocks go down, bonds go up, and suddenly your fund is overweight fixed income. So when and how do you rebalance? Countless tools have been developed to help determine an optimal allocation, yet committees often "fly by the seat of their pants" when it comes to the rebalancing decision.

First of all, is it even necessary to rebalance? Won't market fluctuations even out in the long run? The answer to these questions is that rebalancing is one of the most important things you must do. Markets tend to be mean reverting. Periods of outperformance tend to be followed by periods of underperformance. If you ride your winners up and then back down again you have lost a marvelous opportunity to harvest and recycle those gains. In fact, a disciplined and systematic rebalancing strategy can "engineer" additional return into the portfolio. (You take some of the chips from winning asset classes and feed them to losing classes that have become underweight. When the former losers become winners in the next cycle, you profit.)

TRADITIONAL REBALANCING METHODS

Institutional investors employ a handful of rebalancing techniques. Each has its own benefits and drawbacks. These methods include the following:

- *Arbitrary.* Rebalancing based on gut feeling or emotion. The investment committee sits around a table and asks each other, "Well, do you think it's time to reallocate back into stocks?" Of course, it is human nature to want to wait until all information is known (and the markets have already re-acted).

- *Tactical.* Rebalancing based on short-term fundamental or technical considerations.
- *Time-dependent.* Rebalancing every month, quarter, or year.
- *Percentage Bands.* This is the favored methodology for most consulting firms.
  - *Fixed Percentage Band.* For example, "rebalance if the asset class is plus or minus 5% from the target allocation" (e.g., your fixed-income target is 20%, so you rebalance at 15% or 25%).
  - *Percentage Change Relative to Target Allocation.* For example, rebalance if the asset class is 10% different from the target. If your fixed-income target is 20%, you rebalance at plus or minus 2% (10% of 20%). So you rebalance when the allocation falls outside an 18% to 22% band.
  - *Standard Deviation.* Rebalance as a function of a *multiplier* times the asset class expected standard deviation. The larger the multiplier, the less frequently you will rebalance. With the help of your consultant, your investment committee may define the multiplier. Here is an example that assumes a 1.25 multiplier:
    - Asset class trigger = (asset class standard deviation) × (multiplier)
    - Equity trigger = 20% (standard deviation) × 1.25 = ±25% (of the allocation)
    - Debt trigger = 10% (standard deviation) × 1.25 = ±12.5% (of the allocation)
    - Cash trigger = 1% (standard deviation) × 1.25 = ±1.25% (of the allocation)

Considerations

The *arbitrary* method has severe drawbacks. Humans seem to be "hard-wired" to lose money when investing based on gut reaction (see Chapter 17). There is no evidence that investment committees are more immune to emotion than individuals.

Tactical rebalancing might be effective if the decision makers are armed with superior information and employ a thoughtful and contrarian strategy. Unfortunately, tactical rebalancing often turns out to be indistinguishable from the arbitrary method. For one thing, fear and greed typically govern short-term investment decision making. Second, frequent and costly trading is required to make tactical bets; excessive trading is the enemy of long-term portfolio return. Third, most investment committee structures require some degree of consensus among the committee members. Consensus building takes time and can lead to a "worst of all possible worlds" outcome. In other words, the tactical rebalancing strategy that results from a compromise may be worse than that of either party. Remember the old saw, "A camel is a horse built by committee!"

The *time-dependent* and *percentage band* methods are disciplined rebalancing strategies. As such, they are superior to arbitrary and tactical rebalancing methodologies. But they don't factor in the interaction of the various asset classes. Of the three percentage band rebalancing strategies, the *standard deviation method* makes the most sense. At least it factors the volatility of the assets into the rebalancing decision. However, none of these methods account for the correlations among the assets.

An effective rebalancing strategy should seek to minimize rebalancing frequency and transaction costs while keeping expected return and risk objectives constant. In other words, only rebalance when you *must*. And you must rebalance only when the risk/return profile of the entire portfolio changes. The key is the correlations among the asset classes in the portfolio.

There is a trade-off between maintaining the portfolio's risk and return objectives and minimizing trading expenses. If we rebalance infrequently, transaction fees will be lower, which is a good thing. On the other hand, the less frequently we rebalance, the farther the portfolio drifts away from the policy's stated return and risk objectives, which is a bad thing. Therefore, a compromise is required. We must rebalance only frequently enough to make sure the portfolio doesn't drift too far.

A NEW APPROACH

Portfolio decisions should be made to maximize return while minimizing risk and expenses. Frequent rebalancing can dampen returns by pulling money away from strong-trending asset classes too soon. The *Portfolio Engineer*™ is a rebalancing overlay that seeks to generate optimal rebalancing trigger points. The goals are to maximize return, hold risk constant, and minimize transaction expenses. The Portfolio Engineer is a proprietary product; to the best of our knowledge, there are no commercial programs that perform the same function. However, we will explain how to approximate at least some of the functionality of the overlay.

Underlying Premise

As discussed in Chapter 7, the efficient frontier is generated based on three input assumptions: risk, return, and correlation among asset classes. Because we are uncertain about those three inputs, we should be skeptical of the apparent precision of our target asset allocation. Mixes that at first glance appear to be off the efficient frontier may, in fact, be efficient. We have no way of knowing. You should not rebalance unless you are *certain* that the portfolio has really moved from the target; in other words, until the risk and return characteristics become statistically *meaningfully* different. Think of a band of uncertainty around your target asset allocation. As long as the portfolio stays within the band you have no way of knowing whether the risk and return characteristics have really changed. Therefore, you don't rebalance.

The Key Difference

Unlike traditional rebalancing methods, the model's rebalancing trigger is based on the risk/return parameters of the target and current portfolios rather than the weightings of individual asset classes. The Portfolio Engineer looks at how far from the target the current portfolio has drifted on an expected risk/return graph. If the current portfolio strays from the target portfolio by the critical distance, you rebalance back to your targets (Exhibit 12.1). One of the great benefits of such a systematic approach is that committee members don't have to second guess their timing or reasoning when making the rebalancing decision.

In Exhibit 12.1, the hollow dot represents the expected return and risk of the target allocation. The small dots represent monthly historical return/risk snapshots as the asset allocation has fluctuated around the target (between January 1988 and November 2003). The large circle represents the band of uncertainty around the target allocation. Only if the portfolio drifts outside the circle do we deem that the risk and return have become statistically different from the target allocation. This constraint circle is set with a radius (R) of 0.40% from the center (or target portfolio); 0.40% was chosen for this portfolio because the target allocation and all portfolios with risk and return characteristics that fall within the circle have been statistically indistinguishable based on historical analysis.

Exhibit 12.2 shows results for that period (January 1988 to November 2003). The vertical axis is risk. The horizontal axis represents *degree of portfolio drift prior to rebalancing*. Think of the left side as constant rebalancing and the right side as never rebalancing. The graph illustrates the impact of waiting to rebalance until the portfolio touched the R constraint (the vertical line). Up until that point, risk

EXHIBIT 12.1 HISTORICAL PORTFOLIO OBSERVATIONS

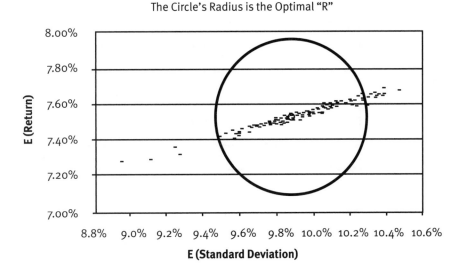

The Circle's Radius is the Optimal "R"

stayed constant (actually there was a statistically insignificant decline in volatility). Once the portfolio drifted beyond R = 0.4%, volatility increased.

Exhibit 12.3 shows that by waiting to rebalance until the R constraint was reached, there was an increase in return as well. Not only would the fund have saved on transaction expenses by rebalancing less frequently than most other dis-

EXHIBIT 12.2 ANNUALIZED STANDARD DEVIATION (1/1988–11/2003)

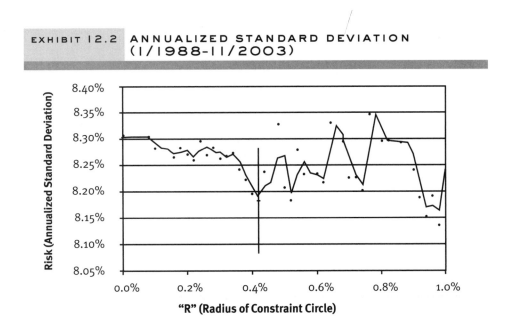

EXHIBIT 12.3   CUMULATIVE ANNUALIZED RETURNS
(1/1988–11/2003)

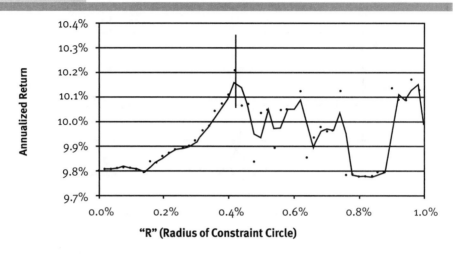

"R" (Radius of Constraint Circle)

ciplined rebalancing methods would suggest, but it also could have generated excess return. By rebalancing when R reached 0.40%, the fund would have added 0.40% of return per year compared with the index benchmark (which is rebalanced monthly). It is worth noting that you did not have to pinpoint a single specific R for the constraint circle to add value. As you can see from the positive slope of the chart in Exhibit 12.3, you could have rebalanced at any point between R = 0% and 0.40% and still increased portfolio return. Of course, when R was greater than 0.40%, risk increased, and when R was less than 0.20%, the portfolio was rebalanced frequently, resulting in unnecessary transaction fees.

The upward sloping line we see when R is between 0% and 0.40% is fairly predictable and consistent over a variety of portfolio mixes, market environments, and time intervals.

In Exhibit 12.4, ABC's portfolio would have been rebalanced about once per year. The greater the market volatility, the more frequently you rebalance. For ABC's portfolio, two rebalances occurred in back-to-back quarters (September 2001 and December 2001). Over another period (February 1992 to August 1994), there were 10 quarters (or 2.5 years) between rebalances. At the model's rebalancing trigger points, the actual stock/bond asset class weightings can vary dramatically (Exhibit 12.5).

At dates 1 and 3, the portfolio was more than 5% from its target of 60% stocks and 40% bonds, but no rebalancing was triggered. However, in time periods 2 and 4, the aggregate allocations were still at the overall 60/40 stock/bond target allocation, but rebalancing was warranted. Why? The answer is that not all stocks and

ABC'S REBALANCING FREQUENCY (1/1988–11/2003)

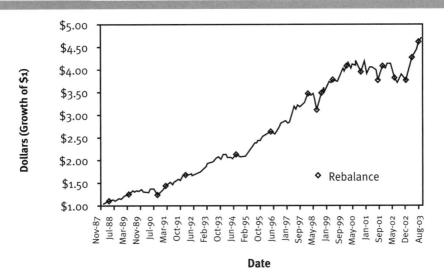

Date

bonds are created equal! Emerging markets being overweight relative to their target allocation pushed the portfolio toward higher risk (and higher expected returns) more than large-cap domestic equities being overweight. On the other hand, being overweight in investment-grade intermediate bonds pulls the risk/return characteristics of the portfolio down more than if high-yield bonds are overweight. If emerging markets and investment grade bonds are overweight at the same time, you have a netting effect on risk and return.

Disclaimer

The results described above are those of a statistical back test. Although the logic is intuitively compelling and actual results have been encouraging, past performance does not guarantee future results.

BUILDING YOUR OWN MODEL

If you don't own a software package like the Portfolio Engineer, you can still approximate the output. You can use features already offered in most commercial mean variance optimization software. The manual process can be somewhat tedious, but should be well worth the effort.

Most software packages allow you to input a *current portfolio*. This feature is de-

EXHIBIT 12.5 PORTFOLIO ENGINEER RADIUS CALCULATOR

*Overview

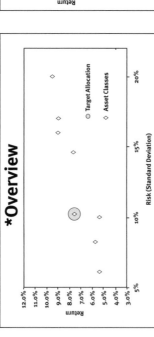

Circle Radius = 0.40%

Asset	Cash	Inter-mediate Bond	Foreign Bond	Large-Cap	Small-Cap	Inter-national Equity	Emerging Market Equity	Real Estate	High-Yield Bond	Inflation Indexed Bonds	% Equity	% Fixed	Return	Risk	Present Distance from Target	Should You Rebal-ance?	
Target	0%	14%	10%	18%	10%	17%	7%	8%	8%	8%	60%	40%	7.61%	10.20%	N.A.	N.A.	100.0%
Risk and Return Declines																	
Date 1	0%	16%	12%	15%	14%	12%	8%	5%	8%	10%	54%	46%	7.46%	9.97%	0.27%	No	100.0%
Date 2	0%	16%	10%	20%	8%	17%	5%	10%	6%	8%	60%	40%	7.54%	9.75%	0.46%	Yes	100.0%
Risk and Return Increases																	
Date 3	0%	12%	8%	21%	10%	19%	5%	11%	7%	7%	66%	34%	7.76%	10.47%	0.31%	No	100.0%
Date 4	0%	13%	10%	15%	13%	15%	9%	8%	10%	7%	60%	40%	7.65%	10.66%	0.45%	Yes	100.0%

*Emerging markets and cash are out of "overview range."

signed to allow you to compare the current portfolio to the efficient frontier, but can also be used to calculate current portfolio expected risk and return. Follow these steps:

1. Calculate your target asset allocation, choosing a specific mix on the efficient frontier. Implement the asset allocation and monitor the shifts in portfolio weights caused by market action.

2. Every month (or at least quarterly), input your new portfolio asset class weights as "current portfolio." The software will generate risk (standard deviation) and return numbers for the current portfolio.

3. Using the Pythagorean Theorem, you can calculate the R. That is, $R =$ the square root of $[(r_t - r_c)^2 + (\sigma_t - \sigma_c)^2]$.

   Where: r_t = expected return of the target portfolio

   r_c = expected return of the current portfolio

   σ_t = expected standard deviation of the target portfolio

   σ_c = expected standard deviation of the current portfolio

4. Define a critical rebalancing trigger between 0.3% and 0.5%. [Note: the actual optimal R should be calculated for each separate asset allocation. That is, a 60/40 target mix will have a different optimal R than will a 55/45 target. However, the vast majority of optimal Rs lie between 0.3% and 0.5%. Knowing that there is a benefit to this approach even if your rebalance trigger is not the most optimal, you can arbitrarily pick a number within that range. An R of 0.3% will result in more frequent rebalancing; an R of 0.5% will result in less frequent rebalancing.]

5. If the R that you calculate exceeds your trigger, rebalance the entire portfolio back to target.

The Portfolio Engineer leads to contrarian rebalancing. This is one of its inherent strengths. We've observed that investors are most reluctant to rebalance during periods of market stress or periods of market exuberance. However, rebalancing is most necessary in both of those environments. During bear markets, an unrebalanced portfolio automatically becomes less aggressive because higher risk/return assets decline as a percentage of total assets. This reduces your chance to benefit from an eventual recovery. The opposite happens during periods of "irrational exuberance." In the absence of a rebalancing strategy, your portfolio will be too conservative at market bottoms and too aggressive at market peaks. In volatile markets, the Portfolio Engineer preserves stable risk and takes advantage of both pessimism and exuberance by rebalancing back to the targets.

CONCLUSION

For every asset allocation along the efficient frontier, a scenario analysis can be used to determine an appropriate rebalancing constraint circle with radius, R. Unfortunately, there is no single best R for every portfolio structure. Typically, the more evenly diversified a portfolio is, the larger the R can become without creating a meaningful risk/return shift. Even portfolios with the same target allocations might be managed using different Rs. For example, a fund using separately managed accounts that have larger implicit and explicit rebalancing costs may be better suited by a larger R. On the other hand, an endowment using mutual funds will have lower transaction expenses. So, a smaller R may be appropriate.

Your committee can define an optimal R and write it into the investment policy statement. Each quarter, the committee quickly compares the present R to the optimal trigger point. If the "distance" has become greater than the constraint circle's R, simply rebalance to target. This provides unambiguous direction.

## CHAPTER 13

Performance Measurement and Evaluation

$\mathbf{I}$t's the fifth game of the NBA finals. The Pistons and the Wizards (this is fantasy) are tied two games apiece. Commissioner Clinton calls a press conference to announce a new policy: "These young men become too stressed about the outcome of a simple game. Some may even suffer psychological damage. Starting today we are removing the scoreboards. Henceforth teams will play for the love of the game; there will be no winner or loser. And another thing: we won't keep track of fouls either. Certain players have developed low self-esteem by constantly fouling out."

Can you imagine the reaction? This would be an extraordinarily bad approach for a professional sports league—or for fiduciaries of an investment fund.

Performance measurement is a critical part of a sound investment program. Once managers have been selected, fund fiduciaries have an ongoing duty to monitor the quality of the manager's performance. Although this responsibility has always existed under the Employee Retirement Income Security Act (ERISA), the bear market of the early 2000s highlighted the importance of these duties for fiduciaries of other fund types as well. Your nonprofit organization should monitor the investment portfolio to ensure that each manager adheres to his or her investment policy guidelines and stated philosophy. By effectively monitoring performance, you will be in a position of strength in moments of crisis. During volatile markets or when occasional problems arise, you will know about it promptly and will be better positioned to take appropriate action.

For many people, evaluating investment performance has meant answering a single question: "Am I beating the market?" (usually defined as the Standard & Poor's [S&P] 500 index). This simple-minded approach was prevalent during the bull market of the 1990s. Domestic large-cap stocks soared, particularly technology stocks. As the U.S. economy raced into the Internet era, investors exuberantly jumped on the bandwagon, only to see many of those gains evaporate. Your fund should focus less attention on "beating the market" and more on achieving reasoned financial objectives. However, investors still need to know whether their return and risk expectations are reasonable. Investment objectives should be specific and need to be outlined in an investment policy statement (see Chapter 6). Objectives typically include an appropriate index benchmark, stated returns above inflation, and performance versus a peer group of similar investment managers. However, return is only half the equation. Investors must also consider risk. Typically, an investment policy statement includes a risk measure, for example, that the manager produce positive annualized *alpha*. (Alpha is excess performance above the index—as adjusted for *beta* or market sensitivity.)

PERFORMANCE CALCULATIONS

Performance measurement begins with the calculation of a rate of return. The total rate of return can be calculated on a *dollar-weighted* or a *time-weighted* basis. The dollar-weighted method, also known as *internal rate of return*, includes the impact of cash flow on total performance. It explains how the portfolio increased or decreased in value from one point in time to another, including cash flows. However, because contributions and distributions are outside the manager's control, it is not an appropriate measure of investment manager performance.

The time-weighted method eliminates the impact of cash flow and therefore allows the investor to evaluate the decisions of the investment manager. This method determines the rate of return for the periods between cash flows and then links those periods together to calculate longer-term returns.

The two methods can produce very different "snapshots" of performance. For example, suppose the XYZ Foundation places a million dollars with a new money manager. In the first year the manager returns 35%. The foundation investment committee is ecstatic and gives the manager an additional $8,650,000. Unfortunately, in the second year the manager loses 15%. When the manager meets with the investment committee to review performance he proudly announces, "Last year was tough. But, since I've been working with you I've returned 7.1% per year—not bad for this environment!"

At this point the foundation's president leaps to his feet and shouts, "You crook! What are you trying to pull? We gave you a total of $9,650,000 and we only have $8,500,000 left. You didn't have a gain, you lost over a million!" ($1,000,000 + $350,000 + $8,650,000 - $1,500,000 = $8,500,000).

The problem is that the manager is using a time-weighted calculation while the foundation president uses a dollar-weighted method. As we said, the time-weighted method best measures a manager's abilities

Occasionally there are return discrepancies between the investment manager and the account custodian. While not all-inclusive, here are the most common reasons for discrepancies:

- Trade date valuation versus settlement date reporting
- Accrued income calculations, particularly for fixed-income investments
- Pricing differences for individual security positions
- Frequency of return linking (monthly vs. quarterly)
- Weighting of transactions, particularly large cash flows

A few spectacular implosions have been triggered when mispriced securities were eventually "marked to market" (adjusted to their true market value). These disasters might have been prevented if accounts were independently verified and reconciled regularly.

After returns are calculated and reconciled, you need to determine whether to look at returns gross or net of management fees. *Gross of fees* means performance calculated before the deduction of management fees. Performance calculated after the deduction of management fees is considered *net of fees*. Fees are a significant factor because they reduce the overall value of the portfolio. Therefore, net-of-fee returns reflect the actual return earned by the investor. However, net-of-fee evaluations can be misleading. Because managers charge different management fees for clients with different asset levels, gross-of-fee comparisons are generally more appropriate. However, a manager's fee schedule should accompany gross-of-fee returns.

BENCHMARKS

The purpose of a benchmark is to provide a frame of reference for manager analysis. You want to know if the rate of return is reasonable when compared with that of similar investment managers and the appropriate index. The most effective benchmarks are widely known, representative of the asset class or mandate, and have a clear construction methodology.

In addition to peer group and index benchmarks, each asset class has an embedded expected return. This expected return is expressed in two ways: a nominal return expressed as a single number, and an inflation-adjusted return (return above inflation). The consumer price index (CPI) is the most common measure

EXHIBIT 13.1 MANAGER XYZ OBJECTIVES: EVALUATION BENCHMARKS

Over a rolling three-year period, the manager's performance is expected to exceed at least three of the established benchmarks:

1. Before inflation benchmark:		10.5%
2. After inflation (CPI) benchmark:	CPI +	7.4%
3. Appropriate universe benchmark (return): broad large cap		Median
4. Appropriate index benchmark: S&P 500 index		
5. Appropriate risk-adjusted performance versus the policy		Positive annualized alpha

of the impact of inflation. Since spending policy is ultimately concerned with purchasing power, outperforming the CPI is a relevant investment objective. As an example of the use of benchmarks, when evaluating a large-cap equity manager, the appropriate index could be the S&P 500. The nominal target might be 10.5%[1] (the long-term average return for large cap stocks). The *real* target would then be 7.4%, adjusting for inflation.[2] These absolute targets should be part of the performance evaluation process. While good starting points, these simple comparisons by themselves are insufficient, and further benchmark comparisons are necessary. Additional benchmarks should include a style-specific market index and a universe or peer group. Exhibit 13.1 gives an example of such benchmarks as outlined in the investment policy statement for a large-cap growth manager.

A common mistake is to compare the manager with the wrong benchmark. This paints a false picture of manager skill and can create unrealistic return expectations. Investors who make the mistake of using the wrong benchmarks can end up terminating a perfectly good manager. This can be both costly and cumbersome. *Style* is the key determinant of performance at the manager level (see Chapter 9). It is crucial to measure each manager against a style-specific index instead of a single benchmark like the Nasdaq Composite or the Dow Jones Industrial Average. By using an appropriate benchmark, you can better understand whether an investment manager has added value.

In addition to providing a useful tool to portfolio measurement, benchmarks

---

[1]Calculated by DiMeo Schneider & Associates, L.L.C. using data presented in *Stocks, Bonds, Bills, and Inflation® 2004 Yearbook,* © 2004 Ibbotson Associates, Inc. Based on copyrighted works by Ibbotson and Sinquefield. All rights reserved. Used with permission.
[2]Ibid.

play critical roles in performance attribution, asset allocation, and style reliability. They also provide a mechanism for passive investing.

MARKET INDEXES

An index is a basket of securities selected to represent a broad market segment. You determine the appropriate blend of index benchmarks during the asset allocation process. The closer the market benchmark fits the style of the investment manager being evaluated, the more useful it becomes for comparison purposes. Investors should recognize that all indexes have limitations, particularly during times of extreme market movement.

Performance benchmarks now exist for virtually every sector and subsector. Indexes can be *broad based*, which means they are composed of a large number of securities and designed to represent an entire market's price movement. The most widely used broad-based index is the S&P 500 composite index. A *narrow-based* index consists of a small number of securities and is designed to avoid overlap with other indexes.

One of the most important factors in benchmark construction is the system used to determine the relative influence, or weight, each security has in the index. In a *cap-weighted* index, each stock is held in proportion to its capitalization relative to that of the entire stock market. "Capitalization" means the price per share times the number of shares outstanding. In an *equal-weighted* index, each security is assigned an equal weight regardless of its relative market capitalization. A cap-weighted index will be dominated by a handful of relatively large stocks, often in a few sectors or industries. On the other hand, an equal-weighted index may be unduly influenced by the performance of small, relatively unimportant companies.

STYLE

Many investment managers follow one of two basic investment styles: *value* and *growth*. Value managers attempt to buy "a dollar's worth of assets for 50 cents"; they are very concerned with the price they pay for a security. Growth managers, on the other hand, seek companies growing faster than the economy; they are less concerned with price.

Nowadays, equity indexes are constructed based on market capitalization and investment style. So, for example, the Russell 1000 index (representing the 1000 largest domestic companies) is sorted into growth stocks and value stocks (the Russell 1000 Growth and the Russell 1000 Value indexes). The securities are sorted based on relative valuation and forecasted earnings growth. Value stocks have prices that are low relative to their earnings, dividends, or assets. Earnings growth for these stocks tends to be relatively modest and often is heavily influenced by short-term fluctuations in the economy. Growth stocks, on the other hand, tend to have prices that are high relative to their current earnings, dividends, or book value. Usually their earnings are projected to grow faster than the market average. Typically this growth is driven by specific industry trends, such as rapidly rising demand for a new product or service. Therefore, earnings of growth companies are less influenced by economic cycles.

Style-based indexes are broken down into medium and small capitalization components. The *Russell Midcap Value, Russell Midcap Growth, Russell 2000 Value,* and *Russell 2000 Growth* indexes perform similar functions for mid- and small-capitalization stocks.

Fixed-income indexes are based on the sector, maturity, and creditworthiness of the issuer. Indexes exist for government, mortgage, and corporate debt securities. One index widely used as a proxy for the entire investment-grade bond market is the Lehman Brothers Aggregate Bond (LBAG) index. It includes government, corporate, and mortgage-backed securities.

There are also benchmarks for below investment-grade or *high-yield* securities. These low-rated bonds are also called "junk bonds." *Moody's* and *S&P* are independent agencies that rate bonds. Below investment grade means below one of the top four ratings.

There are also sector- and industry-specific indexes. Country and regional indexes focus exclusively on a single country or region of the world. *Hedged* and *unhedged* foreign stock and bond indexes also exist. A hedged benchmark reflects the effect of strategic hedging of currency exposure. Unhedged indexes reflect the effect of currency swings.

PICKING THE RIGHT INDEX

R-squared is a statistic that measures how closely correlated an investment manager's returns are with those of the market index. Investors should choose a market index benchmark which has a high R-squared (0.8 or higher) to the manager. A basic style analysis of the investment manager can help you select an appropriate market index benchmark (see Chapter 9).

A number of financial companies create domestic equity market indexes, including Wilshire Associates, S&P, and the Frank Russell Company. Morgan Stanley and Citigroup are leading vendors of international index data. Citigroup, Lehman Brothers, and Merrill Lynch are the dominant index vendors for the fixed-income markets.

MULTIPLE BENCHMARKS

In some cases, investment managers do not limit themselves to a particular segment of the market, but rather invest in a mix of asset classes or styles. For example, a balanced fund may be invested 50% in equities and 50% in fixed income. Or you may have multiple managers of differing styles, each representing part of the overall composite. In such instances, a blended index would be appropriate. For example, you might benchmark the manager against a blend of 50% S&P 500 and 50% LBAG.

Sometimes it becomes necessary to *roll* a benchmark if an investment manager's mandate changes. For example, a small-cap manager may be forced into buying midcap stocks due to his portfolio's growing size. In that instance, the historical benchmark would be rolled to the new benchmark at the time of the change.

PRESENTING THE DATA

Although you should review the investment manager on a quarterly basis, no one thinks that three months is long enough to decide whether or not to fire a manager. The general rule of thumb is that you should evaluate a manager over the course of a market cycle that includes up and down periods. Convention has shortened this "market cycle" evaluation to three years. Exhibit 13.2 shows a large-cap BLEND equity manager compared with the S&P 500 index and nominal and real targets of 10.5% and 7.4%, respectively.[3]

UNIVERSE COMPARISONS

It's all well and good to compare the manager to the market, but it's equally important to compare your results to those of other similar managers. This is called a *peer group* or *universe* comparison. For example, compare fixed-income managers to other fixed-income managers and domestic equity managers to other domestic equity managers. A universe provides a *range* of returns for a given period, unlike a market index, which represents just a single return number. It's helpful to know your investment manager's performance rank. Was he top quartile? Bottom quartile? Average?

Exhibit 13.3 shows a typical universe comparison. In this example, the manager is represented by the white diamond and the index by the triangle.

---

[3]Ibid.

EXHIBIT 13.2 MANAGER XYZ: OBJECTIVE COMPARISON

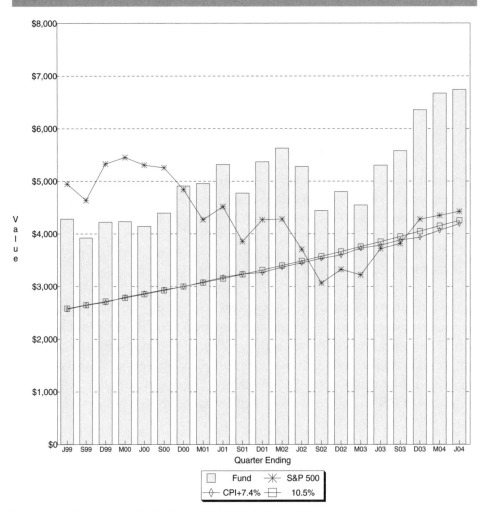

Inception date is December 31, 1989. All dollar values are shown in thousands.

The results are normally reported in terms of percentile rankings of managers. A percentile ranking of 1 is the best, and 100 is the worst. A ranking of 50 means the manager outperformed half of the peer universe. A ranking of 25 means the manager was in the top 25% of the universe. A ranking above 50 is acceptable, whereas above 25 is considered excellent. High rankings over all time periods are ideal, however, it is more important to rank highly over longer rather than shorter periods. A manager who scores consistently above median in shorter periods will end up in the top quartile over longer periods. This is because managers who

EXHIBIT 13.3 MANAGER XYZ: UNIVERSE COMPARISONS
(BROAD LARGE CAP)

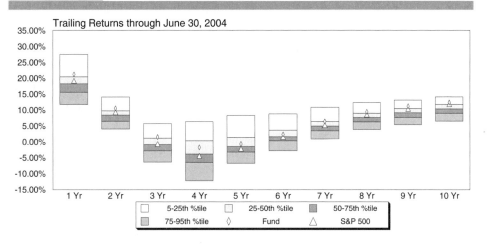

Trailing Returns through June 30, 2004

Trailing Returns through June 30, 2004

	1 Yr	2 Yr	3 Yr	4 Yr	5 Yr	6 Yr	7 Yr	8 Yr	9 Yr	10 Yr
Fund										
Return	21.16	10.51	1.52	-1.77	-0.69	2.33	6.40	9.42	11.19	12.34
%-tile	20	19	23	36	43	38	25	20	17	17
S&P 500										
Return	19.11	9.27	-0.69	-4.43	-2.20	1.57	5.24	8.53	10.35	11.83
%-tile	35	32	48	57	59	50	40	32	27	24
Universe										
5th %-tile	27.46	14.07	5.72	6.36	8.27	8.77	10.83	12.32	13.09	14.11
25th %-tile	20.36	9.71	1.15	0.33	1.39	3.65	6.37	8.96	10.43	11.75
50th %-tile	18.18	8.40	-0.89	-3.87	-1.50	1.57	4.94	7.63	9.09	10.32
75th %-tile	15.52	6.47	-2.86	-6.51	-3.25	0.28	3.45	6.23	7.63	8.95
95th %-tile	11.69	4.02	-6.39	-12.25	-6.76	-2.83	0.89	3.85	5.38	6.50

Returns are percentages, "%-tile" is the percentile ranking within the universe.
Returns for periods exceeding one year are annualized.
Incept is December 31, 1990, to June 30, 2004.

"shoot the lights out" for one or two quarters often fall into the bottom quartile in subsequent quarters.

Universes have certain limitations, including the fact that results are not available in real time. It usually takes at least two weeks after the end of a quarter to compile the universe data. Universes are also subject to *survivor bias*. Over time, some investment managers are removed from the universe—typically the worst performers. Poor-performing managers may go out of business. Or, more frequently (at least in the case of mutual funds), poor performers are merged into better performing but similar funds so that the better track record survives. Managers may also fail to report their returns to the firms that maintain the peer universes and are therefore dropped. As a result, the historical performance of the universe actually overstates the performance of the peer group.

Universes can be purchased from organizations that collect, maintain, and analyze data on a large number of investment managers. A partial list of such organizations includes eVestment Alliance, InvestorForce, Checkfree Investment Services/Mobius Group, Plan Sponsor Network, and Zephyr Associates (see Resources in Appendix G).

PORTFOLIO ANALYSIS

Portfolio analysis, including *attribution analysis,* helps you to understand what specific actions created the fund's returns. Many databases provide quarterly or month-end portfolio holdings for each reporting manager. Analyzing those holdings can help build an accurate picture of the characteristics of the portfolio. Was performance achieved through asset allocation or security selection? Was it accomplished by skillfully picking individual securities or by selectively taking on more risk than the benchmark? Did the manager overweight or underweight industry sectors? If you understand how the manager's track record was generated, you will have some basis for expectations going forward.

Attribution analysis attempts to identify and quantify the contributions that asset allocation, stock selection, currency, country, and sector weightings made to overall portfolio performance. Knowing how an investment manager produces returns can be just as important, if not more important, than knowing how large or small those returns were. Portfolio attribution compares a manager's returns sector by sector to the same sectors of the appropriate benchmark. Sectors may be economic or statistical. For example, did the manager overweight or underweight a particular industry, or did the manager favor stocks with higher price-earnings ratios? Exhibit 13.4 shows such an analysis for a large-cap growth manager.

Attribution analysis programs provided by companies such as *StokTrib, Vestek, and Baseline* can help you determine whether the investment manager's results were based on skill or luck.

STYLE ANALYSIS

Style analysis is related to performance attribution in that it seeks to explain why a manager performed in the way he did. Style analysis is used to determine port-

| | Portfolio | | | Analysis of Skill | | | | |
	A Commitment	B Return	Rank	Benchmark C Commitment	D Return	(D - b)	(A - C) Sector	A(B - D) Selection
Staples	4.89	-3.78	95	11.83	1.11		0.06	-0.24
Discretionary	36.61	8.58	8	22.80	0.20		-0.25	3.07
Health Care	19.12	5.77	13	15.14	1.74		-0.01	0.77
Materials	0.00	0.00		5.99	0.60		0.08	0.00
Info Tech	25.34	5.04	26	19.72	2.09		0.01	0.75
Energy	0.00	0.00		1.70	7.99		-0.10	0.00
Industrial	6.82	2.47	97	10.31	9.96		-0.28	-0.51
Telephone/Utilities	0.00	0.00		1.77	4.41		-0.04	0.00
Finance	7.22	-9.08	99	10.74	-1.33		0.12	-0.56
		4.85	16	5.20	1.98		-0.41	3.28
Activity		0.25			b			
		5.10	14					

161

folio exposures to various investment styles. Because recent research shows that over 90% of a manager's performance is attributable to its style, we have devoted a complete chapter to style analysis (see Chapter 9). *Growth* style managers seek to identify companies with the best prospects for rapid earnings growth, whereas *value* style managers seek to buy stocks at a discount to their true value. Historically, both styles have produced similar returns over longer periods of time, but one style is usually in favor while the other is out of favor, depending on market conditions. Investors often shift from out-of-favor to in-favor styles just at the wrong time. They often end up selling low and buying high, a recipe for disaster.

In 1984, DALBAR Inc., an independent research firm, began a continuously running study of investment behavior and market performance called the Quantitative Analysis of Investor Behavior (QAIB). In the most recent update of this study, DALBAR examined the 19-year period ending on December 31, 2002. Over that time, the S&P 500 index earned an average annual return of 12.2%. The "average" individual equity mutual fund investor, however, had a fund holding period of just over 2 years, and earned an average annual return of just 2.6% over the same period of time (less than the 3.1% average rate of inflation). The inference is that by chasing the best *recent* performance, investors ended up shooting themselves in the foot.

An investment manager should exhibit a clear, consistent, definable style. In Exhibit 13.5, closely clustered symbols show style consistency. A manager whose style has not remained consistent is said to drift. The exhibit shows two different managers with similar investment styles. However, one has shown style consistency, while the other clearly exhibits style drift.

RISK ANALYSIS

There are many definitions of risk: the chance of losing money, the probability of not meeting your objectives, or the likelihood of being criticized. However, most investment professionals view risk as the volatility of returns. It is crucial to measure the risk that a manager has taken to produce the return. It is an underpinning of *Modern Portfolio Theory* (MPT) that the returns of various asset classes are related to their risk. The greater the expected volatility, the greater return investors should expect for taking that risk. MPT holds that the markets are relatively efficient and that over time the returns of specific asset classes will reflect their relative volatility. MPT uses statistical concepts to define risk. These include risk measures such as beta, alpha, and standard deviation.

Beta measures risk relative to the benchmark. A portfolio with a beta of 1 has

EXHIBIT 13.5 ZEPHYR STYLEADVISOR: MANAGER STYLE

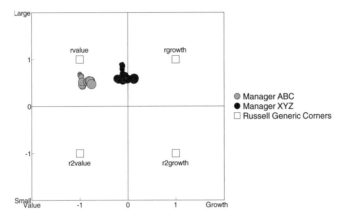

risk equivalent to that of the benchmark. If the market were up 5%, one would expect the portfolio also to be up 5%. A portfolio with a beta greater than 1 has more risk than the index. For example, a portfolio with a beta of 1.5 would be up (or down) 50% more than the index (relative to the risk-free rate). *Alpha* measures the return adjusted for beta. Positive alpha implies that the manager's decisions added value. *R-squared* measures the validity of the relationship between the benchmark and the manager. The higher the R-squared, the more reliable the alpha and the beta. R-squared may range from 0 to 1.00. Beta, alpha, and R-squared are derived from statistical regression analysis using the manager and the benchmark returns as the dependent and independent variables, respectively.

Standard deviation measures the total volatility of the manager by measuring the dispersion of returns. Unlike beta, which measures market risk, standard deviation is a measure of total risk (market risk and security-specific risk). A high standard deviation means greater volatility.

The Sharpe ratio measures return per unit of standard deviation. Developed by William Sharpe, the Sharpe ratio is simply the ratio of the portfolio return in excess of the risk-free rate (Treasury bills) to the portfolio's standard deviation. The higher the Sharpe ratio, the more return per unit of risk. A similar method, the *Treynor ratio,* was developed by Jack Treynor. The Treynor ratio is the ratio of the reward, again defined as the portfolio return minus the risk-free rate to the portfolio beta. Again, a higher Treynor ratio is better. Exhibit 13.6 shows a risk analysis for a specific manager.

RECENT DEVELOPMENTS

In the past few years, consultants and academics have developed new techniques to plug the holes in traditional manager benchmarks. Index and universe comparisons are almost always flawed. For example, an underperforming manager often complains, "True, I trailed the Russell 1000 value index, but I only buy stocks with a market cap above $10 billion, less than 20% debt, dividends above 3%, and with positive earnings. So you can see that the benchmark really isn't a good fit." The *normal portfolio* attempts to solve the problem of index misfit.

To construct a normal portfolio, you list all the securities that fit the particular manager's buy criteria. In the example in the preceding paragraph, screens would include market cap above $10 billion, debt below 20%, dividends above 3%, and positive earnings. You can then calculate the total return for each of the securities and the normal portfolio as a whole. The manager's results can then be compared with those of the normal portfolio (the stocks he or she *could* have bought). Albeit a stronger benchmark than a standard index, there is still a drawback. The manager either beats the normal portfolio or he doesn't. There is no ranking system.

Portfolio opportunity distribution sets (PODS) are artificial universes created from the normal portfolio. Developed by Ronald J. Surz, PODS universes are designed to rank managers. They also do away with the problem of *survivor bias*. As we mentioned, the "bad" track records vanish from the universe data. The result is that the median of the universe appears higher than it should. One might say that "raising the bar" is not necessarily a bad thing. However, your investment policy may force you to fire managers who seem to fall into the bottom half over a three-year period. This results in increased cost to the fund (to sell manager A's positions and replace them with manager B's picks can cost 2%).

According to Ron Surz, "Peer groups suffer from a collection of biases, only one of which is survivor bias, and each peer group has its own unique set of idiosyncratic distortions. As a result, the exact same performance number will rank differently against different peer groups, even when all of the peer groups are for the same management mandate, such as large cap growth."

PODS universes start with the normal portfolio. You then apply the manager's *portfolio construction rules*. For example, the manager might build portfolios with "40 to 50 equal-weighted positions, with no sector more than $1\frac{1}{2}$ times the index weight." The normal portfolio is then sorted into individual, randomized portfolios based on the portfolio construction rules. Results for each are calculated and sorted into quartiles just as are traditional manager universes. Although the PODS approach avoids the problem of survivor bias, it is labor intensive. Creating customized PODS universes for a specific manager may be too costly for smaller funds. An evolutionary step has been the creation of generic

EXHIBIT 13.6 ZEPHYR STYLEADVISOR

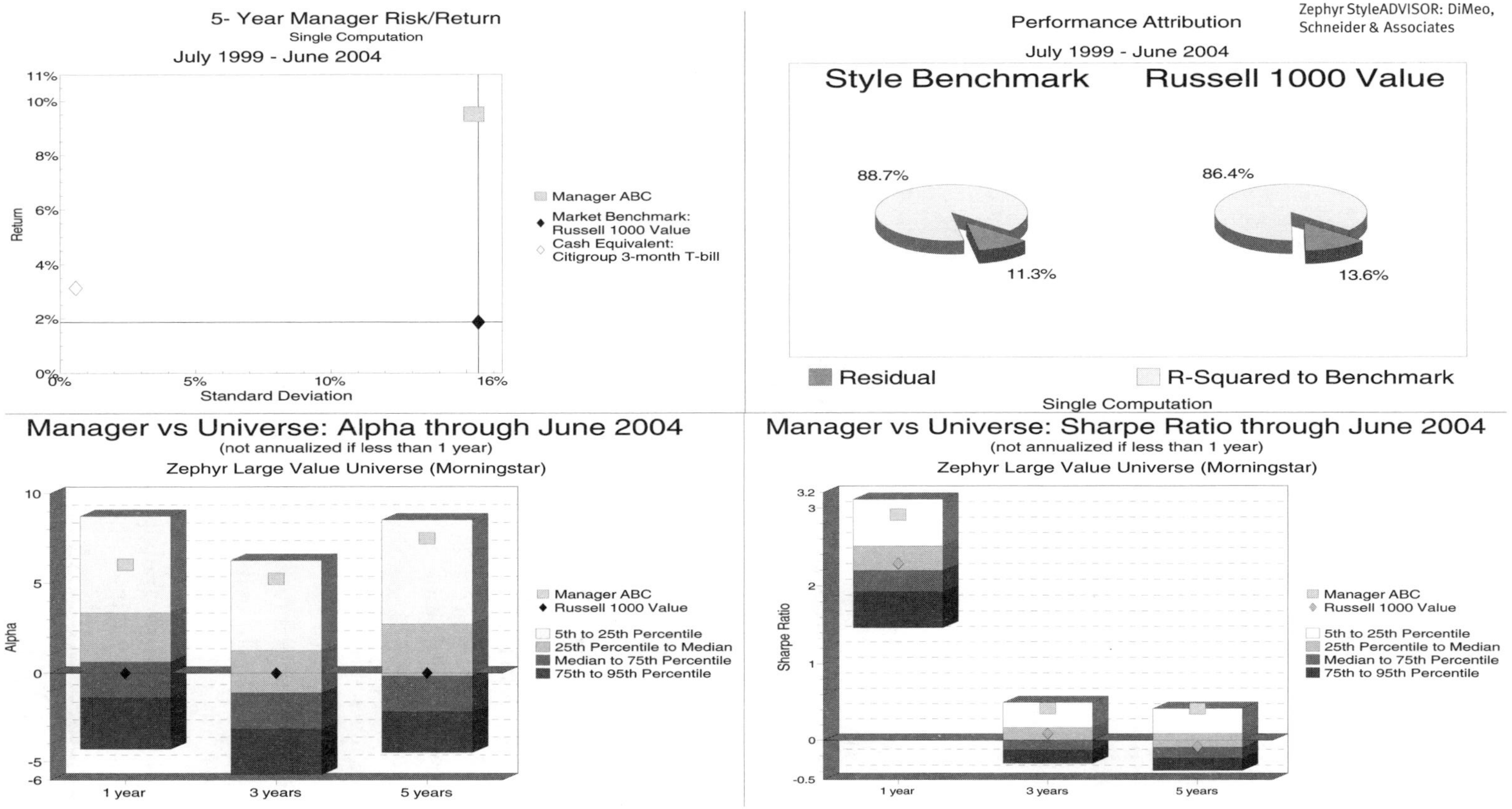

Performance Attribution
July 1999 - June 2004

Zephyr StyleADVISOR: DiMeo,
Schneider & Associates

Style Benchmark · Russell 1000 Value

Single Computation

■ Residual ■ R-Squared to Benchmark

88.7% 11.3%

86.4% 13.6%

5- Year Manager Risk/Return
Single Computation
July 1999 - June 2004

■ Manager ABC
♦ Market Benchmark:
   Russell 1000 Value
   Cash Equivalent:
◇ Citigroup 3-month T-bill

Return
11%
10%
8%
6%
4%
2%
0%
0% 5% 10% 16%
Standard Deviation

Manager vs Universe: Sharpe Ratio through June 2004
(not annualized if less than 1 year)
Zephyr Large Value Universe (Morningstar)

■ Manager ABC
♦ Russell 1000 Value

□ 5th to 25th Percentile
□ 25th Percentile to Median
□ Median to 75th Percentile
■ 75th to 95th Percentile

Sharpe Ratio
3.2
3
2
1
0
-0.5
1 year   3 years   5 years

Manager vs Universe: Alpha through June 2004
(not annualized if less than 1 year)
Zephyr Large Value Universe (Morningstar)

■ Manager ABC
♦ Russell 1000 Value

□ 5th to 25th Percentile
□ 25th Percentile to Median
□ Median to 75th Percentile
■ 75th to 95th Percentile

Alpha
10
5
0
-5
-6
1 year   3 years   5 years

Created with Zephyr StyleADVISOR. Manager returns supplied by: Morningstar, Inc.

PODS universes called *PIPODS*—popular index PODS. These are style-specific universes created in the same manner as the customized PODS universes, but using portfolio rules common to most managers of a particular style. Although acceptance of PODS and PIPODS is growing, as of this writing their use is not widespread.

PERFORMANCE REPORTING

Performance reports should provide a clear and concise evaluation of a portfolio's performance. These reports measure and analyze investment performance in a format that answers the following questions:

- Has the manager achieved the expected return and investment objective?
- Is the manager abiding by the intended investment policy?
- What factors contributed to the total return of the portfolio?
- How does performance compare with the appropriate market benchmark and peer group?
- Is the content of the report adequate to make the necessary evaluations, or is additional information necessary?
- Is continued use of this manager prudent given the responses to these questions?

Regular performance evaluation encourages a proactive rather than reactive approach. Quarterly evaluation should generally be sufficient.

TERMINATING A MANAGER

Performance evaluation extends to more than preparing performance reports and reviewing performance. You should routinely ask the managers if there have been any changes at their firms that could impact future performance. It is a good practice to require managers to report any such changes, without exception. It is also recommended that fund fiduciaries regularly meet with the managers, at least on an annual basis. In general, the following events warrant placing a manager on "watch list" status:

- Is the manager trailing two of three of the stated investment policy guidelines over a trailing three-year period?
- Is the manager exhibiting style drift?
- Has there been a change in the firm's investment process or philosophy?

- Has there been a significant change in assets under management?
- Have any senior investment professionals left the firm?
- Has a lead portfolio manager and/or two or more members left the team?
- Has there been an organizational change or change in ownership due to merger or acquisition?
- Is the firm facing any legal or compliance issues?

Once a manager is on watch list status, fiduciaries should implement strict due diligence procedures including:

- Discussions with current and new portfolio manager or team.
- In cases of mergers and acquisitions, discussions with individuals from both firms involved.
- Analysis of current fund strategy and holdings relative to historical positioning.
- Gathering and reviewing related news items and press releases.

After rigorous due diligence, fiduciaries face two choices: retain or terminate the manager. If you are not confident that the changes may, in fact, have a positive impact on future performance, then terminating the manager is appropriate. The "correctness" of the decision to terminate or retain a manager will not be known until the manager's future returns are reviewed. The important point is that no matter what the outcome, the decision-making process is prudent.

Although not all-inclusive, a list of performance analysis software and data providers can be found in Appendix G.

## CHAPTER 14

Socially Responsible Investing

J udging by recent trends, many nonprofit organizations have already begun *socially responsible investing* (or may be having the discussion soon). Socially responsible investing (SRI) has evolved considerably in the past few decades and is no longer strictly the province of religious organizations. SRI investors tackle concerns far beyond simple restrictions on holdings in tobacco, alcohol, and environmentally unsafe companies. Due to recent high-profile corporate scandals, SRI has expanded to include issues of corporate governance, business ethics, financial responsibility, and transparency. More and more investors are concerned not only with the financial and economic performance of companies, but also how their policies and practices contribute to our society. With interest in SRI on the rise and the expanding range of issues, asset growth has followed. According to the Social Investment Forum, from 1995 to 2003, assets invested according to socially responsible guidelines have grown 40% faster than all professionally managed assets.

SRI can be loosely defined as the use of social, moral, or ethical guidelines in evaluating investments *in addition* to considering financial metrics. SRI is also sometimes referred to as "socially conscious investing," "values-based investing," and "ethical investing."

HISTORY

Socially responsible investing had it origins in the beliefs of various religious faiths. Dating back several hundred years, religious investors' belief in peace and nonviolence led them to avoid investments in products that could cause harm, such as alcohol, tobacco, guns, and gambling. With the passage of time, those concerns evolved, and the focus of SRI expanded. Civil Rights, women's rights, the environment, and nuclear energy concerns all came to the forefront during the period of activism in the 1960s and 1970s. The anti-apartheid movement (opposing investments in South Africa) and opposition to the Vietnam War were two causes that greatly increased awareness of SRI. More recently, SRI has expanded to include labor relations and corporate governance issues. SRI asset levels continue to grow, along with the causes that SRI strategies seek to address. According to the Social Investment Forum's *2003 Report on Socially Responsible Investing Trends in the United States*, $2.16 trillion in assets was identified as professionally managed in SRI strategies, accounting for "more than one out of every nine dollars" under professional management in the United States. SRI assets increased 7% in 2001–2002, a period when the markets suffered through a difficult downturn and the broader universe of all professionally managed portfolios fell by 4%. During the eight-year period 1995 to 2003, "portfolios involved in SRI grew by more than 240%, compared with 174% growth of the overall universe of assets under professional management."

SOCIALLY RESPONSIBLE INVESTING STRATEGIES

Most investors may think of SRI purely in terms of screening, or excluding, companies that don't fit the desired social criteria. However, there are other methods to effect social goals. Many investors pursue SRI through active ownership strategies often referred to as *shareholder advocacy*. Shareholder advocacy can be implemented through *corporate dialogue, shareholder resolutions,* and *proxy voting.* Through these methods, investors don't simply exclude companies whose activities they may disagree with, they become shareholders in these companies and try to effect change in the policies or practices with which they disagree.

A third SRI strategy, *community investing,* is less common, but is also experiencing growth. Community investing strategies provide support for economic development in disadvantaged or financially impoverished communities. Economic development is generally accomplished through community development banks, credit unions, and loan funds that offer savings and investment options as well as loans and access to capital that may not otherwise be available in low-income areas.

Screening

The exclusion of stocks due to social criteria is the oldest method of SRI implementation. In order to follow this or any other SRI strategy, you need to begin with a thoughtful discussion regarding the values that your organization wishes to be reflected in the portfolio. Common exclusions include alcohol, tobacco, gaming, militarism, pornography, and environmentally "unfriendly" companies. Other exclusions may involve human rights, labor relations/employment equality, abortion, and birth control.

Some religious organizations have written guidelines for their various affiliated organizations. For instance, the U.S Catholic Conference of Bishops (USCCB, www.usccb.org) has offered guidelines that may be used by Catholic organizations. The USCCB investment policies include specific areas of concern under six broad social goals:

1. Protecting human life
   - Abortion
   - Contraceptives
   - Embryonic stem cell/human cloning
2. Promoting human dignity
   - Human rights
   - Racial discrimination
   - Gender discrimination
   - Access to pharmaceuticals (e.g., HIV/AIDS)
   - Curbing pornography
3. Reducing arms production
   - Production and sale of weapons
   - Antipersonnel landmines
4. Pursuing economic justice
   - Labor standards/sweatshops
   - Affordable housing/banking
5. Protecting the environment
6. Encouraging corporate responsibility

Once you have identified the areas of social concern, the process of screening may seem somewhat straightforward. However, an individual company's SRI conformity is rarely a clear-cut case. Many larger corporations have businesses and affiliates in diverse industries and geographic regions. These subsidiaries may manufacture myriad products that are unrelated to the parent company's primary revenue sources and commonly known lines of business. For instance, a company such as General Electric is involved in such business lines as media and entertainment (NBC Universal), consumer and commercial finance, health care (including medical imaging and diagnostic technologies), transportation (such as the manufacture of aircraft engines), consumer and industrial products (appliances, lighting), and insurance and investment products—just to name a few. At any given point in time, such a conglomerate may have a business line involved in activities that violate a nonprofit organization's stated SRI policies. These policy violations may or may not be readily apparent to an outside observer.

Another consideration is the supply and end-product relationships that companies may have. Suppose a paper company that has an otherwise exemplary environmental and labor relations track record produces products that are ultimately used by tobacco companies to manufacture cigarettes? Should holdings in a large grocer be excluded simply because they sell alcohol and tobacco products? What about an apparel company that is an active contributor to its community, but uses fabrics and materials produced by underage workers overseas in a sweatshop?

Ultimately, reasonable allowances can be built into an SRI policy so that companies with significant noncompliant activities are screened out, but lesser involvement can be considered tolerable. It's possible with certain social screening tools to set a revenue threshold such that companies that derive greater than x% of their total revenues are excluded. In any case, the nonprofit organization's consultant and/or investment managers can help sort through these issues.

Shareholder Advocacy

Some socially conscious investors pursue a strategy of *shareholder advocacy*. The three main components of an activist shareholder strategy are *corporate dialogue, shareholder resolutions,* and *proxy votes.*

Corporate dialogue is generally the first step in shareholder advocacy. Through this dialogue, shareholders convey their concern on social issues directly to the company. By articulating the position in a thoughtful and consistent manner, investors have the potential to shape policy in areas such as the environment, employment equality, and corporate governance. Lobbying shareholders need to be persistent. It may take several years of dialogue to change a given policy. However, your conversations can be successful if you can convince the company that the issue, if unresolved, will ultimately be brought to a shareholder resolution.

A shareholder resolution is a formal request made to a company by a current shareholder. The resolution seeks or recommends action by the company on a specific issue. The Securities and Exchange Commission (SEC) has set forth certain regulations regarding the eligibility, timing, and filing of shareholder resolutions. Each shareholder is limited to one resolution per year, so it is quite common for several shareholders to join together and coordinate their resolution efforts, choosing a designated sponsoring shareholder. Organizations that provide proxy research services and shareholder advocacy support include the Investor Responsibility Research Center (IRRC, www.IRRC.org) and the Interfaith

Center on Corporate Responsibility (ICCR, www.ICCR.org). They can be helpful resources in building a network of support.

Proxy Voting

The initial goal of a shareholder resolution is to get the issue on the proxy statement so that all shareholders can vote on it at the company's annual meeting. If the resolution fails to meet certain guidelines, the company has the right to omit it. This prevents the issue from reaching a shareholder vote. If the resolution is successfully placed on the proxy statement, then it will be voted on at the annual shareholder's meeting. Depending on the shareholder vote, the company may move to adopt or change their policies in accordance with the resolution. However, regardless of the support level, the shareholder resolution is generally not binding on a company's board of directors. They can simply choose to ignore it. For example, in 2004, 54% of Intel Corporation's shareholders voted in favor of adopting the practice of expensing stock options,[1] but Intel's board disagreed with the majority vote and the resolution was not implemented. At General Electric's 2004 shareholder meeting, the board rejected a resolution supported by 68% of voting shareholders[2] calling for annual board elections. According to Institutional Shareholder Services (ISS), of the 172 shareholder proposals that received a majority vote in 2003, only 70 of them were acted upon by company management.[3] Conversely, it's possible for a resolution to be successful with as little as 10% of the shareholder vote if the board believes the recommendations have merit. Guidelines sometimes restrict the resubmittal of failed shareholder resolutions. Generally, first-time resolutions must receive at least 3% of the vote to be considered for the following year's proxy statement. Second-year resolutions must receive at least 6% of the vote, and third-year resolutions must receive 10% of the vote in order to be eligible to continue on the proxy statement.

For shareholders other than the resolution's sponsor, the proxy voting process provides an opportunity to voice their opinion, either for or against the resolution. You need to understand the company-specific proxy issues in order to vote in a consistent, thoughtful manner that reflects the values of your organization. While keeping track of numerous proxy voting issues may seem a daunting task, there are several organizations such as ISS, the IRRC, the ICCR, and many

---

[1]William Baue, "Companies Ignore Majority Votes on Shareowner Resolutions," *Socialfunds.com*, May 20, 2004.
[2]Ibid.
[3]Barry B. Burr, "All Investor Eyes On Busy Proxy Season," *Pensions & Investments*, 14 June, 2004, p. 3.

others that provide research and recommendations on individual company proxy votes.

Current high levels of shareholder activism should make 2004 a record year for shareholder resolutions, surpassing even 2003. According to data from ISS, 1,050 shareholder resolutions were filed in 2003, and estimates for 2004 are at 1,100 resolutions.[4] Given the recent focus on corporate governance, shareholders are likely to keep the pressure on companies for greater transparency and board independence.

If corporate dialogue and shareholder resolutions fail to bring about the desired change in policy, shareholders can still resort to divesting, or selling, a stock holding. A small shareholder may not have much leverage in suggesting this alternative, but a group of shareholders, especially large institutions, may command attention. (Significant selling pressure will drive the price down, impacting incentive stock options and management bonuses.)

Community Investing

Although generally not the centerpiece of most nonprofit organizations' SRI programs, *community investing* plays a small yet meaningful role. Community investing supports low-income and disadvantaged communities by providing financial services for individuals and small business enterprises that may not otherwise have access. Community investing also provides loans and access to capital for local businesses and organizations to provide services in the community such as day-care centers and affordable housing. These resources are created when nonprofit and other investors open certain savings and checking accounts, money market accounts, certificates of deposit, and other investment options. Investment options are generally available through four types of vendors: community development banks, community development credit unions, community development loan funds, and community development venture capital funds.

The simplest form of community investment is to merely open a checking, savings, or money market account at a community development bank or credit union. The accounts are federally insured, similar to traditional banks and credit unions, and generally offer rates that are competitive with traditional banks. These deposits can then be used by the community bank to extend credit or to fund small business loans and worthwhile projects in the community.

Community development loan funds pool investors' resources and extend loans that are generally below market interest rates to those within the commu-

---

[4]Ibid.

nity. These investments are not federally insured and usually require an investment commitment of several years. Though these types of investments produce lower returns than available elsewhere, proponents of community investing argue that even a 1% commitment from individual investors and institutions, if followed broadly, would have a tremendous impact in disadvantaged communities. In essence, the nonprofit organization gives up some portfolio gain in an effort to "prime the pump" of grass roots capitalism. Proponents argue that the performance impact from a 1% community investment allocation has a minimal overall affect on portfolio returns.

SEPARATE ACCOUNTS VERSUS MUTUAL FUNDS

Depending on the overall size of your organization's portfolio, the asset classes you've selected, and their corresponding weights, *separate account management* may offer significant advantages in implementing an SRI strategy. Separate account management means that your portfolio managers run stand–alone accounts containing only your organization's assets. The management of these accounts can be tailored to follow your specific investment directions. This customization means that the portfolio will follow the exact social screens you desire. In addition, you can set limits on cash or foreign exposure, sector weighting, and acceptable credit quality, to name a few. In addition to customization, separate account expenses are frequently lower than those of mutual funds or commingled trusts. Virtually every investment manager will run assets in a separate account (if you meet their minimum), so you have a broad universe of managers from which to choose.

If your nonprofit organization has a small amount of assets, mutual funds may offer the most practical solution. Although the universe of SRI mutual funds is not nearly as large as the universe of SRI separate account managers, the number continues to grow. According to the 2003 Report on Socially Responsible Investing Trends in the United States, there are 200 socially screened mutual funds as of 2004, up from 139 in 1997.[5] Available mutual funds use all three primary SRI methods: screening, shareholder advocacy, and community investing. Some may offer only one or two of the three strategies.

Another key differentiator among SRI mutual funds is the screening criteria that each may use. The most commonly used mutual fund screens are (in order of prevalence) tobacco, alcohol, labor relations, environment, and gambling. Other less common screens include pornography, abortion, and animal testing. Many SRI mutual funds use five or more individual screens; and the vast majority use at

---

[5]Social Investment Forum, "2003 Report on Socially Responsible Investing Trends in the United States," (December 2003); p. ii.

least two. One drawback to using mutual funds is that finding a fund that incorporates the exact screens that your organization desires (within a given investment discipline) may prove to be very difficult. If screening in a certain area is important, you may have to accept screening in other areas that your organization does not feel as strongly about.

Another consideration is cost. SRI mutual funds usually have higher investment expenses (as a percentage of assets) compared with similar separate account managers. Since mutual funds expenses are largely driven by economies of scale, funds that have been around longer and have larger asset bases are more likely to have lower expenses than newer, smaller funds.

You should also consider commingled products. Even fewer in number than mutual funds, some investment firms offer these products as a means of offering their SRI capabilities to prospective clients who are too small for separate account management. These commingled products are similar to mutual funds in some key ways. The manager pools investors' assets and runs the portfolio according to a uniform set of guidelines. Similar to mutual funds, custom screening is not available through a commingled product. Unlike a mutual fund, commingled funds usually offer monthly, rather than daily, liquidity. Certain SRI commingled products may limit liquidity to once per quarter. If the ability to move cash quickly is important, you'll want to clarify this during the due diligence process.

Depending on the commingled fund, the expenses may be lower than a comparable mutual fund, because commingled funds are designed with institutional investors in mind. Institutional investors don't generally require the ancillary services that mutual fund companies provide, for example, toll free phone lines staffed around the clock with investment representatives.   So, the additional costs of those services aren't built into the expense ratio.

PERFORMANCE IMPACT OF SOCIALLY RESPONSIBLE INVESTING

For some nonprofit organizations, adhering to specific social guidelines in investing is not a subject for serious debate. To them, it is critical that their portfolios reflect the values and beliefs of their organization. However, other nonprofit organizations may fear being "penalized" with lower returns for following socially responsible guidelines. In reality, much of the research conducted over the past 10 to 15 years points to no discernable "penalty" for following socially responsible guidelines.

Some research done during the 1990s found that much of the difference in performance of SRI versus traditional investing could be accounted for by differences in market cap, style, and risk. Generally speaking, social screens have resulted in portfolios characterized by smaller market capitalizations, higher beta (market-related risk), and higher growth characteristics (e.g., higher price-earnings ratios) when compared with traditionally managed portfolios that lack social guidelines. When the market favors these characteristics, SRI portfolios benefit.

By taking into account the impact of these characteristics, two significant studies completed in the past several years concluded that an SRI approach does not underperform traditional investing approaches. Rob Bauer, Koedijk Kees, and Roger Otten wrote a paper titled "International Evidence on Ethical Mutual Fund Performance and Investment Style" in January 2002.[6] Bauer, Kees, and Otten analyzed a database of more than 100 socially screened mutual funds using multifactor models to examine returns and investment style from 1990 to 2001. Their research affirmed that SRI mutual funds tend to be more growth oriented than value oriented due to their screening process. However, their research also found that, after accounting for investment style, there was no significant difference in returns on a risk-adjusted basis between SRI strategies and traditional strategies. Bauer, Kees, and Otten concluded that SRI (or ethical) funds "do not under-perform relative to conventional funds."

Another important piece of research in this area reaches a similar conclusion. Bernell K. Stone, John B. Guerard, Jr., Mustafa N. Gultekin, and Greg Adams wrote a research piece in 2001 titled "Socially Responsible Investment Screening: Strong Evidence of No Significant Cost for Actively Managed Portfolios."[7] This research examined the impact of *size, risk, growth,* and *dividend yield* on socially responsible investment returns. Stone and co-authors concluded that, after adjusting for these factors, there was "no significant cost to social screening." Moreover, their research also found that the conclusion of "no significant cost" also held over many shorter-term periods as well as the entire 1984 to 1997 period on which they conducted their research.

The Social Investment Forum looked at the Morningstar ratings of SRI mutual funds versus the overall universe of mutual funds. According to the methodology behind Morningstar's rating system, a four- or five-star rating is awarded to the top 32.5% of mutual funds based largely on risk-adjusted returns. According to the Social Forum, from 2001 to 2003, anywhere from 38% to 43% of all SRI funds were awarded four- and five-star rankings in those years. The conclusion is that a higher percentage of SRI funds received four- and five-star rankings than would be expected relative to the entire mutual fund universe.

---

[6]Rob Bauer, Koedijk Kees, and Roger Otten, "International Evidence on Ethical Mutual Fund Performance and Investment Style," Working Paper, January 2002.

[7]Bernell, K. Stone, John B. Guerard, Jr., Mustafa N. Gultekin, Greg Adams, "Socially Responsible Investment Screening: Strong Evidence of No Significant Cost for Actively Managed Portfolios," *Journal of Investing,* forthcoming.

INCORPORATING SOCIALLY RESPONSIBLE INVESTING INTO INVESTMENT POLICY

A nonprofit organization's desired approach to SRI (screening, advocacy, etc.) should be incorporated in the investment policy statement (IPS). This language can be either detailed or general, depending on the specific issues to be screened, the desired level of adherence, and whether separate accounts, commingled trusts, or mutual funds are used. If the portfolio's size allows for the use of separate accounts, and the nonprofit organization subscribes to various research and proxy voting services, they may have access to company-specific data that would allow the formulation of a list of individual company restrictions to be included in the investment policy. However, that process is likely to be too time consuming and cumbersome for many nonprofit organizations. For this reason, broader language is commonly used to convey the types of business and activities that should be restricted from the portfolio. Separate account managers often subscribe to software and various research services to ensure that the holdings in the portfolio adhere to the IPS objectives (and exclude holdings that don't). Provide your SRI separate account managers with an individual IPS that is specific to your desired portfolio guidelines. As with traditional separate accounts, managers should sign the IPS, acknowledging their understanding of the guidelines.

When your overall portfolio size precludes the use of separate accounts, apply even more general language in the main IPS. Because mutual fund investors have virtually no control over the screening decisions made in mutual funds, it's important that the IPS does not require screening to which your mutual funds managers may not adhere. Your mutual fund or commingled trust investments will be pooled with the investments of others and be screened according to predetermined criteria identified in the fund's prospectus.

Each manager or fund in the portfolio should be incorporated into the main IPS. Also list your criteria for oversight, selection of managers, and ongoing performance evaluation measures. The same performance measures that are used to evaluate traditional managers should be applied to SRI managers. For instance, a large-cap value equity manager following SRI guidelines should be measured against the Russell 1000 Value index or the Standard & Poor's Barra Value index (large-cap value stocks) and against a peer group of other large-cap value managers.

The inclusion of screening criteria in the IPS helps ensure that the values and beliefs of your nonprofit organization are consistently reflected in the portfolio. In addition to the other aspects of an IPS, the SRI screening criteria should receive periodic (annual) review by your investment committee.

## CHAPTER 15

Selecting Other Vendors

In addition to all the other important decisions you have had to make, your nonprofit organization may need to select a trustee or custodian for the investment portfolio, a record keeper for your retirement plan assets or charitable trusts, or a broker to execute trades.

A custodian holds most, if not all, of the assets of your fund. Custodians can be banks (local, regional, or global), trust companies, and even brokerage firms. They hold the securities in safekeeping, facilitate or execute transactions, and provide an accounting of assets and any activity in your accounts. Many banks and trust companies may also provide trustee services. Trustee status means that they assume a fiduciary role in the oversight of the funds. The use of such an outside trustee can provide some comfort to your nonprofit organization's decision makers.

A record keeper can be a bank, trust company, mutual fund company, or independent third-party administrator. There are many financial institutions that administer 401(k) or 403(b) (defined contribution) retirement plans, as well as DB pension plans. Record keepers can also handle the administration of charitable remainder trusts and other annuity trusts that may be gifted to your organization. They track individual accounts and process distributions.

Finally, brokers/dealers execute and clear transactions. They also sell investments and custody assets. However, because of the sales component, you need a complete understanding of the services offered, the broker's capabilities, and any potential conflicts of interest.

STEP ONE

Your first step should be to completely assess your organization's needs. There are various types of vendors, with different areas of specialization. It is important that you have a clear sense of exactly where you need help before embarking on the search process. There is no "one size fits all" solution; it is rare that one vendor can excel in providing multiple services to nonprofit organizations. A firm that does a terrific job administering 401(k) or 403(b) plans may not have the capabilities to custody/trustee and administer a DB pension plan. A firm that handles custody of your assets may not provide record keeping for charitable trusts. Many vendors offer ancillary services so that they can manage the investments. Money management is where the profits lie. See Exhibit 15.1 for a sample questionnaire that can help you clarify your goals.

Let's assume that your organization needs trust and custody services; you can consider a number of different types of firms. Perhaps your local bank provides these services. If your needs are more complex, larger regional and national banks or trust companies have robust trust and custody operations and provide these same services for large numbers of clients. Also, your nonprofit organization's financial adviser or investment management consultant may have an affiliation with a broker/dealer that can provide custody services for little or no cost. You can start with a list of such firms as potential recipients for your request for proposal (RFP).

STEP TWO

The next step is to draft the RFP. Your specific needs will determine if the RFP should be shorter and simpler, or if it needs to include great detail. In general, the smaller the portfolio, the simpler your trust and custody needs may be, particularly if the portfolio predominantly holds mutual funds. If your portfolio is larger, or you use separately managed accounts, your custody needs may be greater. Separate accounts holding foreign securities present an additional layer of complexity.

The RFP should address a few broad areas, with detailed questions in each section. You need to understand the background of each firm and their experience in providing trust and custody services. How many clients do they service? What level of assets does that represent? How many clients similar to your size and needs? How committed is this firm to the trust/custody business? Are they likely to exit this business (do they have critical mass)?

Along with the firm background, it is important to learn about the individuals who will service your account. What is their average industry and firm experience? What is the level of personnel turnover? How do they compensate these people? What incentives do they have to provide superior service?

A second area of importance in the RFP relates to the capabilities of the potential custodian. Can they provide master trust administration? In other words,

EXHIBIT 15.1 VENDOR SEARCH NEEDS ASSESSMENT SAMPLE QUESTIONNAIRE

1. Identify the most important items that should be addressed as they relate to the custody/administration/record keeping of your funds.

_____

_____

_____

2. What are the distribution (cash flow) requirements of the organization? Are there any complexities associated with these requirements?

_____

_____

_____

3. Is "master trust" accounting desired? Are there numerous subaccounts within the larger fund(s) that require detailed reporting?

_____

_____

_____

4. Does your organization have charitable annuities? If so, is assistance needed in their administration?

_____

_____

_____

5. Does your organization have retirement plans that require record keeping? If so, what type of plan? Defined benefit (pension) plan? Defined contribution [401(k) or 403(b)] plan? What is working well and what could be improved?

_____

_____

_____

6. Identify any other obstacles, goals, or thoughts you have about improving the efficiency of administration of these funds.

_____

_____

_____

Source: DiMeo Schneider & Associates, L.L.C.

can a portfolio be managed as one large pool, even though the custodian has the capability to track several subaccounts as individual segments? Does the custodian have global custody capabilities? For larger portfolios, can they facilitate securities lending? (Securities are loaned to various brokers in exchange for a fee. Securities lending can provide an additional source of revenue to your fund.) If they do, what is the minimum account size they'll consider for lending? Generally, the individual separate accounts need to be fairly sizeable ($50–75 million or more depending on the asset class). If you have a small portfolio, can the custodian work with a large universe of mutual funds? Is it a finite list or do they have the capability to custody and place transactions in any publicly traded mutual fund? What do their statements look like? Do they provide the level of reporting that your nonprofit organization desires? How often are the statements generated and how promptly after each period will you receive yours?

A third area you need to examine is technology. How much does the firm invest annually in technology? Can clients access account data via the Internet? What functions can you perform via the Internet? How is your data protected? What are their disaster recovery contingency plans? What new capabilities are on the horizon?

The fourth major section of the RFP should address fees. Describe your expected investment structure. Provide an estimate of the number and types of separate accounts and mutual funds; this will allow the potential vendor to gauge the complexity of their trust/custody duties. The vendor may propose a flat-dollar fee, a percentage of assets, and transaction fees. If the fee is a percentage of assets, it should include break points. The RFP should require details on any transaction fees. For how long will they guarantee their fees? Is there a service guarantee?

The fifth section of the RFP should include a request for references. It is most productive to ask for references that are similar to your organization. Presumably they face many of the same issues that you do. Three or four current client references should be sufficient. See Exhibit 15.2 for a sample RFP.

STEP THREE

Send the RFP with a brief introduction. Describe a bit about your organization, its history, and mission. Include specific instructions about how and to whom to respond. It's a good idea to clearly set a response deadline no later than three weeks from the date you send the RFP. Also communicate the name and contact information for a point person who can respond to vendors' questions. Clearly state that any questions should be directed to this person. This will prevent vendors from hounding board members.

REQUEST FOR PROPOSAL: TRUSTEE/
CUSTODY SERVICES

Background Information

1. Please state the name, title, address, and telephone number of the person we may contact with questions about your responses to this request for proposal.
2. Please provide a brief overview of your firm's trustee/custody department including these specifics:
   - Date founded
   - Total employees in the department
   - Total trust assets
   - Number of clients
   - Number of clients by size:
     —Under $20 million
     —$20–$100 million
     —$101–$500 million
     —$501 million +
   - From where would the account be serviced?
   - Any parent/subsidiary relationships
3. Please provide a brief overview of the account officer who would be assigned to the account:
   - Name of account officer
   - Background and experience
   - Number of clients serviced
   - Who is this person's backup?
4. Please describe forms of insurance regarding errors and omissions.
5. What is your firm's commitment to the trust/custody area for the future?

Technological Capabilities

1. Do you provide online services to your customers? How long has this been offered?
2. How current is online information and how many hours per day is this available?
3. Please describe your backup process and your disaster recovery plan. How often is your backup system tested?

Accounting Systems

1. Explain your process for pricing portfolio securities (also discuss your reconciliation process).
2. What services do you use for pricing held securities?
3. Describe your firm's process in resolving errors. How are they corrected?
4. How are global custody services provided?
5. Are there any specific requirements of international managers?
6. Does your firm have any special concerns with emerging markets? Small or illiquid securities?

Reports

1. Please describe your standard reporting package. Provide a complete description and copies of all reports available to clients. Which standard reports are available online?
2. Are you willing and able to prepare special reports from available data? Is there an additional charge for this service?
3. Is reporting provided on a trade date or settlement date basis?

(continued)

EXHIBIT 15.2 (CONTINUED)

4. Can you integrate the two outside trust assets into your reporting?
5. When are the reports sent out?
6. Please provide a sample statement.

Disbursements

1. What information (and in what format) is required to make disbursements? What is the minimum time required to issue a payment once information is received?
2. What is the charge for checks? Wires?
3. Will you coordinate and assist in planning timelines for disbursements?

Fees

1. Are you willing to offer service guarantees and to put your fees at risk?
2. How long will you guarantee fees?
3. Please describe any costs incurred for terminating the agreement prior to contract expiration?
4. Please provide an estimate of overall first year fees.
5. Please provide an estimate of overall ongoing fees (after first year).
6. Please be specific on base fee versus transaction fees. Will you cap transaction fees?
7. Can trades be placed through your firm? If so, what are the trading costs?
8. Are transaction costs waived or reduced when placed through your firm?
9. Please detail fees associated with custody of mutual plan and commingled trusts.
10. What are the conversion/set-up fees if any?
11. What are the trustee fees?
12. Is there a set-up and/or annual fee for online access?
13. Are there global custody fees?
14. Please provide a detailed estimate of *all* fees for administration, custody and trustee services. Include in your fee quote all assumptions used.

Source: DiMeo Schneider & Associates, L.L.C.

STEP FOUR

When the RFP responses are received, it is helpful to place the individual vendor responses into a matrix. This will make it easier for you to compare and contrast vendors' responses, question by question. This method is particularly helpful when reviewing proposals in a committee setting. Time may be limited, and efficiency is important. You will find it easier to compare vendors if you set up a grid where each type of fee is broken out line by line. When preparing this analysis, carefully consider any transaction-related fees. Estimate a total annual fee. Compare those bottom-line numbers side-by-side. Also, estimate any asset-based fees based on a recent market value of the portfolio. See Exhibit 15.3 for a sample of such a matrix.

With this information in hand, your committee's review will be more organized and efficient.

EXHIBIT 15.3 SAMPLE CUSTODY/TRUSTEE FEE SUMMARY

	Vendor A	Vendor B	Vendor C
Conversion Fee	Waived	$5,000	$0
Asset-based fee Rate	$0	0.10%–$30,000 0.10% of market value of assets	0.05%–$15,000 0.05% of market value of assets
Account/trustee fees	$8,400 $350 annually per mutual fund account (24) = $8,400	$15,000 Monthly maintenance of $50 per subfund (chapter, scholarship accounts). 25 total subfunds. $50 × 12(mos) × 25 = $15,000/year	$7,200 $300/mutual fund account (24) = $7,200
Internet access	$0	$0	$0
Estimated total fees	$8,400	$50,000	$22,500
Minus: Estimated 12b-1 fee credit	$0	$0	$28,575
Estimated net cost	$8,400	$50,000	$0

Assumptions:
$30 million in assets.
Trustee will serve as custodian.
Likely to be all mutual funds with as many as 12 per fund.
Accounts will be valued at least monthly.

12b-1 fee estimates:
ABC Mutual Fund (0.35%) = $9,450
DEF Mutual Fund (0.25%) = $7,125
XYZ Mutual Fund (0.25%) = $12,000

Source: DiMeo Schneider & Associates, L.L.C.

RECORD KEEPERS

Your nonprofit organization may also need to perform a search for a record keeper. If you offer a 401(k) or 403(b) plan for staff members, you need a firm with record-keeping abilities. Record keepers need to account for numerous individual accounts within a larger plan. They have to process purchase and sales transactions as well as contributions to the plan and distributions from the plan.

You can access retirement plan record keepers in several different ways. Bundled providers offer record keeping, compliance and regulatory reporting, participant and plan level servicing, and investment management "bundled" into one product. Large mutual fund families, insurance companies, and banks often dedicate significant resources to the retirement plan business.

An alternative is the semibundled approach. In a semibundled plan, record keeping and some investment management is typically provided by one firm. However, they may also allow outside mutual funds. In a semibundled approach, the compliance testing and regulatory reporting may also be outsourced by the record keeper.

A third alternative is to search for an unbundled record keeper. In an unbundled environment, you usually have the greatest investment flexibility since the record keeper does not manage any competing offerings. Also, compliance testing and regulatory reporting are usually separate functions performed by other firms. Firms that specialize in providing unbundled record keeping solutions are sometimes referred to as third-party administrators.

The entire record-keeping vendor search process (from the very beginning to conversion to the new vendor) can often take six months. Because there are many important steps along the way, it is important to start the process by putting together a time line. This time line lists specific actions, their due date, and the responsible party. In creating this time line, consider the work, preparation, and all of the intermediate steps involved. Allow enough time to create the RFP, develop the recipient list, await vendor responses, summarize their answers, schedule semifinalist presentations, conduct on-site finalist visits, negotiate fees, and prepare for plan conversion. See Exhibit 15.4 for a sample time line.

The RFP should include many of the same broad categories addressed in a trustee/custodian RFP. The vendor's background, the people, the capabilities, commitment to technology, and the fees are all important issues to be addressed. However, record keeping is more complex than trust/custody services. There are several other important areas you need to include.

Most likely the record keeper will provide services directly to plan participants. Be sure to inquire about the availability of toll-free customer service representatives, and Internet functionality. Are there participant research and advice tools?

EXHIBIT 15.4 RECORD-KEEPING REQUEST FOR PROPOSAL (RFP) TIME LINE: SAMPLE WORK PLAN

Action Item	Responsibility	Date	Completed
Solicit plan information and committee input	Consultant	Week 1	
Provide plan information and committee input	Nonprofit	By week 3	
Analyze and resolve committee input	Consultant	By week 4	
Provide draft RFP	Consultant	By week 4	
Provide potential candidate list	Consultant	By week 4	
*Meet to discuss and finalize: • Committee objectives/goals • RFP • RFP recipient list	Nonprofit and consultant	Week 6	
Forward final RFP to potential candidates	Consultant	Week 7	
Receive completed RFPs from candidates	Vendor candidates	Week 10	
Produce RFP summary of all services and costs	Consultant	By Week 13	
*Meet to review RFP summary and select semifinalist candidates	Nonprofit and consultant	Week 13	
*Arrange and facilitate semifinalist presentations	Nonprofit and consultant	Week 16	
Select finalists	Nonprofit and consultant	Week 16	
Arrange on-site due diligence and check references	Consultant	Week 17	
*Conduct on-site visits	Nonprofit and consultant	Week 18	
Negotiate fees and contract issues	Nonprofit and consultant	Week 19	
Provide final recommendation letter/report	Consultant	Week 20	
*Select new vendor (a meeting may be necessary)	Nonprofit	Week 22	
Negotiate and finalize vendor agreement	Nonprofit and consultant	Week 22	
*Meet to select specific funds to fill menu slots	Nonprofit and consultant	Week 23	
Recommend changes/updates to investment policy statement (IPS)	Consultant	Week 24	
Approve and adopt IPS	Nonprofit	By conversion date	
Conversion begins (initiate contributions to new vendor)	Nonprofit	Week 36	
Oversee conversion	Consultant	Week 36	
Monitor plan rollout	Consultant	Ongoing	
Commence investment performance evaluation	Consultant	Ongoing	

*Indicates meeting.

Participant education services should also be addressed in the RFP. Will the vendor do in-person education meetings? If so, how many per year? How many days of initial enrollment meetings are included in their proposal? Can they provide targeted education campaigns for different segments of the participant population?

You also need to inquire about investments. Manager/fund selection and menu design are two crucial areas. Do they have proprietary investment products? If so, must you use a minimum number of their funds? Are there a percentage of assets that need to be invested in these proprietary products? What other funds can they accommodate? How large is this universe? Do they offer lifestyle funds? Do they offer a stable value fund? How many funds are allowed in the lineup without an increase in record-keeping costs? Ask them to recommend a specific fund in each of the following categories: large-cap U.S. equity (in value, growth, and blend styles), small-cap U.S. equity (value and growth), international equity, real estate (i.e., real estate investment trusts), and intermediate bonds. Ask them to provide information on returns, risk, and expenses for each of the proposed funds. A sample RFP can be found in Appendix F.

Once the RFP responses are received, again summarize the individual responses in a grid. The table should have a column for each vendor, with the RFP questions in the far left column and the individual vendor responses across each row. This can be time consuming, but it is time well spent. Also, create a spreadsheet comparison of the proposed fund lineups for each vendor. Reflect annual returns, risk and expenses in individual columns on the spreadsheet. This type of analysis allows the committee to easily make comparisons.

NARROW THE FIELD

Using this summary information, the committee should narrow the field to three or four semifinalist firms. Invite the semifinalists to present to the committee. It is best to have the vendors in one after the other or, at worst, on two consecutive days. The presenting firms should be encouraged to bring along the people who will service you. Presentations should be limited to one hour and allow sufficient time for questions. If possible, provide the vendors with topics that are most important to the committee. It can be helpful to distribute a rating sheet to the committee members before the presentation. This rating sheet covers the major elements you'll use to judge the vendors and allows committee members to score each vendor on a scale of 1 to 5. This is an especially helpful tool after you have listened to three or four different presentations over the course of a day. See Exhibit 15.5 for a sample rating sheet.

EXHIBIT 15.5 SAMPLE PROVIDER RATING WORKSHEET

1. Define the importance of each selection criteria (based on percentages).
2. Rank each provider in each selection criteria area (highest 5; lowest 1).
3. Calculate weighted score for each selection criteria (criteria score x criteria weighting).
4. Total weighted scores at bottom of page.

Selection Criteria	Criteria Weighting %	Vendor A	Vendor B	Vendor C	Vendor D
Organization	____%	_____	_____	_____	_____
• Capability					
Client service	____%	_____	_____	_____	_____
• Participant services					
• Plan sponsor services					
Record keeping/administration	____%	_____	_____	_____	_____
• Technology					
• Efficiencies					
Education/communication	____%	_____	_____	_____	_____
• Education meetings initial/ongoing					
• Quality/quantity of materials					
People	____%	_____	_____	_____	_____
• Training/experience					
• Account coverage					
Investments	____%	_____	_____	_____	_____
• Quality					
• Quantity					
• Ability to use outside funds					
• Lifestyle/asset allocation funds					
• Other					
Cost	____%	_____	_____	_____	_____
• Initial					
• Ongoing					
Total weighted score	**100%**	_____	_____	_____	_____

FINAL STEPS

After the vendor presentations are complete, try to narrow the field to two vendors for on-site visits. We encourage the on-site visit, but many nonprofit organizations simply select a winner on the basis of the presentation. On-site visits can be particularly helpful if the field has been narrowed to two vendors but the committee has no clear preference. On-site visits typically involve a half or full day of tours and meetings at the vendor's record-keeping facility. Committee members get a look at the vendor's infrastructure, view the service team in action, and can spend more time getting to know the people who will service the plan.

Check references when you've decided on the finalists. Depending on staff resources, you may perform this reference check yourselves or delegate it to your investment consultant. Before placing calls, formulate a list of reference questions. Make sure you pose the same question to each reference. You'll get more information if you "loosen up" the reference. Start out with general information such as the person's position and details about the plan size and demographics. Then ask about particular services that the vendor provides. First, ask the reference to describe the vendor's strengths. Then ask "where is there room for improvement?" People generally don't like to start out by saying anything bad about someone.

Probe specific areas such as plan conversion, blackout periods, and payroll integration. How have problems been resolved? Does the main contact respond in a timely and efficient manner? Has there been turnover among the individuals working on the account? Have they increased fees? If so, what was the rationale? Exhibit 15.6 provides some sample questions.

As part of fee negotiations, also discuss related issues such as the number of nonproprietary funds allowed or the number of education meetings to be provided. If the vendor won't budge on the overall fee structure, perhaps there are additional services that they could include? This is the time to address any element of the proposal that you don't like.

Ideally, fee negotiations should take place before the winner is selected. This is your time of maximum leverage; use it to your advantage.

DEFINED BENEFIT PLANS

You may also need to search for a provider of trust/custody and administration for a defined benefit (DB) pension plan. Although DB plans are a dying breed, some older organizations, including many hospitals, still have them. DB plans are similar to other trustee/custodian searches, but they have the added wrinkle of ongoing benefit payments to retirees. Organizations with trust departments (banks, trust companies, and some mutual funds companies) are equipped to provide this service.

In the RFP you should include the number of estimated monthly benefit payments. Request details on processing or transaction-related fees. Will the vendor handle tax reporting such as providing a W-2 or 1099 to the beneficiaries? Will they provide federal and state tax withholding? The investment structure of the pension may also have some bearing on fees. Does the vendor have proprietary investment products? If so, would inclusion of any of those products in the pension's asset allocation impact the overall fee structure?

GIFT ANNUITIES

You may also need an administrator for gift annuities that have been donated to the organization. Donors often make gifts that ultimately pass to your nonprofit organization but provide the grantor with an income stream in the interim. The grantor enters into a contract that stipulates the amount to be paid back to the grantor on an annual basis as an annuity. These are irrevocable gifts that may pay income for life or a specific period of years. The payments are generally fixed. When both the grantor and surviving beneficiary pass, the remaining funds become the sole property of the nonprofit organization. There are tax advantages for the grantor as well as the comfort of a steady income stream.

Your organization undoubtedly appreciates such gifts, but they come with the responsibility to oversee the investment strategy, remit payments, handle tax reporting, and issue statements to the donors. Administration of these annuities can be complex, particularly if you oversee a large number. It's possible for the annual payments to represent taxable income, taxable capital gains, or even nontaxable income to the grantor. A nonprofit organization has to either hire staff to administer these annuities or find a record keeper or administrator to perform these duties for them. Outsourcing is a growing trend because many schools, hospitals, and religious organizations recognize the liability and complexity in servicing these annuities.

If the annuities are custodied at a large trust company or bank, they may provide software to help you manage the accounting and general administration. But if the process has become too cumbersome, you may want to search for a vendor to take over the administration.

The search process can begin with local financial institutions that have trust servicing capabilities. But generally only large banks with significant trust operations offer these planned giving services. If your bank says that they offer this

EXHIBIT 15.6 SAMPLE REFERENCE QUESTIONS

Provider:
Company Name:
Contact Name:
Date:

1. Are you the individual who works most frequently with this vendor within your company?
2. What industry is your company in? How do you classify your work force (blue collar, professional, etc.)
3. How many participants are in your plan?
4. How many total employees are in your company? Of those, how many are eligible to participate?
5. What is the total asset value of the plan?
6. How long has _____ been your vendor?
7. What are their strengths?
8. Where are there areas for improvement?
9. Have they been able to do everything that they initially said they could do?
10. Are they doing everything that they said they would do?
11. Did you feel the conversion process and steps were well communicated to you? To participants?
12. Was the conversion completed on time?
13. What was the biggest problem encountered in the conversion process? How was it resolved?
14. How long was the blackout period? Overall, did you feel like a partner in the conversion process?
15. Who was your former provider and what was your reason for leaving?
16. Did you receive accurate statements on a timely basis the first quarter after conversion? Subsequent statements?
17. Comment on the usefulness of the statements. Were they able to customize them?
18. How are record keeping/administrative issues resolved?
19. Do you use _____ for your payroll? If so, are they integrated with the vendor?
20. How would you describe your employees' understanding of retirement planning concepts?
21. Do communication materials address all segments of your population?
22. What do participants think of the voice response system? Internet?
23. What do you as an administrator think of the Internet capabilities and voice response system?
24. Do you feel phone representatives are knowledgeable and well-trained? Have there been any participant comments regarding phone representative service?
25. Does this vendor conduct annual on-site education meetings?
26. Were enrollment meetings conducted in a professional and lively manner? (Did they "sell" the plan to the participants?)
27. How did your employees view these meetings?
28. Did they customize the ongoing education meetings for you?
29. How effective were/are the communications pieces? Did you realize an increase in participation? A decrease?
30. Do you feel you receive accurate and timely responses from your main contacts?

31. Do you feel your account manager is knowledgeable? Do you have confidence in the answers to your questions?

32. Has there been any turnover among the individuals working on your account? If so, has this caused any problems?

33. Have they increased fees? What has been the frequency or motivation behind the increases?

34. If you had it to do over, what would you have done differently?

35. Given the benefit of hindsight, would you have:
    A. Selected this provider?
    B. Retained your previous provider?
    C. Selected a different provider?

36. Do you believe there is any reason to seek a new vendor today or at some point in the near future?

37. Did you feel that the relationship was and continues to be important to them?

38. On a scale from 1 to 10 with 10 being the highest, how would you rate this vendor on the following?
    A. Plan sponsor service
    B. Participant service
    C. Record keeping/administration
    D. Communications
    E. Investments
    F. Overall

39. On a scale from 1 to 10 with 10 being the highest, how do you think participants would rate this vendor on the following?
    A. Internet services
    B. Phone services
    C. Statements
    D. Communications
    E. Investments

40. Would you or have you recommended this vendor to other companies?

41. Notes:

---

service, ask for a list of clients they currently serve. Some smaller trust companies may claim that they can perform these duties, when in reality they are geared to service individual trusts and are not structured to administer a hundred or more annuity trusts for one client.

Modify the custodial RFP to focus on the key services needed to administer these annuities. How will the bank perform tax reporting? How timely can they process payments to donors? How often will statements be sent to donors? What do the statements look like? What type of investment flexibility is allowed in these annuity accounts? Is there a proprietary investment requirement?

Fees for this service can be paid directly out of the annuity trusts. By virtue of the workload relief, outsourcing this service can actually reduce your institution's costs. Fees are generally quoted as a percentage of assets. Fees in the 0.5% to 0.75% range are quite common.

Large nonprofit organizations that hold hundreds or even thousands of these annuity accounts may find that the larger financial institutions with great processing capabilities are the best fit for their needs. However, if your nonprofit organization only has a few, banks and trust companies below that top tier may work.

BROKERS

You may also consider using brokers/dealers for some of these functions. When considering utilizing a broker's services, it's important to understand the nature of their business and how they are compensated. Individual brokers are, first and foremost, sales people. Most are paid based on transactions. These transactions can generate a commission on a stock purchase or sale, the markup or spread on a bond that is purchased or sold, or the front-end loads (sales charge) that are assessed on mutual fund transactions. Brokers also receive compensation on a trailing basis as 12b-1 fees that are embedded in some funds' expenses. If it seems as though a broker (or anyone for that matter) offers a host of services at little or no cost, chances are that there may be hidden fees or commissions.

When considering a broker for custody services, be conscious of the fact that while the custody costs may be "free," you need to keep a close eye on trading costs. You should make a distinction between institutional brokers and the traditional retail firms. The institutional firms are generally accessed through independent registered investment advisers or money managers. They are characterized by salaried service people. The retail Wall Street firms tend to actively pursue your business. They are characterized by commissioned sales people. (More and more firms now seek to compensate their sales people via a "wrap fee" as a percentage of assets.)

Brokers/dealers are generally not well suited for trust/custody of a DB pension plan. Unless they own a trust company, they cannot accomplish the important functions of benefit payment processing and tax reporting.

## CHAPTER 16

Hiring an Investment Management Consultant

Once nonprofit organizations cross a certain financial threshold, they are well advised to obtain assistance in the management of their assets. The problem is that there are far more pretenders than players. Most vendors offering "help" have a product to sell that may or may not provide a solution.

Nonprofit organizations tend to be passionate about their programs and missions. This is good. Their desire to manage their money prudently sometimes takes a back seat. This is not good. However, a nonprofit organization's ability to fulfill its mission is almost always constrained by financial resources. Higher investment returns translate directly into accomplishing more.

IDENTIFYING THE NEED: A TALE OF THE TYPICAL NONPROFIT ORGANIZATION

Investment for nonprofit organizations, at least in the beginning, is practically an afterthought. The portfolio is small and the organization's dependency on it is minimal. But over time, assets grow and the portfolio takes on greater importance.

An investment committee is eventually formed, and its members include key individuals on staff as well as successful businesspeople gracious enough to volunteer their time. The committee considers suggestions and adopts policies on everything from asset allocation to the hiring of managers to socially responsible investing.

A local bank is hired to "handle" the investments. The portfolio continues to grow. A shrewd committee member contends that diversification is good and a second local bank is hired. Over the years, the committee continues to diversify.

Money is placed with a mutual fund that uses social screens, a money manager that a staff member met at a conference, and a well-intentioned broker, the brother-in-law of a committee member.

Is the nonprofit fund prudently diversified? Hardly! Although each decision was made with the best of intentions, committee members did not truly possess the information and expertise to make good decisions. Unless you are knowledgeable in all of the following areas, it may make sense to hire a consultant:

- *Investments*. Working at a financial institution in an unrelated role does not qualify. Do committee members possess direct knowledge and experience in the capital markets? Do they oversee similar investment pools for other nonprofit organizations?

- *Fiduciary Stewardship*. Do committee members understand their legal (and moral) duties and can they effectively document their compliance?

- *Impartiality*. Do committee members apply a completely independent and objective perspective in the decision-making process?

- *Fees and Expenses*. Do committee members understand pricing structures? Are they capable of negotiating favorable terms with investment managers and other vendors?

- *Time*. Can they commit the required time?

THE GENERAL CONTRACTOR—A.K.A. THE INVESTMENT CONSULTANT

You can imagine how difficult if would be to construct a home by haphazardly hiring tradesmen without a clear understanding of the role each plays. Although each carpenter, plumber, and electrician may be a skilled worker and possess good references, they may not be right for the specific assignment. Is there a rationale as to when and how each subcontractor should be hired? Are they capable of following the blueprint? Who coordinates all of this? Every well-run construction project has a general contractor. In the investment world, an investment consultant is the general.

A good investment consultant will help to:

- Crystallize the organization's goals and objectives.
- Develop a "blueprint" (investment policy, spending policy, and asset allocation).
- Hire subcontractors (appropriate investment managers).
- Closely monitor performance to ensure that the project is a success.

- Negotiate fees.
- Coordinate time lines among the various parties.

Simply put, a good investment consultant should help the nonprofit organization to achieve its goals with less time, cost, and burden. Most importantly, a good consultant will accomplish this in a completely impartial fashion. There is neither a product to sell nor an axe to grind. Each and every recommendation should be the result of independent analysis. Developing the very best solution should be a good consultant's only goal.

There are several resources that list consulting firms. The Investment Management Consultants Association (IMCA) can provide references and The Nelsons' Consultants' Directory is quite comprehensive (see Resources in Appendix G).

Exhibit 16.1 is a questionnaire that can help one decide if it makes sense to seek outside expertise.

Although properly overseeing the management of a nonprofit fund may not be rocket science, it is time consuming. And the stakes—the long-term existence of the fund—are high!

An experienced consultant has probably already dealt with every challenge the organization faces. And there's no substitute for objective advice. Even if committee members happen to be expert and have the time to devote to this task, they still may not have all the resources needed. Good consulting firms have all the necessary hardware, software, and, most importantly, people.

EXHIBIT 16.1 DO WE NEED A CONSULTANT?

Do I have the expertise to handle this project?	yes	no
Do I understand all the fiduciary requirements?	yes	no
Am I clear on all the players and their exact duties (e.g., custodian, trustees, asset manager, etc.)?	yes	no
Can I establish successful spending and investment policies?	yes	no
Do I understand portfolio theory and asset allocation?	yes	no
Do I have the expertise to analyze investment managers or funds?	yes	no
Do I adequately understand risk as well as return?	yes	no
Do I understand the operational/administrative procedures?	yes	no
Do I have enough time to devote to this project?	yes	no
Do I have staff to work on this?	yes	no
Do I have the budget for this (data sources, software, etc.)?	yes	no
Do I even want to do this on my own?	yes	no

Key: Two or more "no" answers—find a consultant!

Source: DiMeo Schneider & Associates, L.L.C.

Identifying a Qualified Investment Consultant

Assuming that you have made the decision to seek outside help, it rapidly becomes apparent that every salesperson with a financial product to push now is identified as "consultant" or "adviser." How can a fund fiduciary identify the real thing?

It's relatively easy. A true consulting firm derives virtually all of its revenue from consulting; it is not a part-time occupation. A good consultant does not recommend proprietary money management or financial products. The firm should be able to provide numerous references from current clients similar in structure. The IMCA Code of Professional Responsibility (Exhibit 16.2) provides a good sense of the proper mind-set.

Exhibit 16.3 is a sample request for proposal (RFP) that you can adapt. As with all RFPs, shorter is better. Ask only for information that will help the committee make a decision. Identify only needed services.

EXHIBIT 16.2   INVESTMENT MANAGEMENT CONSULTANTS ASSOCIATION CODE OF PROFESSIONAL RESPONSIBILITY

Each professional investment management consultant shall:

- Serve the financial interests of clients. Each professional shall always place the financial interests of the client first. All recommendations to clients and decisions on behalf of clients shall be solely in the interest of providing the highest value and benefit to the client.

- Disclose fully to clients services provided and compensation received. All financial relationships, direct or indirect, between consultants and investment managers, plan officials, beneficiaries, sponsors, or any other potential conflicts of interest shall be fully disclosed on a timely basis.

- Provide to clients all information related to the investment decision-making process as well as other information they may need to make informed decisions based on realistic expectations. All client inquiries shall be answered promptly, completely, and truthfully.

- Maintain the confidentiality of all information entrusted by the client, to the fullest extent permitted by law.

- Comply fully with all statutory and regulatory requirements affecting the delivery of consulting services to clients.

- Endeavor to establish and maintain excellence personally and among colleagues in all aspects of investment management consulting and all aspects of financial services to clients.

- Support and participate in the activities of the Investment Management Consultants Association to enhance the investment management consulting profession.

- Maintain the highest standard of personal conduct.

Source: Investment Management Consultants Association.

EXHIBIT 16.3 REQUEST FOR PROPOSAL

I. Background Information
   A. Name and address of firm.
   B. Name, address, telephone numbers, and e-mail address of key contact.
   C. Business focus/client base.
      1. Provide a brief history of your firm and parent organization and a current organization chart.
      2. Discuss the ownership structure of your firm. Are there unique attributes in the ownership structure that act to encourage the retention of key personnel?
      3. What is the median and mean size of the portfolio of your foundation/endowment clients?
      4. List any senior level hires and departures over the past two years. Indicate reasons for departure.
      5. What is the number of clients the consultant has that would be handling our account? What is the maximum number of clients you allow each consultant to service?
      6. List the personnel you would expect to assign to the foundation. Please provide brief biographical information on each individual including position in the company, education, years and type of experience in investment management.
      7. Is your firm affiliated with a brokerage firm or other financial service enterprises? Do you manage money for any clients?
      8. What percentage of your income comes from consulting activities?
      9. Identify other sources of income.
      10. How many clients have you added in the past two years?
      11. How many clients have you lost in the past two years?
      12. Indicate any future plans, which your firm has regarding investment consulting, investment management, or other business activities?

II. Investment Management Process
   A. Asset allocation methodology
      1. How are projections of your capital markets derived?
      2. Is your asset allocation software developed in-house or externally? Please provide a sample.
   B. Investment Policy Statements
      1. Describe in detail the process you undertake to analyze and make recommendations regarding our investment policy statement. Please provide a sample statement.
   C. Money manager structure and search (see attached list of current investment managers)
      1. Does your firm maintain a database of money management organizations? If so, is the database compiled internally or purchased from an outside source? Does the database include minority- and female-owned firms?
      2. How many managers do you currently track?
      3. How do you gather your money manager information and how often is the data updated?
      4. Are managers required to pay a fee for inclusion in your database?
      5. Please describe your due diligence/search process for manager selection.
      6. How often does your staff visit money managers, both in house and on site? What type

(continued)

EXHIBIT 16.3 (CONTINUED)

      of reports do you provide the client after meetings with the money manager? Do you have a proprietary quality rating system for managers in your database?

    7. What guidelines do you use with respect to a possible money manager termination?

D. Performance measurement

    1. Describe your process of monitoring money managers for a client.

    2. List comparisons, including databases, used to analyze the performance of portfolios. What peer groups would you propose and what are the characteristics of those groupings (foundations, endowments, pension funds, etc.)? Do you have information on endowment funds comparable to us?

    3. How soon after the quarter end are your reports available?

    4. Please provide a sample report that includes performance measurement and other portfolio analysis.

    5. What is your position on the effectiveness of performance fees?

III. Conflicts of Interest

Please disclose any potential conflicts of interest, or appearance of conflict, which might arise if selected to represent the foundation.

IV. References

Please provide a list of at least five references, preferably including any INSERT YOUR TYPE OF PLAN clients. Please indicate contact name, address, and phone number.

V. Fee Schedule

A. Please outline your proposed fee structure for the foundation, including fixed and variable fees, and any performance-based fees. Please indicate all services you propose to provide and their associated fees. Assume participation at quarterly meetings of the Investment and Finance Committee.

B. The stated fee schedule must include all charges associated with your service provisions.

C. If hired, will firm receive any other form of compensation, including soft dollars, from working with this account that has not yet been revealed? If so, what is the form of compensation?

D. Do you provide modified or specialized fee schedules for foundations and/or philanthropic organizations?

Useful Hints

Send the RFP only to viable candidates. For example, if the committee would not really consider the consulting department of a large broker-dealer, don't waste the committee's time or the broker's. One should narrow the list of candidates before sending out the questionnaire.

Keep the RFP short and insist on complete but concise responses. Describe minimum selection requirements—"deal-killers." This will keep noncandidates out of the process.

Exhibit 16.4 may prove useful when you check references. These questions are designed to help solicit information that the reference might not volunteer.

EXHIBIT 16.4 CONSULTANT REFERENCE QUESTIONNAIRE

1. How long have you worked with _____ [the consulting firm]?
2. What do they do best?
3. Where is there room for improvement?
4. Describe how they reduce your workload.
5. What could have been streamlined?
6. Rate their capabilities in each of these areas from highest (5) to lowest (1):
   - General expertise
   - Goal setting/fund design
   - Spending policies
   - Asset allocation
   - Manager search
   - Performance evaluation
   - Pricing
   - Overall client service

Note: This is designed for a phone interview. Although the list of questions is short, it is designed to uncover areas of weakness. It's important to keep the questions in this order.

Once the committee has sent out the RFPs and evaluated the answers, it is time to narrow the field. The goal should be to perform face-to-face due diligence on no more than four finalist candidates. It is best to interview all candidates on the same day or at least during a two-day period. If too much time elapses between interviews, distinctions among the finalists will blur.

The Interview

Your committee already knows most of the quantitative information about the finalists before the face-to-face meeting. Presumably all are competent. What, then, is the purpose of the interview?

First, which of the candidates best fits the organization's objectives? Personal compatibility is important as well. The committee will work closely with the consultant on important projects with tight deadlines. You shouldn't be too quick to overlook personality quirks that may become hugely irritating with constant contact.

Try to understand the philosophy of the firm. If the nonprofit organization and the consultant share a common point of view, many of the details will fall into place. Philosophical differences can lead to friction.

The interview is the time to confirm, or deny, initial perceptions developed earlier in the process. For example, several years ago our firm, a midsize Midwest-based consult, was in competition for an assignment for a $60 million foundation. Close to a dozen consulting firms were in the RFP process, and the firm was selected as one of two finalists to be interviewed by the committee.

Although we enjoy a strong reputation for client service and "outside the box" proactive thinking, the other finalist was a very large East Coast firm. They enjoy a fine reputation and an absolutely star-studded list of endowment and foundation clients.

As the process unfolded, we interviewed with the committee, our references were checked, and we were fortunate enough to be hired. After the fact, it came to light that, before the interviews, one of the committee members strongly felt that meeting with us would be a waste of time. Why wouldn't the committee simply make the "IBM decision" and hire the big firm with the sterling client list?

It turns out that, during the interview, the committee members truly appreciated the time we had spent preparing for the meeting and some of the potential solutions presented. It was also only in the meeting that the committee learned they'd work with principals of the firm compared with relatively junior professionals from the big firm.

So what is the message? Not that the big firm was bad or even that they could not have done a nice job. The lesson is that fit is important and that certain things can only be learned in these important face-to-face meetings.

Proof

In the interview, the committee should ask for demonstrations or specific examples. For each area of service, don't let the candidates claim to be good—make them prove it. Each candidate should review the fund specifics prior to the meeting and make observations and suggestions. The investment committee will be able to easily judge the candidates' level of preparation and expertise.

Verification

What have the finalists done for other clients? How have the strategies they've recommended performed? Get the numbers.

Exhibit 16.5 provides some sample interview questions. Make certain to ask each finalist the same questions. Keep the list of questions relatively short. You won't get through a long list anyway. Finally, open-ended questions ("essay questions") will help the committee understand how the consultant candidates think.

EXHIBIT 16.5 CONSULTANT INTERVIEW QUESTIONS

1. Why do you want to do business with us?
2. Describe your ideal client.
3. What sets you apart?
4. What is your greatest shortcoming?
5. How would you foresee helping us?
6. When you don't win a competition, why do you lose?
7. How many clients have you lost in the past year?
8. Why did they leave?
9. If I were to hire two consulting firms, what would I hire you for?
10. What would I hire the other firm to do?
11. What steps have you taken to eliminate conflict of interest with regard to fund or manager selection?

Note: Most factual information should come from the response to the RFP. Of course, any questions that are raised by a response should be addressed.
Source: DiMeo Schneider & Associates, L.L.C.

The On-Site Visit

Often nonprofit investment committees want to skip this step. They are well advised not to. It is very telling to visit the finalists in their shop. Anyone can talk about their capabilities, but it is quite another thing to demonstrate the hardware and software. Reading a biography is a poor substitute for actually meeting the personnel who will provide the work.

The Agreement

Once the committee has made its decision, it's necessary to get the agreement in writing. What services will be provided? Is there a satisfaction guarantee? What are the remedies if the consultant fails to meet expectations? What is the term of the contract? How do they bill?

The client should have the right to end the contract with 30 days written notice and to be obligated only for services rendered up to that point. The nonprofit organization's attorney should review the contract. We are not in the business of rendering legal advice, and so have intentionally excluded a sample contract or worksheet. Suffice it to say, legal review is not the area in which to cut costs.

Fees

Fees are typically quoted in one of three ways:

1. *Project Basis.* There is a fee for each specific service; e.g., X dollars for an investment policy, Y dollars for a manager search, and so on.

2. *Fixed Retainer.* There is an annual fee to include all services. If the organization's needs are fairly broad, the retainer may be more cost effective than are project-based fees. Retainer fees quoted as a set dollar amount are generally more restrictive in terms of the services covered than the asset-based retainer.

3. *Asset-Based Retainer.* The annual fee is quoted as a percentage of assets. This is generally the broadest contract in terms of services ("all services, when needed"). The asset-based retainer has the advantage that your committee will make full use of the consultant without worrying about "starting the meter." This arrangement is most advantageous if the organization may have stable or even declining asset balances or if the committee is concerned about the market outlook.

EFFECTIVE USE OF A CONSULTANT

How does the organization get its money's worth after it has hired a consulting firm? First, think of them as an extension of staff, and help them understand what is expected. Also, someone on the committee should help them understand the organization, including the personalities of the players.

Next, give them as much of the work as possible. They'll make it obvious if they don't consider a certain task to be a part of their assignment. If the committee is unsure of which way to go at key turning points, let the consultant research the alternatives. Instruct them to succinctly present the pros and cons. Let them create the detailed backup.

Ask them to explain their process. How do they come to their conclusions? For instance, in conducting an investment manager search, get the details. How are candidates to be screened? The committee may want to add or subtract certain criteria.

Use their experience. They probably know what works and what doesn't. Trust them. For example, if the committee wants 11 different fund choices, but the consultant says that 5 or 6 will be sufficient and a more manageable number, listen. Obviously, the client controls the decision, but it pays to be open minded.

If committee members don't understand something, they should make the consultant explain. Part of their job is to educate the committee so you can be better trustees.

SUMMARY

A good investment consultant should add value many times its fee by:

- Improving investment performance.
- Helping committee members satisfy their fiduciary responsibilities.
- Reducing expenses.
- Providing continuity for a committee with regular changes in its membership.
- Increasing contributions to the nonprofit organization by helping to communicate well-founded investment and spending policies.

## CHAPTER 17

Behavioral Finance

Every Wall Street trader knows that "fear and greed move markets." This stark reality, that human emotions are a major driver of the global financial markets, flies in the face of the "rational investor" assumptions rooted deep in Modern Portfolio Theory and the *Efficient Market Hypothesis*. Over the years, academic researchers have built mathematical models to describe financial markets. William Sharpe developed the *Capital Asset Pricing Model* to explain security and portfolio price movements. Other models such as *Arbitrage Pricing Theory* attempt to further refine the theories. For years the Efficient Market Hypothesis has ruled academia. Its basic tenet is that all known information is already reflected in security prices. The implication is that it is impossible for an investor to "beat the market" over time. The entire index fund industry is built on that premise.

But there have always been nagging questions. There is some evidence that value stocks tend to outperform over long periods. Why? Is there a measurable "January effect"? What causes it? What leads to market bubbles . . . and crashes?

Academics have claimed that long-term successful investors like Warren Buffet, Peter Lynch, Bill Miller, and Bill Gross are merely the lucky survivors. But others have had their doubts. Some basketball players are better than others. You can identify superior ballerinas, singers, actors, business people, even politicians. Why should investing be the only human activity where it's impossible to be skillful?

Over the past 10 or 15 years a new line of research has developed a theory that is 180 degrees opposite to the Efficient Market Hypothesis. *Behavioral finance* takes a psychological view of market behavior. Professors Richard Thaler at the University of Chicago, Terence O'Dean at the University of California-Berkley, Hersh Shefrin at Santa Clara University, and others have developed a body of work that has gradually come to ascendancy. Their basic premise is that humans are *not* rational when it comes to investing. Furthermore, investors are not only irrational, but they are irrational in predictable ways.

In this chapter we will identify some of these human tendencies. Over millennia people have evolved mental short-cuts called *heuristics* to deal with the complexities of existence. These heuristics, while generally helpful, sometimes result in conceptual flaws. Think of these flaws as "bugs" in a computer program. Hopefully this overview will help your committee avoid some of the all too human tendencies to shoot ourselves in the foot.

TRYING TO BREAK EVEN

As an addicted gambler can attest, people often prefer large uncertain losses to smaller certain ones. This is clearly not logical, either for a gambler or an investor. Yet investors often behave like desperate gamblers, trying to quickly break even after sour bets by increasing portfolio risk. A rational investor would be guided by portfolio objectives and constraints that do not change based on short-term portfolio fluctuations.

SNAKE BITTEN

An investor may become "snake bitten" after suffering portfolio losses. The opposite of trying to break even, a snake-bitten investor may suddenly reduce or eliminate portfolio risk in order to avoid making the same mistake twice. Before the recent bear market, many investors overestimated their risk tolerance. Only after they experienced the loss did they adopt a more conservative posture, thereby guaranteeing that they wouldn't participate in the rebound. They experienced the entire downside consequence of risk-taking activities while missing the longer-term upside potential.

BIASED EXPECTATIONS AND OVERCONFIDENCE

Many investors have too much confidence in their ability to forecast the future. Believing their expectations are more likely to be realized than those of others, overconfident investors tend to discount any information that doesn't support their opinions. An investment committee member once stated, "Since the dollar is going to rise relative to the euro and yen next year, we should sell all of our international investments." Notwithstanding the facts that exchange rate forecasting is notoriously difficult and there has often been low or negative correlation be-tween domestic currency returns and foreign asset performance, the committee member was absolutely certain about his expectations and discounted any infor-mation to the contrary. By the way, he was forecasting 2004, a year in which the dollar declined precipitously. Overconfident investors often "put too many eggs in the wrong basket."

HERD MENTALITY

Investors sometimes blindly follow the majority position or the "loudest" high-conviction idea. They fall prey to the *herd mentality*. Psychological studies show that people often have a difficult time dissenting within a group. In a committee-driven investment process, groupthink can be damaging. Such portfolios tend to have poor risk controls and to be poorly diversified.

ASSET SEGREGATION OR MENTAL ACCOUNTING

Instead of evaluating an investment's return and risk impact on the overall port-folio, investors often fixate on individual asset return and risk characteristics. This can lead to a breakdown in effective portfolio construction principals. For exam-ple, if you fixate on the risks of high-yield bonds you might ignore their diversi-fication benefits for the portfolio as a whole.

Investors apply the mental accounting heuristic to returns as well. An invest-ment committee member once stated, "Since the target return of our portfolio is 9% per year, we should eliminate all asset classes that won't get at least 9%, in-cluding all of our investment-grade bonds." This is an example of naïve mental accounting. This committee member has fixated on individual assets when the objective return of 9% is for the whole portfolio. As we saw in Chapter 7, by blending noncorrelating assets, you produce portfolios with higher expected re-turns at each risk level.

Another example of mental accounting is "playing with the house's money." Gamblers are willing to take greater risk with their winnings than their prin-cipal. They don't view a dollar of winnings as equal to a dollar of principal. Like the gambler, investors are often more willing to lose what they view as the "gain" rather than what they view as "principal." Asset segregation like this results in suboptimal total portfolio risk-adjusted returns. There's a reason casi-nos thrive.

COGNITIVE DISSONANCE

Cognitive Dissonance Theory was developed in 1957 by former Stanford University Psychology Professor Leon Festinger. Festinger proved that the brain records historic *feelings* more vividly than facts. Cognitive dissonance is created when people's actions differ from their beliefs. People are driven to be consistent and therefore to avoid cognitive dissonance. They either alter the behavior or, more commonly, they alter their beliefs. Festinger's thesis is that people often conveniently avoid or ignore information that might cause cognitive dissonance. Because investors want to believe they are successful, they tend to recall investment successes more vividly than investment failures. Cognitive dissonance explains many irrational tendencies. For example, at least half of the world's investors have below average ability, yet most believe they are in the top half!

ANCHORS

An *anchor* is a reference point that shapes thought. Professor Thaler demonstrates anchoring during group lectures. He asks audience members to write down their birthday as a number. If someone was born on December 20, they would write down 1220. He then asks the audience to estimate Charlemagne's year of birth. Since most people don't study history, they are relegated to guessing. An interesting phenomenon occurs; people tend to make their estimates as a function of their own birthday. In other words, an audience member who was born on May 19 would be likely to guess Charlemagne lived in the sixth century. Someone who was born in November might guess the 12th century! (He was actually born in 742—the 8th century.)

Quantitative and *moral anchors* often end up overwhelming the investment decision-making process. Quantitative anchors measure an investment relative to some arbitrary reference price. For example, an investor buys a stock at $100 and watches it decline precipitously to $50. In the investor's mind, the stock remains a $100 stock. The investor is anchored to $100 and is unwilling to sell at $50 regardless of the fundamental outlook for the stock.

Moral anchors center around qualitative factors such as narratives, stories shared with others, and rationalizations. In 1999, "pie in the sky" stories about the Internet kept hyperventilating investors buying, even though some of their purchases were trading at multiples of 100 or 200 times earnings. (In fact, companies with no earnings whatsoever did best.) The moral anchor overwhelmed fundamental considerations and even common sense.

FEAR OF REGRET AND SEEKING PRIDE

Fear of regret refers to the pain felt after making a bad investment decision. It causes investors to hold on to losers too long. "If I haven't sold, I haven't taken a loss." Conversely, investors *seek pride*. They want the joy of making a wise investment decision. Seeking pride can lead investors to sell too quickly so they can brag about the associated profit.

REPRESENTATIVENESS

Investors often rely on certain characteristics to be representative of future investment success. For example, the "value expressive" investor might view a "good" company as a "good" investment. However, good companies are often bad investments if the market's optimistic expectations are already factored into the current stock price. You are better off buying an underpriced "bad" company than an overvalued "good" one. But to the value expressive investor, the good company is always preferred over the bad company, no matter what the valuation.

FAMILIARITY

Investors often choose investments they are most familiar with. They feel more comfortable with things they recognize. This can lead to poorly diversified portfolios that are overly concentrated in domestic blue chip stocks and domestic investment-grade bonds. It also often leads to little or no allocations to small-cap stocks, foreign stocks, high-yield bonds, real estate, foreign bonds, inflation indexed bonds, emerging market stocks or bonds, or alternative asset classes or investment strategies.

INVESTOR PERSONALITY TYPES

You can categorize individuals within broad investor personality types. This can be helpful in understanding the way they make investment decisions. Look around at your committee. There are at least four broad investor personality types:

- *The Suspicious Investor.* Suspicious investors are very cautious and exhibit a strong desire for financial security. They are the most risk averse. They focus on very safe investment vehicles with little potential for loss. Individuals in this category tend to overanalyze investment opportunities, but once they make investment decisions, their portfolios exhibit relatively low turnover and low volatility.

- *The Process-Oriented Investor.* Process-oriented investors are methodical and maintain a keen eye on risk. They perform their own research and rarely make emotional investment decisions. Their investment decisions tend to be conservative or risk averse. Working with these investors on investment committees can be difficult due to the confidence they place on their own investment processes.

- *The Structured Investor.* Structured investors are the most individualistic. They do their own homework and are confident in their abilities. They are capable of questioning inconsistencies in analyst or consultant recommendations or conclusions. They are unlikely to get caught up in a herd mentality. Structured investors are less risk averse than process-oriented investors.

- *The Unstructured Investor.* Unstructured investors are spontaneous. They often chase the latest hot investments. They are also often risk seeking rather than risk averse. Their portfolios typically exhibit high turnover, and superior investment decisions are often negated by high transaction costs. Risk considerations are often secondary to their investment decision-making process. Investment decisions are often attributed to "gut instinct."

RISK-SEEKING BEHAVIOR

A fundamental tenet of Modern Portfolio Theory is that all investors are rational, preferring less risk. In reality, investors are often risk seeking as they search for short-term "lottery-type" payoffs rather than long-term superior risk-adjusted returns. Risk seekers get caught up in the hype of the latest hot investment. The gambling culture in the United States or a powerful adrenaline rush might explain why investors frequently seek risk rather than work to minimize it. "Get rich quick" stories told by successful risk seekers (e.g., dot-com millionaires in the late 1990s) can cause others to seek out similar low-probability investment opportunities. Unsuccessful risk seekers are either less vocal or they block out their failed investment decisions.

NATURALLY OCCURRING PONZI SCHEMES AND MARKET BUBBLES

According to the Merriam-Webster Online Dictionary, a Ponzi scheme is "an investment swindle in which some early investors are paid off with money put up by later ones in order to encourage more and bigger risks." Charles Ponzi concocted a scheme in 1909 to sell notes promising a 40% profit in 90 days. Instead of actually investing the money, Ponzi used new investor dollars to pay out prior investors. As the number of new investors grew, it eventually became impossible to continue the scheme. The highly publicized collapse led to the term *Ponzi scheme*.

Speculative bubbles are naturally occurring Ponzi schemes. Later investors hear success stories from early-stage investors and eagerly jump into the market. As share prices keep going up, the irrational exuberance of the rising prices themselves causes a positive feedback loop. When the world runs out of "new investors," the market collapses. Once the collapse begins, a negative feedback loop is created and prices fall faster and faster. In 1928, apparently Joseph Kennedy (details of the story vary) got a stock tip from his shoeshine boy and decided to sell all his holdings. If the shoeshine boy was in stocks, he figured there must be nobody left to keep the Ponzi process going.

Bubbles in specific market sectors (e.g., technology stocks in the late 1990s) or within a whole stock market (e.g., 1929) can take years to form. Value-conscious investment professionals who remain on the sidelines during the early stages of the positive feedback loop are often ostracized by clients and peers for missing the boat. They are often compelled to join the party in later stages to save their investment jobs. Unlike in the 1920s, a large percentage of investment professionals don't own the assets they manage.

CONCLUSION

It is important to balance the logic-driven tenets of Modern Portfolio Theory against the irrational human tendencies that are revealed in Behavioral Finance Theory. After all, the human beings that drive global financial markets are not robots designed to be logical. Harry Markowitz, the father of Modern Portfolio Theory himself, described his own investment strategy: "I should have computed the historical covariances of the asset classes and drawn an efficient frontier. Instead, I visualized my grief if the stock market went way up and I wasn't in it—or if it went way down and I was completely in it. My intention was to minimize my future regret. So I split my contributions fifty-fifty between bonds and equities." If the father of Modern Portfolio Theory can fall prey to behavioral finance tendencies like fear of regret, your investment committee should be careful as well.

## CHAPTER 18

Legal Aspects of Investing Charitable Endowment, Restricted, and Other Donor Funds

OVERVIEW

Although it is difficult to generalize about the legal issues involving every aspect of investing charitable endowment, restricted, and other donor funds, fiduciaries involved in such activities should be aware of several legal parameters and guidelines.

Factors that may influence legal consequences include whether the investing is being done by a corporation or trust; whether the donor of gifted funds has effectively restricted the nature of the investments; whether the gift is for "endowment," restricted, or unrestricted purposes; the applicability of a wide variety of common and statutory laws, including the application of the "prudent man" rule, the Uniform Prudent Investor Act, the Uniform Principal and Income Act, and the Uniform Management of Institutional Funds Act; and the "Private Foundation" restrictions imposed by Chapter 42 of the United States Internal Revenue Code of 1986 and equivalent state statutes.

This chapter does not discuss the Employee Retirement Income Security Act (ERISA) or other rules applicable to investments by fiduciaries of pension or other employee benefit plans or the applicability of rules of jurisdictions outside the United States (see Chapter 19).

This chapter also does not discuss extensively the issue of legal "standing," that is, who has the right to enforce the rules applicable to investing by fiduciaries of charitable and similar endowment or restricted funds. However, it should be noted that (depending on the laws of a particular state) attempts to enforce the rules may be brought by a state's attorney general or other public official; by the institution as beneficiary or, in the case where the institution is itself doing the investing, by members of the Board of Trustees, clients (such as students or patients) of the institution, or other legally interested parties; or, in what may be a growing trend in the law, by donors or their heirs.

THE NATURE OF ENDOWMENT OR RESTRICTED FUNDS

When a donor writes a check to an institution for unrestricted purposes (such as the annual operating campaign), the institution typically segregates and normally spends those funds for ordinary operating purposes. If a donor writes a check for restricted capital purposes, the institution typically segregates and normally spends those funds over time for the intended capital purposes. In both cases the institution typically invests the funds in such a manner that market risk is minimized and the funds remain available for the intended purposes.

However, when a donor makes a contribution for "endowment" or custom-designed "restricted" purposes, particularly if the restriction includes restriction on investment, a variety of legal issues may arise. The word "endowment" is often used fairly loosely, but in fact the legal nature of an "endowment" reflects a variety of different circumstances.

ENDOWMENTS CREATED BY THE BOARD

Perhaps the most common type of endowment is one created by resolution of the governing board of the organization (which may be called a Board of Directors or some other designation). Sometimes the resolutions are quite broad, and often they are quite old (in fact, the original resolution and its several amendments may often be difficult to locate). Several endowments might be created over a period of years.

The original resolution is an important document, but so are the many varieties of fund-raising letters and materials submitted to potential donors over the years. All of these form the basis for defining how the endowment has been presented to the donors and what self-imposed restrictions on investment exist.

For instance, an endowment may simply have been created that said "income" shall be used for the benefit of the institution (or in some cases departments or programs) and "principal" shall not be used.

The endowment may have been created as a separate "trust" (complete with a mechanism for naming trustees or stating or implying that the Board of Trustees as it is constituted from time to time acts as trustees) or it may simply be a component part of the institution's asset base.

DONOR-CREATED ENDOWMENT FUNDS

Sometimes donors create their own "endowment" funds for particular purposes, such as a named scholarship or support of a department or program. These donor-created endowment funds typically have a separate gift instrument, which may be very specific as to distributions of income and principal, investment restrictions, and so forth. However, they may, at times, be simple one-paragraph letters or provisions in wills or other estate planning documents (for example, "I bequeath $XXX to Boola Boola University for endowment in support of the fine arts department").

The endowment may be created as, or purport to be, a separate trust either in general language (for example, "I bequeath $XXX in trust to Boola Boola University for endowment purposes") or in specific language naming trustees (for example, "I bequeath $XXX to my friends Bill and George as trustees of a trust to be used in support of Boola Boola University").

DONOR-CREATED RESTRICTED GIFTS OR FUNDS

A donor may make a gift to a charitable institution with program restrictions ("to fund a chair of capitalism and economic freedom") that may not constitute a trust and that may or may not be regarded as an "endowment." For instance, gifts with time restrictions ("to be used to build a new gymnasium within 10 years") are rarely treated as "endowment" but rather as "restricted" gifts, all of whose funds and earnings thereon can be expended at the free discretion of the institution for the stated purposes.

And, of course, often it is difficult to tell what the legal nature of the gift is at all!

GENERAL STATEMENT ABOUT INVESTING ENDOWMENT AND OTHER FUNDS

Although the legal rules applicable to investment of endowment or similar funds may be influenced by whether the fund is or is not a separate "trust," the standards to which fiduciaries and managers should pay attention will not differ materially between the two and neither will the possible confusion about which standards or rules apply. What those standards are may also vary from state to state and are subject to ongoing change as states modernize their applicable statutes and rules.

THE PRUDENT MAN RULE

For instance, the classic Massachusetts Supreme Court case of *Harvard v. Amory* established in 1830 the standard that trustees "should observe how men of prudence, discretion and intelligence manage their own affairs, not in regard to speculation, but in regard to the permanent disposition of their funds, considering the probable income, as well as the probable safety of capital to be invested."

This was in its time a radical extension of the trustee's duties, particularly considering that trusts (once called "uses") were created in England to avoid the rule that the eldest son would inherit the family property, and that for several centuries the primary role of the trustee (usually a friend burdened by the responsibility since corporate trustees were not permitted until the late 18th and early 19th centuries) was to maintain the family farm and deliver it after a period of years to one or more named beneficiaries. This system for escaping the reins of feudalism has developed into a vehicle for the investment of vast sums of personal wealth!

This so-called "prudent man" rule became part of American common law and was enacted as legislation in varying forms in the several states. Some state laws went further and prohibited (in the absence of language in the applicable instrument) investments in common stocks in excess of certain percentages of value.

The prudent man rule is still the law in many states, although it is being supplanted over time and in several states by the "prudent investor" rule.

THE PRUDENT INVESTOR ACT

Many states have adopted some version of what is called the Uniform Model Prudent Investor Act developed by a group called the National Conference of Commissioners on Uniform State Laws in 1994. Of course, as various states adopt slight variations to this "uniform" act, the uniformity disappears. Thus, the general statements in this chapter need to be evaluated by reference to the specifics of each state's laws in those states that have adopted some form of the Uniform Prudent Investor Act.

As in the case of the prudent man rule discussed in the preceding section, the application is technically to fiduciaries of "trusts" and the application of the prudent man rule to investment of board-created and other nontrust endowments is by analogy. The reader should also refer to the discussion later in this chapter of the Uniform Management of Institutional Funds Act, which has clear and direct application to endowment funds that are not in the form of trusts with outside trustees.

The prudent investor rule is one that will give investment managers comfort in the sense that it speaks in terms that are familiar to them. Although it may be varied by the terms of particular instruments, the Uniform Prudent Investor Act generally makes what the Commissioners describe as five fundamental alterations in the former criteria for prudent investing (all also found in an important document called the Restatement of Trusts of Prudent Investor Rule):

1. The standard of prudence is applied to any investment as part of the total portfolio, rather than to individual investments. In the trust setting, the term *portfolio* embraces all the trust's assets.

2. The trade-off in all investing between risk and return is identified as the fiduciary's central consideration.

3. All categorical restrictions on types of investments have been abrogated; the trustee can invest in anything that plays an appropriate role in achieving the risk/return objectives of the trust and that meets the other requirements of prudent investing.

4. The long familiar requirement that fiduciaries diversify their investments has been integrated into the definition of prudent investing.

5. The much criticized former rule of trust law forbidding the trustee to delegate investment and management functions has been reversed. Delegation is now permitted, subject to safeguards. In fact, in some circumstances and in varying circumstances in the various states that have adopted the Act, trustees may be able to absolve themselves of personal liability for investing if the responsibility is delegated to and accepted by an investment manager. However, notwithstanding delegation authority, trustees have responsibility for monitoring investment in light of trust goals and guidelines established by the trustees.

The comments to the Uniform Prudent Investor Act state that the Act is centrally concerned with the investment responsibilities arising under the private trust, but that the prudent investor rule also bears on charitable and pension trusts. Furthermore, although the Uniform Prudent Investor Act by its terms applies to trusts and not to charitable corporations, the comments state that the standards of the Act can be expected to inform the investment responsibilities of directors and officers of charitable corporations.

UNIFORM MANAGEMENT OF INSTITUTIONAL FUNDS ACT

The Uniform Management of Institutional Funds Act (UMIFA) was approved and recommended for enactment by the National Conference of Commissioners on Uniform State Laws in 1972. UMIFA is currently being reconsidered by the Commissioners, and a national debate is being aired in the nonprofit community about the potentially extensive changes. Thus, the discussion in this chapter reflects the generally current state of UMIFA, and any consideration of UMIFA in the future must take into account those potential changes.

Application

UMIFA applies to an "endowment fund" held by an institution (whether or not incorporated) organized and operated exclusively for educational, religious, charitable, or other eleemosynary purposes. It does not apply to a "trust" held by a trustee such as a bank or trust company for such an institution (refer to earlier section on the prudent man and prudent investor rules applicable to such a trustee) or to a fund (such as a charitable remainder trust) in which any beneficiary that is not such an institution has an interest (see later discussion about possible application of private foundation rules to such a trust).

An "endowment fund" means such an institutional fund, or any part thereof, that is not wholly expendable by the institution on a current basis under the terms of the applicable gift instrument.

The "gift instrument" by which the terms of an endowment fund can be discerned means a will, deed, grant, conveyance, agreement, memorandum, writing, or other governing document (including the terms of any institutional solicitations from which an institutional fund resulted) under which property is transferred to or held by an institution as an institutional fund.

That means that a board-created endowment fund can become an endowment fund subject to UMIFA if a donor makes a gift to the board-created endowment fund, and the terms of the endowment fund are then discerned not only by reference to the original board resolution but also by reference to agreements, memoranda, or fund-raising materials used to solicit gifts to the endowment fund. It should be no surprise that these are not always consistent!

Investment Authority, Delegation, and Standards

In terms of investment authority, UMIFA states that (in addition to any investment otherwise authorized by law or by the applicable gift instrument, and without restriction to investments a fiduciary may make), the governing board of the institution (subject to any specific limitations set forth in the applicable gift instrument or in the applicable law other than law relating to investments by fiduciaries) may:

- Invest and reinvest an institutional fund in any real or personal property deemed advisable by the governing board, whether or not it produces a current return, including mortgages, stocks, bonds, debentures, and other securities of profit or nonprofit corporations, shares in or obligations of associations, partnerships, or individuals, and obligations of any government or subdivision or instrumentality thereof.

- Retain property contributed by a donor to an institutional fund for as long as the governing board deems advisable.

- Include all or any part of an institutional fund in any pooled or common fund maintained by the institution.

- Invest all or any part of an institutional fund in any other pooled or common fund available for investment, including shares or interests in regulated investment companies, mutual funds, common trust funds, investment partnerships, real estate investment trusts, or similar organizations in which funds are commingled and investment determinations are made by persons other than the governing board.

UMIFA also makes it clear that (subject to the gift instrument) the governing board may delegate investment authority to committees and investment counsel and may contract with and pay investment counsel.

UMIFA provides that in the administration of the powers to appropriate appreciation (see next section), to make and retain investments, and to delegate investment management of institutional funds, members of a governing board shall exercise ordinary business care and prudence under the facts and circumstances prevailing at the time of the action or decision. In so doing, they shall consider long- and short-term needs of the institution in carrying out purposes, its present and anticipated financial requirements, expected total return on its investments, price level trends, and general economic conditions.

Current debates on modification of UMIFA include updating the foregoing investment standard of conduct in light of more current investment trends, the above statement being an advance beyond the prudent man rule but short of the prudent investor rule.

Appropriation of Appreciation

One of the most important aspects of UMIFA is its sanction of the use of appreciation by the governing board of an institution notwithstanding a limitation in the gift instrument that "principal" may not be invaded.

UMIFA accomplishes this by permitting the appropriation of the value of an endowment fund over its "historic dollar value," which generally means the value at the time of each gift to the fund. Funds wholly expendable by the institution are not affected by this limitation. An institution's good faith determination of historic dollar value is respected.

This converts the concept of "principal" used in private trusts. In private trusts, "principal" ordinarily includes not just the value of the original funding but also realized and unrealized investment growth in that value. However, even that concept is being eroded in the case of private trusts through the enactment of a more modern version of the Uniform Principal and Income Act that would permit more flexible definitions of "income" than has been the case in the past.

Recent stock market losses experienced by many institutions have caused this provision to be problematic (intended to free up principal for use by institutions) because the investment value may have fallen below historic dollar value in cases where appreciation has been aggressively appropriated in the past). Much of the current debate over modification of UMIFA by the National Conference of Commissioners on Uniform State Laws revolves around modification of this provision to permit further appropriation of endowment assets.

The standard of conduct for determination of the circumstances under which appreciation should be appropriated by the governing board is the same standard applicable to investments discussed in the preceding section.

In light of potential changes in UMIFA, and in light of the fact that UMIFA has been enacted in a variety of different forms by the various states, reference should always be made to the specific statutory language of UMIFA in each state that has adopted it.

PRIVATE FOUNDATION RULES

For federal tax purposes, all charitable and other organizations classified as tax exempt under Section 501(c)(3) of the U.S. Internal Revenue Code are classified either as "private foundation" or organizations that are not "private foundations."

Organizations that are not private foundations include churches, schools, hospitals, and public fund-raising and membership organizations (such as the United Way, the Boy and Girl Scouts, and organizations such as symphony orchestras) that meet arithmetic fund-raising tests described in Internal Revenue Service rules. All other "Section 501(c)(3)" organizations are private foundations.

The fact that the word *foundation* is included in the organization's name is irrelevant. A typical "community foundation," for instance, is not a "private" foundation. However, the typical family foundation or privately funded charitable trust is a private foundation.

An organization that is a private foundation is subject to Chapter 42 of the Internal Revenue Code (and equivalent state law), which, among other things, contains investment restrictions.

Section 4944 of the Internal Revenue Code (and equivalent state law) provides that a private foundation may not make investments that "jeopardize" the organization's tax-exempt purpose, a provision that is interpreted by the Treasury Regulations as imposing what is effectively a prudent man rule within the tax code. Since these regulations were adopted in 1972, they have not kept up with Modern Portfolio Theory (e.g., puts, calls, and straddles are supposed to be given "special scrutiny"). Excise tax penalties may be imposed on the organization and its officers, directors, and managers for violation of the rules.

Section 4943 of the Internal Revenue Code (and equivalent state law) provides that a private foundation may not hold any investment in a particular business enterprise to the extent it exceeds 20% less the amount held by so-called disqualified persons (essentially the trustees, officers, managers, and substantial contributors to the foundation and members of their families and trusts or other entities in which they hold a requisite interest). Excise tax penalties may be imposed on the organization and its officers, directors, and managers for violation of the rules.

SUMMARY

The investment rules applicable to the investment of charitable funds is dependent on a number of detailed questions about the nature of the fund and the institution for which it is being invested.

## CHAPTER 19

Fiduciary Issues—Retirement Funds

O ffering a retirement plan can be one of the most challenging, yet rewarding, decisions an employer can make. The employees participating in the plan, their beneficiaries, and the employer all benefit when a retirement plan is in place. However, administering a plan and managing its assets require certain actions and involve specific responsibilities.

To meet their responsibilities as plan sponsors, employers need to understand some basic rules, specifically the *Employee Retirement Income Security Act of 1974* (ERISA). ERISA sets standards of conduct for those who manage an employee benefit plan and its assets (called fiduciaries).

This chapter addresses the scope of ERISA's protections for *private sector* retirement plans. (Generally, public sector plans and plans sponsored by churches are not covered by the fiduciary responsibility standards of ERISA.) This chapter provides a simplified explanation of the law and regulations. It is not a legal interpretation of ERISA, nor is it intended to be a substitute for the advice of a retirement plan professional. Finally, this chapter does not cover the numerous provisions of Federal tax law related to qualified retirement plans.

ERISA

ERISA was enacted to protect the assets of workers so that funds contributed to retirement plans during their working lives would be available when they retire. ERISA is a federal law that sets minimum standards for pension plans in private industry. For example, ERISA specifies when employees must be allowed to become a participant, how long employees have to work before they have a nonforfeitable interest in their pension, how long they can be away from their job before it might affect their benefit, and whether a participant's spouse has a right to part of the participant's pension in the event of the participant's death. Most of the provisions of ERISA are effective for plan years beginning on or after January 1, 1975.

ERISA does not require any employer to establish a pension plan or specify any minimum benefit level. It only requires that those who establish plans must meet certain minimum standards. For example, ERISA does the following:

- Requires plans to provide participants with information about the plan, including important information about plan features and funding. The plan must furnish some information regularly and automatically. Some is available free of charge, some is not.

- Sets minimum standards for participation, vesting, benefit accrual, and funding. The law defines how long a person may be required to work before becoming eligible to participate in a plan, to accumulate benefits, and to have a nonforfeitable right to those benefits. The law also establishes detailed funding rules that require pension plan sponsors to provide adequate funding for plans.

- Guarantees payment of certain benefits if a defined plan is terminated, through a federally chartered corporation, known as the *Pension Benefit Guaranty Corporation* (PBGC).

- Requires accountability of plan fiduciaries and provides participants the right to sue for benefits and breaches of fiduciary duty.

The balance of this chapter addresses who is a fiduciary, the fiduciary's responsibilities, the penalties for breaches of those responsibilities, and how an employer can establish prudent procedures to ensure compliance with ERISA's fiduciary duty requirements.

The U.S. *Department of Labor* (DOL) enforces Title I of ERISA, which, in part, establishes participants' rights and fiduciaries' duties. The *Employee Benefits Security Administration* (EBSA) portion of the DOL is the agency charged with enforcing the rules governing the conduct of plan managers, investment of plan assets, reporting and disclosure of plan information, enforcement of the fiduciary provisions of the law, and workers' benefit rights.

Other federal agencies also regulate retirement plans. For example, the Treasury Department's *Internal Revenue Service* (IRS) is responsible for ensuring compliance with the Internal Revenue Code, which establishes the rules for operating a tax-qualified pension plan, including pension plan funding and vesting requirements. In addition, the PBGC guarantees payment of certain pension benefits under defined benefit plans that are terminated with insufficient money to pay benefits. Detailed explanations of the roles of the IRS and the PBGC are beyond the scope of this chapter.

WHO IS A FIDUCIARY?

ERISA requires plans to have at least one fiduciary (a person or entity) named in the written plan, or through a process described in the plan, as having control over the plan's operation. The named fiduciary can be identified by office or by name. For some plans, it may be an administrative committee or a company's board of directors. As one court noted, "the first place courts look to determine whether a defendant is a fiduciary is the plan documents."

Merely because one is not a named fiduciary, however, does not mean that the individual is "off the hook" as far as potential fiduciary liability is concerned. Anyone who uses discretion in administering and managing a plan or controlling the plan's assets is a fiduciary to the extent of that discretion or control. Thus, fiduciary status is based on the functions performed for the plan, not just a person's title. These types of fiduciaries are sometimes referred to as "functional fiduciaries" to distinguish them from named fiduciaries (although note that the term *functional fiduciary* does not exist anywhere in ERISA).

Many of the actions involved in operating an employee benefit plan make the person or entity performing them a fiduciary. A plan's fiduciaries will ordinarily include the trustee, investment advisers, all individuals exercising discretion in the administration of the plan, all members of a plan's administrative committee (if it has such a committee), and those who select committee officials. Attorneys, accountants, and actuaries generally are not fiduciaries when acting solely in their professional capacities. The key to determining whether an individual or an entity is a fiduciary is whether they are exercising discretion or control over the plan. Note that the law makes a person a fiduciary only *to the extent* that the person exercises discretionary authority over the plan. As one court has phrased it, "fiduciary status is not an all or nothing proposition."

Finally, note that there are at least two other broad types of decisions that may affect a retirement plan that are *not* fiduciary decisions. The first type of decisions are so-called "settlor functions," meaning business decisions made by the employer. For example, the decisions to establish a plan, to determine the benefit package, to include certain features in a plan, to amend a plan, and to terminate a plan are business decisions. When making these decisions, an employer is acting on behalf of its business, not the plan, and therefore is not a fiduciary. However, when an employer (or someone hired by the employer) takes steps to *implement* these decisions, that person is acting on behalf of the plan and, in carrying out these actions, may be a fiduciary.

The second type of decisions regarding a plan that are not fiduciary decisions involve individuals who exercise purely "ministerial functions" and who have no power to make discretionary decisions as to plan policies, interpretations, practices, or procedures; these individuals are not fiduciaries. However, any activities that require discretionary judgment are not ministerial. The following are examples of activities that may be ministerial:

- Application of the plan administrator's rules to determine eligibility for participation or benefits
- Calculation of service and compensation credits for benefits
- Calculation of benefit amounts
- Maintenance of participants' service and employment records
- Preparation of reports required by government agencies
- Orientation of new participants and advising participants of their rights and options under the plan
- Collection of contributions and application of contributions as provided in the plan
- Preparation of reports concerning participants' benefits
- Processing of benefit claims
- Making recommendations to others for decisions with respect to plan administration

Because these tasks are ministerial, they may be delegated to others (in accordance with plan provisions or procedures) without creating fiduciary liability for the delegatee. The *key* concern is whether these functions involve discretionary authority or control with respect to management of the plan, management or disposition of plan assets, or formally rendering investment advice with respect to plan funds. If not, the task is likely considered ministerial.

One common question is whether boards of directors are treated as fiduciaries. A company's board of directors *can* be a fiduciary to the extent that the board performs fiduciary functions such as the selection and retention of other plan fiduciaries. However, the mere power to amend or terminate a plan does not give the board of directors fiduciary status because those are settlor functions.

On the other hand, if a board of directors is responsible for the selection and retention of plan fiduciaries or fiduciary committees, but does not have any other discretionary functions, the board will have a fiduciary function to oversee those fiduciaries. In this instance, the board's fiduciary responsibility (and liability) is limited to that delegation function. This means that if fiduciary duties are properly delegated, the board will generally not be liable for any acts undertaken by the delegatee that were within the scope of the delegation, and the board's responsibilities are limited to oversight of the appointed fiduciary (and to avoiding cofiduciary liability, as described below).

FIDUCIARY REQUIREMENTS

Being a fiduciary is significant because fiduciaries have important responsibilities and are subject to standards of conduct because they act on behalf of participants in a retirement plan and their beneficiaries. These responsibilities include the following:

- *Duty of Loyalty (Exclusive Benefit Rule)*. Fiduciaries must discharge their duties solely in the interests of participants and beneficiaries and for the exclusive purpose of providing benefits to participants and beneficiaries and defraying reasonable expenses of administering the plan. This is also known as the exclusive benefit rule. A fiduciary violates the duty of loyalty by placing his or her own interests, or the interests of a third party, including the employer, above those of the plan participants. ERISA's duty of loyalty has been described as "the highest known to the law." This duty is based on trust law principles and according to the U.S. Supreme Court, "The most fundamental duty owed by the trustee to the beneficiaries of the trust is the duty of loyalty. . . It is the duty of a trustee to administer the trust solely in the interest of the beneficiaries."

- *Duty of Care (Prudent Person Rule)*. The duty to act prudently is one of a fiduciary's central responsibilities under ERISA. It requires expertise in a variety of areas, such as investments. Although this rule is commonly referred to as the prudent person rule, the standard is sometimes thought of as that of a "prudent *expert*" or, as one court determined, "a prudent fiduciary with experience dealing with a similar enterprise." As another court has noted, "this is not a search for subjective good faith—a pure heart and an empty head are not enough."

    Practically applied, this means that a fiduciary will have an active duty to understand what actions it is required to take with respect to the ERISA plans for which it is a fiduciary, and how, where, and when to take them. If the fiduciary does not have sufficient understanding of an area, it has the responsibility to conduct appropriate research and take such other measures to gain a proper understanding of the issue. If necessary, a fiduciary must also seek the advice of experts with appropriate background and experience.

Prudence focuses on the process for making fiduciary decisions. Therefore, it is wise to document decisions and the basis for those decisions. For instance, as described later in this chapter, in hiring any plan service provider, a fiduciary may want to survey a number of potential providers, asking for the same information and providing the same requirements. By doing so, a fiduciary can document the process and make a meaningful comparison and selection.

- *Duty to Diversify Plan Investments.* The fiduciary of a funded ERISA retirement or welfare benefit plan has a duty to diversify plan investments so as to minimize the risk for large losses, unless it is clearly not prudent to do so. Accordingly, fiduciaries generally should avoid investing disproportionately in a particular investment or enterprise. Diversification helps to minimize the risk for large investment losses to the plan. Fiduciaries should consider each plan investment as part of the plan's entire portfolio. Fiduciaries will want to document their evaluation and investment decisions. See Chapter 7 for a further discussion of asset allocation and the importance of diversification.

- *Duty to Comply with the Plan Documents (unless inconsistent with ERISA).* Following the terms of the plan document is also an important responsibility. The document serves as the foundation for plan operations. Employers will want to be familiar with the plan document (especially when it is drawn up by a third-party service provider), and periodically review the document to make sure it remains current. For example, if a plan official named in the document changes, the plan document should be updated to reflect that change.

- *Duty to Avoid Prohibited Transactions.* ERISA's *general* duty of undivided loyalty is supplemented by *specific* rules prohibiting fiduciaries from causing the plan to enter into certain transactions with parties affiliated with the plan or plan sponsor (called "parties in interest" and including the employer, the union, plan fiduciaries, service providers, and statutorily defined owners, officers, and relatives of parties-in-interest) who may be in a position to exercise improper influence over the plan. Some of the prohibited transactions are: (1) a sale, exchange, or lease between the plan and party-in-interest; (2) lending money or other extension of credit between the plan and party-in-interest; and (3) furnishing goods, services, or facilities between the plan and party-in-interest. In addition, fiduciaries are prohibited from engaging in self-dealing and must avoid conflicts of interest that could harm the plan.

For example, fiduciaries cannot receive money or any other consideration for their personal account from any party doing business with the plan related to that business.

There are a number of exceptions (called "exemptions") in the law that provide protections for the plan in conducting necessary transactions that would otherwise be prohibited. For example, exemptions are provided in the law for many dealings with banks, insurance companies, and other financial institutions that are essential to the ongoing operations of the plan. One exemption in the law allows the plan to hire a service provider as long as the services are necessary to operate the plan and the contract or arrangement under which the services are provided and the compensation paid for those services is reasonable. Another important exemption—and a popular feature of most plans—permits plans to offer loans to participants. The loans, which are considered investments of the plan, must be available to all participants on a reasonably equivalent basis, must be made according to the provisions in the plan, and must charge a reasonable rate of interest and be adequately secured. The Labor Department has the authority to grant additional exemptions that cover either individual transactions or a "class" of transactions.

- *Duty with Respect to Cofiduciaries.* A fiduciary should be aware of others who serve as fiduciaries to the same plan, since all fiduciaries have potential liability for the actions of their cofiduciaries. For example, if one fiduciary knowingly participates in a second fiduciary's breach of responsibility, conceals the breach, or does not act to correct it, the first fiduciary is liable as well.

- *Bonding Requirement.* As an additional protection for plans, those who handle plan funds or other plan property generally must be covered by a fidelity bond. A fidelity bond protects the plan against loss resulting from fraudulent or dishonest acts of those covered by the bond. A fidelity bond is not the same as fiduciary liability insurance. Fiduciary liability insurance is not mandatory, but is maintained by many employers.

PENALTIES FOR FIDUCIARY BREACHES

When a fiduciary breaches its fiduciary duties, the fiduciary can be *personally* liable for any losses suffered by the plan and subject to such other equitable or remedial relief as a court may determine as follows:

- *Compensatory Damages and Equitable Relief.* A fiduciary is *personally* liable to restore plan losses and any profits made through the improper use of plan assets. The fiduciary may also be subject to such other equitable or remedial relief as the court may deem appropriate. If the fiduciary has benefits under the plan involved, the plan may obtain a judgment or settlement providing for the offset of the amount ordered or required to be paid to the plan against the participant's benefits under the plan. A civil action may be brought against a fiduciary by a plan participant, a beneficiary, the DOL, or by another fiduciary.

• *Statutory Penalties.* The DOL may assess a civil penalty of 20% of the amount recovered in an action brought by the DOL (whether the amount recovered is through a settlement or court order). The DOL may waive this penalty if the DOL determines that the fiduciary (or other person) acted reasonably and in good faith or it is reasonable to expect that the fiduciary (or other person) cannot restore losses to the plan without severe financial hardship unless the waiver is granted. The IRS also can impose an excise tax on any fiduciary duty breach that constitutes a prohibited transaction. The initial tax is 15% of the amount involved. If the transaction is not corrected after notice from the IRS, an additional tax of 100% of the amount involved could be imposed. Finally, criminal penalties also may be imposed on individuals or companies for "willful" violations of ERISA. Under the recently enacted Sarbanes-Oxley legislation, Congress substantially increased the maximum criminal penalty for such violations—conviction may result in fines of up to $100,000 or 10 years in prison for individuals, and fines of up to $500,000 for companies.

• *Removal.* In cases involving serious breaches of trust, courts may exercise their equitable powers and order the removal of a fiduciary and prevent the fiduciary from ever again acting as an ERISA fiduciary or as a service provider to an ERISA plan. One notable recent example is the Enron situation, where, as part of a proposed settlement with the DOL, the members of the Enron board of directors were barred for five years from acting as fiduciaries of any ERISA plan unless they receive DOL permission.

If there is an actual or potential breach of fiduciary duties, there are several available remedial options, including requesting guidance from the DOL in the form of an individual prohibited transaction exemption (which can even be obtained after the fact). Also, to the extent the fiduciary breach involves a prohibited transaction, IRS Form 5330 will need to be completed to report the prohibited transaction and pay the associated excise tax.

The DOL has provided a correction program for certain fiduciary breaches called the *Voluntary Fiduciary Correction* (VFC) program. The VFC program allows fiduciaries to avoid potential civil actions brought by the DOL under ERISA and the assessment of civil penalties by the DOL. The purpose of the VFC and the corresponding class exemption is to encourage the "voluntary and timely correction of possible fiduciary breaches" under ERISA.

In general, a person who has violated certain ERISA requirements may take advantage of the VFC by "correcting" the ERISA violation and completing a VFC filing with the DOL. The VFC is limited to certain specified transactions. As noted in the Preamble to the VFC, the DOL believes that the transactions specified under the VFC are uniform enough that general rules of correction can be stated with respect to them.

A person who satisfies the VFC requirement may also avoid excise taxes under Code Section 4975 with respect to a limited number of prohibited transactions. Prohibited Transaction Class Exemption (PTCE) 2002-51 sets forth the requirements that must be satisfied to avoid excise taxes. The program covers 15 transactions, including failure to timely remit participant contributions and some prohibited transactions with parties-in-interest. The program includes a description of how to apply, as well as acceptable methods for correcting violations. In addition, the DOL gives applicants immediate relief from payment of excise taxes under a class exemption.

PRUDENT PROCEDURES TO LIMIT FIDUCIARY LIABILITY

The following describes several steps prudent fiduciaries can take to manage fiduciary risk.

- *Hold Regular Meetings and Document Findings.* One way fiduciaries can demonstrate that they have carried out their responsibilities properly is by documenting the processes used to carry out their fiduciary responsibilities. In carrying out their duties, plan fiduciaries must review all relevant facts and circumstances ("substantive prudence") and make their decisions in accordance with proper procedures ("procedural prudence"). It is essential to document the procedures followed in making any fiduciary decision (e.g., committee minutes). Plan fiduciaries are not responsible, per se, for the outcome of fiduciary decisions; however, they are responsible for maintaining a proper fiduciary decision-making process that is protective of plan participants' interests.

- *Establish an Investment Policy.* With respect to plan investments, an investment policy should be maintained for each plan. The investment policy should cover the following topics: (1) the role and responsibilities of the fiduciary (and possibly other fiduciaries involved in plan investments, such as the trust manager and the trustee), (2) the overall investment objective of the plan, (3) the asset allocation/investment funds of the plan, (4) investment objectives and guidelines for each investment fund (or portion of the plan's portfolio), (5) performance standards, (6) selection procedures, (7) review procedures, and (8), at least in general terms, termination criteria. An investment policy should be reviewed periodically and modified as necessary. See Chapter 7 for a further discussion of written policy statements.

• *Give Participants Investment Responsibility.* Some plans, such as most 401(k), 403(b), or profit-sharing plans, can be set up to give participants control over the investments in their accounts. For participants to have control, they must be given the opportunity to choose from a broad range of investment alternatives. Under DOL regulations, there must be at least three different investment options so that employees can diversify investments within an investment category, such as through a mutual fund, and diversify among the investment alternatives offered. In addition, participants must be given sufficient information to make informed decisions about the options offered under the plan. Participants also must be allowed to give investment instructions at least once a quarter, and perhaps more often if the investment option is extremely volatile. If an employer sets up their plan in this manner [a so-called "404(c)" plan], a fiduciary's liability is limited for the investment decisions made by participants. However, a fiduciary retains the responsibility for selecting the providers of the investment options and the options themselves and monitoring their performance.

• *Hire (and Monitor) an Outside Expert.* A fiduciary can also hire a service provider or providers to handle fiduciary functions, entering into an agreement so that the service provider assumes responsibility for those functions selected. If an employer appoints an investment manager that is a bank, insurance company, or registered investment adviser, the employer is responsible for the selection of the manager, but is not liable for the individual investment decisions of that manager. However, an employer is required to monitor the manager periodically to assure that it is handling the plan's investments prudently. Note that hiring a service provider is in and of itself a fiduciary function. When considering prospective service providers, plan fiduciaries should provide each of them with complete and identical information about the plan and the desired services so as to permit a meaningful comparison. Some items a fiduciary needs to consider when selecting a service provider include:

  • Information about the firm itself: financial condition and experience with retirement plans of similar size and complexity.

- Information about the quality of the firm's services: the identity, experience, and qualifications of professionals who will be handling the plan's account; any recent litigation or enforcement action that has been taken against the firm; and the firm's experience or performance record.
- A description of business practices: how plan assets will be invested if the firm will manage plan investments or how participant investment directions will be handled; the proposed fee structure; and whether the firm has fiduciary liability insurance.

An employer should document its selection (and monitoring) process, and, when using an internal administrative committee, should educate committee members on their roles and responsibilities.

In addition, the employer must monitor the service provider, establishing and following a formal review process at reasonable intervals to decide if it wants to continue using the current service providers or look for replacements. When monitoring service providers, actions to ensure they are performing the agreed-upon services include:

- Reviewing the service providers' performance.
- Reading any reports they provide.
- Checking actual fees charged.
- Asking about policies and practices (such as trading, investment turnover, and proxy voting).
- Following up on participant complaints.

- *Monitor Fees.* Fees are just one of several factors fiduciaries need to consider in deciding on service providers and plan investments. When the fees for services are paid out of plan assets, fiduciaries must understand the fees and expenses charged and the services provided. Although the law does not specify a permissible level of fees, it does require that fees charged to a plan be "reasonable." In comparing estimates from prospective service providers, plan fiduciaries should ask which services are covered for the estimated fees and which are not. This is important because some providers offer a number of services for one fee (sometimes referred to as a "bundled" services arrangement) while other service providers charge separately for individual services. Plan fiduciaries need to compare all services to be provided with the total cost for each provider and consider whether the estimate includes any unnecessary or unwanted services.

  Plan fiduciaries should also be aware that all services have costs, so even if a service is advertised as "free" or without charge, plan participants likely are paying for the services indirectly. For instance, some service providers may receive additional fees from investment vehicles, such as mutual funds, that may be offered under an employer's plan. For example, mutual funds often charge fees to pay brokers and other salespersons for promoting the fund and providing other services. There also may be sales and other related charges for investments offered by a service provider. As a result, plan fiduciaries should ask prospective providers for a detailed explanation of all fees associated with their investment options.

Once fiduciaries have properly identified the plan expenses, those expenses may be paid by the employer, the plan (if the plan so provides), or both. In addition, for expenses paid by the plan, they may be allocated to participants' accounts in a variety of ways pursuant to DOL guidance. In any case, the plan document should specify how fees are paid.

Finally, after carefully evaluating fees during the initial selection process, plan fiduciaries should make sure to monitor the plan's fees and expenses to determine whether they continue to be reasonable.

DEPARTMENT OF LABOR TIPS TO HELP FIDUCIARIES UNDERSTAND THEIR RESPONSIBILITIES

Finally, because understanding fiduciary responsibilities is important for the security of a retirement plan and for compliance with the law, the DOL has provided some tips (slightly modified below) as a helpful starting point for employers and plan fiduciaries:

- Have you identified your plan fiduciaries, and are those fiduciaries clear about the extent of their fiduciary responsibilities? Are all of the plan documents (i.e., the plan, the trust, the investment manager agreements, etc.) consistent on the identification and roles of various fiduciaries?

- If participants make their own investment decisions, have you provided sufficient information for them to exercise control in making those decisions, and have you notified participants that the plan is a so-called "404(c)" plan designed to limit the fiduciaries' liability for the investment decisions made by participants?

- Are you aware of the schedule to deposit participants' contributions in the plan, and have you made sure it complies with the law?

- If you are hiring third-party service providers, have you looked at a number of providers, given each potential provider the same information, and considered whether the fees are reasonable for the services provided? Have you documented the hiring process? Are you prepared to monitor your plan's service providers?

- Have you identified parties-in-interest to the plan and taken steps to monitor transactions with them? Are you aware of the major exemptions under ERISA that permit transactions with parties-in-interest, especially those key for plan operations (such as hiring service providers and making plan loans to participants)?

- Have you reviewed your plan document in light of current plan operations and made necessary updates? After amending the plan, have you provided participants with an updated summary plan description (SPD) or summary of material modifications (SMM)?

- Are all individuals handling plan funds or other plan property covered by a fidelity bond?

## CHAPTER 20

Final Thoughts

By now, we hope you feel that you have a handle on the oversight of your not-for-profit investment portfolio.

SUMMARY

We have explored:

- *Challenges* that will be faced by nonprofit organizations in the 21st century: increasing demand for your services, reduced funding, lower investment return expectations, and increased fiduciary scrutiny.

- *Special Issues Facing Hospitals,* including retirement plan considerations and the increasing importance of endowment funds.

- *Considerations for Religious Institutions:* The decline in the numbers of young people choosing to enter religious life, and cash flow problems.

- *The Total Return Approach* as a superior spending methodology.

- *Investment Style:* The key determinant of manager performance.

- *Newer Asset Classes,* including real estate investment trusts (REITs), high-yield bonds, non-U.S. fixed-income and inflation indexed bonds (Treasury inflation protection securities, or TIPS) and how these assets can increase your opportunity for diversification.

- *Alternative Investments,* including hedge funds, private real estate, timberland, private equity, structured products, and managed futures, and some of their benefits and drawbacks and why you may need to use them.

- *Socially Responsible Investing:* Creating you own screens or using prescreened funds and managers to match your investment portfolio to your core values.

- *Selecting Other Vendors:* How to find custodians, trustees, record keepers, and brokers.

- *Hiring Investment Management Consultants:* How to tell if you need one; how to identify the real thing (as opposed to the many salespeople disguised as "advisers"); and how to select a consultant who fits your needs.

- *Behavioral Finance:* A new financial world-view—identifying the mental errors that humans make can help avoid "shooting ourselves in the foot."

- *Legal requirements for endowments and other donor funds:* A brief overview of prudent procedures for fund fiduciaries.

- *Employee Retirement Income Security Act (ERISA):* Legal requirements for retirement plan sponsors.

- *Fees:* How to establish investment programs that are cost effective and how to negotiate with vendors to help reduce fees.

THE PRUDENT STEWARD

There are six steps involved in the effective management of your investment fund. These six steps are followed by virtually all of the largest, most successful, non-profits:

1. Set goals.
2. Allocate assets.
3. Develop a written investment and spending policy statement.
4. Select managers.
5. Implement a rebalancing strategy.
6. Monitor performance.

TAKE AWAYS

If you take away only two ideas from this book, they should be:

- Asset allocation is far and away the most important decision you make. It accounts for over 90% of your investment results. Get this right and you are miles ahead of the game. The new probabilistic models avoid some of the drawbacks inherent in traditional mean variance optimization and can help you create an "all-weather" portfolio.

- If you don't have the time or expertise to follow the steps outlined in this book, hire someone who does. Good investment consultants should be able to pay for themselves several times over. (If they can't, find someone else.)

CONCLUSION

Your role in overseeing nonprofit investments is both noble and material. Like most fiduciaries, you do what you do to try to make a difference. Maybe you're a volunteer board member or a donor who has created a private foundation. In any case, you recognize you have a responsibility and you are likely reading this book because you care deeply about your mission. You want to give your organization every opportunity to succeed.

Hopefully the information in this book will help you to reach that worthy goal.

Sample Investment Policy Statement[1]

INTRODUCTION

The Investment Policy for the ABC Hospital Fund ("Fund") has been established to facilitate a clear understanding of the investment policy, guidelines, and objectives between the committee and its investment managers, including those funds held for anticipated disbursements. The Policy also sets forth the guidelines and restrictions to be followed by the investment managers. It is the intention of this Policy to be sufficiently specific to be both meaningful and flexible enough to be practical.

PURPOSE

The ABC Hospital Fund exists to provide funding for the growth and maintenance of the ABC Hospital as it strives to be a quality provider of healthcare services. ABC Hospital is a nonprofit institution established in 1946 to provide high quality healthcare services and research to its members and surrounding community. The Fund will be utilized to establish or maintain programs that are consistent with the aims of the ABC Hospital and the Spending Policy found in the next section. Those aims may include, but are not limited to: providing funds for

---

[1]The following investment policy statement has been adopted by the ABC Hospital Fund and may be amended as necessary from time to time.

specific research projects approved by the board; providing clinical support to staff doctors; and providing funds for resident and internship programs.

SPENDING POLICY

The ABC Hospital Fund will spend 4.5% of its assets each year. These funds will be spent on programs submitted to and approved by the board of trustees. The Spending Policy shall be implemented with the intent not only to provide funds for the Hospital's immediate aims but also to preserve and grow assets to meet future spending needs.

INVESTMENT POLICY

The Fund shall be invested to provide for total return. The Fund shall be invested in a diversified portfolio, consisting primarily of common stocks, bonds, cash equivalents, and other investments, which may reflect varying rates of return. The overall rate of return objective of the portfolio is a reasonable "real" rate, consistent with the risk levels established by the Finance Committee ("Committee"). The minimum acceptable rate of return over a full market cycle (3 to 5 years) is that which equals or exceeds the assumed spending rate, plus the rate of inflation. The Committee has also established a target return objective, which may be changed from time to time, but is currently 8.0%, net of fees, assuming a 3.1% inflation rate (an assumption which may be adjusted from time to time and whose forecast is based on long-term historical rates of inflation).

INVESTMENT OBJECTIVES

Return

The total return objective, measured over a full market cycle (3 to 5 years), shall be to outperform, net of fees, the custom index, made up of 30% Standard & Poor's 500; 15% Russell 2000; 30% Lehman Brothers Aggregate Bond; 15% Europe, Australia, and the Far East (EAFE); and 10% Wilshire Real Estate Index.

Risk

The Plan should experience less risk (volatility and variability of return) than that of a custom index made up of the following indices: 30% Standard & Poor's 500;

15% Russell 2000; 30% Lehman Brothers Aggregate Bond; 15% Europe, Australia, and the Far East (EAFE); and 10% Wilshire Real Estate Index.

ASSET ALLOCATION

The target asset allocation for the investment portfolio is determined by the Committee to facilitate the achievement of the Fund's long-term investment objectives within the established risk parameters. Due to the fact that the allocation of funds between asset classes may be the single most important determinant of the investment performance over the long run, the Plan's assets shall be divided into five major asset classes as follows:

Class	Maximum Percent	Minimum Percent	Target Percent
Fixed Income	40.0	20.0	30.0
Large-Cap Domestic Equities	40.0	20.0	30.0
Small-Cap Domestic Equities	22.0	8.0	15.0
International Equities	22.0	8.0	15.0
Real Estate	10.0	5.0	10.0
Cash	39.0	0.0	0.0

The actual asset allocation, which will fluctuate with market conditions, will receive the regular scrutiny of the Committee. The Committee bears the responsibility for making adjustments in order to maintain target ranges and for any permanent changes to policy.

CASH FLOWS/REBALANCING

The Committee shall allocate net cash flows (contributions) to investment managers. As a general rule, new cash will first be used to rebalance the total fund in accordance with target asset allocation policy. If one asset class reaches the maximum or minimum limit, the entire portfolio will be rebalanced to long-term asset allocation targets. The purpose of rebalancing is to maintain the risk/reward relationship implied by the stated long-term asset allocation targets. This process may result in withdrawing assets from investment managers who have performed well in the latest year or adding assets to managers who have lagged in the most recent period. This policy may necessitate the purchase and/or sale of securities, which may create transaction costs to the account and the recognition of capital losses.

TRANSACTION GUIDELINES

All transactions should be entered into on the basis of best price and execution. All fees, commissions, and other transaction costs shall be reported as requested by the Committee.

SELECTION OF INVESTMENT FUNDS/MANAGERS

In selecting the funds or managers, the Committee will examine the following:

A. *Firm Quality and Depth.* Investment companies should have a history of reliability and a sound financial background.

B. *History of Adherence to Investment Objective and/or Approach.* Portfolio managers should consistently invest according to the investment objectives stated in their prospectus and investment policy statement.

C. *Performance Measured against an Appropriate Benchmark.* Based on the investment objective, holdings, investment style, and market capitalization, an appropriate benchmark should be used for relative investment performance evaluation.

D. *Diversification.* Portfolio managers will employ investment strategies that show sufficient diversification.

E. *Performance and Risk.* Investment performance should be competitive on a long-term basis and on a risk-adjusted basis within each appropriate asset class.

F. *Fees.* Selected funds/managers should have reasonable fees competitive with those of similar offerings.

PERFORMANCE MONITORING

All guidelines and objectives shall be in force until modified in writing. If, at any time, investment managers believe that a specific guideline or restriction is impeding the ability to implement their process or meet the performance objective, they should present this fact to the Committee.

Each investment manager's performance will be reviewed quarterly by the Committee. Investment managers (when requested) will report portfolio holdings and quarterly performance. Additionally, the managers should provide a written update concerning current investment strategy and market outlook at least every quarter. Managers are required to inform the Committee of any change in firm ownership, organizational structure, professional personnel, accounts under management, or fundamental investment philosophy within three months of such event.

TERMINATION OF MANAGERS

Managers will be reviewed by the Committee for possible termination if, over a rolling three year period, they fail to outperform at least three of the five benchmarks enumerated in the attached appendices. In addition, managers may be terminated at any time, at the discretion of the Committee. Events that may trigger such termination include but are not limited to:

- Illegal or unethical behavior on the part of the manager.
- Failure to follow the guidelines established in this investment policy statement.
- Change of key management personnel.
- Style drift.
- Insufficiency of manager's infrastructure to keep pace with asset growth.
- Any other event which might prevent the manager from effectively carrying out their duties.

PROXY VOTING POLICY

Separately managed accounts will be voted in accordance with the procedures established in their respective Investment Policy Statements.

Mutual fund accounts will be voted in accordance with established procedures in place at their respective mutual fund families.

RESPONSIBILITIES OF THE INVESTMENT CONSULTANT

The investment consultant will provide performance measurement and evaluation reporting for each investment manager and/or fund as well as for the total fund(s). Performance will be evaluated relative to stated policy objectives, appropriate benchmarks, and a universe of investment returns appropriate to the investment manager or fund evaluated. Performance will be evaluated over different time periods, including the latest quarter, as well as latest one-, three-, and five-year periods. In addition to performance, the consultant will provide reporting and evaluation regarding the level of risk associated with a manager's performance as well as the manager's consistency and adherence to the specific style which they were hired to implement.

The investment consultant will also report to the Committee with the data available on the compliance of a manager or fund to the guidelines of these policies.

MEETING SCHEDULE

Performance reviews will be held on a quarterly basis.

This document is adopted as the Investment Policy for the ABC Hospital Fund.

ABC HOSPITAL FUND

Name: _____

Title: _____

Date: _____

MANAGERS' INVESTMENT OBJECTIVES AND GUIDELINES

Dated: May 2002

GENERAL GUIDELINES FOR ALL MANAGERS

The investment managers shall have complete discretion in the management of the assets subject to the guidelines set forth herein.

Mutual funds or commingled funds may be used in any category of investment management. When one is selected, however, it is expected that the fund(s) will, in general, comply with the guidelines set forth herein. No fund may be used without approval of the Committee. Any exceptions to these Guidelines shall be listed in the following Investment Manager Objectives section.

Cash equivalents may be held in any manager's portfolio at the manager's discretion so long as the securities used comply with the guidelines established for fixed-income managers. Managers will be evaluated, however, based on their performance relative to the appropriate index benchmark, regardless of the amount of cash equivalents held during any performance-measuring period.

Investment managers shall be required to provide quarterly reports. Performance shall be reviewed each quarter with emphasis on mid- to long-term objectives, generally defined as three and five years, respectively.

SPECIFIC GUIDELINES

Guidelines are included in the attached investment policy statements for each manager. Mutual fund benchmarks are listed in the Investment Manager Objectives section.

Implementation

The portfolio will be reviewed on a quarterly basis to assure compliance with the guidelines.

INVESTMENT MANAGER OBJECTIVES: EVALUATION BENCHMARKS OF SELECTED MANAGERS

Over a rolling three- to five-year period, each manager's performance is expected to exceed at least two of the three established benchmarks:

1. ABC Fixed Income Manager

   a. Appropriate Universe Benchmark (Return):   Median
      Intermediate Fixed Income
   b. Appropriate Index Benchmark:
      Lehman Aggregate Bond Index
   c. Appropriate Risk-Adjusted Performance   Positive
      versus the Policy   annualized
              alpha

2. ABC Domestic Equity Manager

   a. Appropriate Universe Benchmark (Return):   Median
      Large-Cap Core
   b. Appropriate Index Benchmark:
      S&P 500 Index

    c. Appropriate Risk-Adjusted Performance   Positive
       versus the Policy   annualized
                                                           alpha

3. ABC International Equity Manager

    a. Appropriate Universe Benchmark (Return):   Median
       International Equity

    b. Appropriate Index Benchmark:
       MSCI EAFE Index

    c. Appropriate Risk-Adjusted Performance   Positive
       versus the Policy   annualized
                                                           alpha

Investment Manager Questionnaire

1. Firm Name: _____
   Address: _____
2. Primary Contact: _____
3. Telephone Number: _____
   Fax Number: _____
   Web Site & Password (if applicable): _____
   Email address: _____

Organization

1. When was the firm formed?   Month: _____
                                 Year: _____
2. Please provide the requested information regarding your firm's assets under management:

| Period | Domestic Equity | | International Equity | | Fixed Income | | Total Assets |
	# of Accts	Assets	# of Accts	Assets	# of Accts	Assets	Under Mgt.
2003							
2002							
2001							
2000							
1999							

3. Provide the name, relationship and percentage ownership of:
   a. each parent organization
   b. other affiliated organizations

4. Please provide a brief history of your organization. Be sure to include the ownership structure and a list of all offices (along with the number of investment professionals at each location).

5. Please provide a detail (including the percentage ownership) of current owners of the firm. Include the titles of employee owners.

6. Does your firm have a succession plan? If so, please outline in fewer than 150 words.

7. Does the firm have errors and omissions insurance? Please indicate the extent of coverage.

8. Does the firm have fiduciary liability insurance? Please indicate the coverage.

9. In the past 10 years, has the firm, its parent, or another subsidiary been subject to any litigation or censure by a regulatory body? If yes, please explain.

10. Has the firm or any of its employees ever been the subject of any sanction or disciplinary action by any state or federal regulatory body? Are there any SEC or *other legal inquiries* pending against the firm? If so, explain.

11. Please detail *all* relationships for which the firm or its employees receive compensation or pay for referrals.

12. Provide a copy of the firm's Form ADV Parts I & II.

Assets Under Management

1. Please provide a breakdown of the firm's assets under management as of the most recent quarter:

   Total Assets: _____

   Total Tax-Exempt Assets: _____

2. Identify any area of the firm's business that is receiving additional marketing emphasis at this time.

3. What are the goals for growth of assets under management for the organization? Please discuss total assets, total accounts, addition of staff, and new products.

4. Is there a dollar amount of assets under management in any product where you expect to close to new investors? (Please list product and dollar amount).

5. Please provide the names of all accounts with over $1 million in assets that were lost in the past three years, and list the reason.

Client Name/Account Size	Reason for Loss

Professional Staff

1. Please provide the total number of employees of the firm.
2. Please provide the number of investment professionals by function.

	Total number of Professionals (Firm)	Number of Professionals (Product)
Equity portfolio managers		
Fixed-income portfolio managers		
Equity research analysts		
Fixed-income research analysts		
Marketing and client service		
Chief investment officers		
Economists		
Equity traders		
Fixed-income traders		
Administration		
Other (explain)		

3. Provide biographies on your key portfolio managers and analysts.
4. Describe the compensation package available to your professional staff, including any incentive bonuses (i.e., performance or asset based), stock options, and equity participation.
5. Describe and explain any departures or additions in investment personnel that have taken place during the past three years? If changes in staff have occurred, please indicate the functional titles (e.g., portfolio manager) of each and describe the changes.
6. What is the average number of accounts per portfolio manager? Please indicate whether your firm has an established maximum number of accounts per manager, and if so, what that maximum is.

7. List the average years at the firm and in the industry for both your analysts and portfolio managers.

8. Is the research analyst position a career path for future portfolio managers or is it considered a career path by itself? Have any research analysts been hired as portfolio managers?

9. Who is responsible for relationship management activities? Describe how client servicing responsibilities are divided between portfolio managers and client servicing/marketing personnel.

Investment Philosophy/Strategy

1. Strategy: _____

2. Date of first actual account: _____

3. Total product assets (in Millions): _____

4. Total product accounts: _____

5. Please provide the following information for this product.

	Product Totals		Accounts Gained		Accounts Lost	
	# of Accts	Assets ($)	# of Accts	Assets($)	# of Accts	Assets ($)
2003						
2002						
2001						
2000						
1999						
1998						

6. Minimum account size for separately managed: _____

7. Minimum fee for separately managed: _____

8. Fee schedule for separately managed accounts.

   # of Basis Points   Amount of Assets

   _____   On the first $ _____

   _____   On the next $ _____

   _____   On the next $ _____

   _____   On the next $ _____

9. Minimum account size for pooled/commingled: _____

10. Minimum fee for pooled/commingled accounts.

    # of Basis Points   Amount of Assets

    _____   On the first $ _____

    _____   On the next $ _____

    _____   On the next $ _____

11. Will you negotiate fees on this product?   yes___ no___

12. Do you currently have any accounts using performance-based fees with this product?   yes___ no___ If yes, how many accounts?_____

13. Please describe in detail your firm's investment philosophy and strategy.

14. Explain your buy discipline, including economic analysis, initial screening of securities, screening steps and criteria, number of securities followed, etc.

15. Does your firm use an equity investment committee to select specific securities? If so, indicate the members of the committee, frequency of meetings, and the implementation process of committee decisions. If not, describe the decision-making process employed by your firm.

16. Provide the names of all investment professionals associated with this product (include the name, title, years with the firm, and years in the industry).

17. What is the number of industries covered per analyst (or portfolio manager)?

18. How often do investment professionals meet with companies?

19. Please describe your equity research capabilities and the extent to which you rely on external sources for research.

20. Describe your sell discipline (price targets, market cap restrictions, portfolio percentage guidelines, individual holding restrictions, etc.). What events typically trigger a sell signal?

21. How are portfolios constructed? Please discuss the sector, industry, and individual security weighting process. Also include the benchmark that sector exposure is measured against.

22. What are the normal, minimum, and maximum percentages of a total portfolio that would be invested in any one sector, industry, and stock (absolute or relative to the benchmark)? Has this philosophy been altered over the past five years? Can the portfolio manager override any of the guidelines? If so, how often has this happened?

23. Do you use a model portfolio? If so, who is responsible for maintaining and updating the model portfolio?

24. Do you have liquidity screens for smaller cap stocks?

25. Please provide the following portfolio characteristics:

	06/2004	12/2003	06/2003	12/2002	06/2002	12/2001	06/2001	12/2000
P/E								
P/B								
Yield								
Debt/Equity								
3 Year EPS Growth Rate								
% in Top 10 Holdings								
Cash								
Medium Market Capitalization								
# of Securities								
% Foreign								

26. Do you use derivative financial instruments, IPOs, or ADRs in the portfolio? If leverage is used, discuss in detail the use and methodology behind the strategies employed.

27. Please provide sector distributions for the past eight quarters.

28. What do you consider to be the most appropriate benchmark for this strategy?

29. What is the annual turnover range in a typical portfolio?

30. Over a market cycle, what is the typical cash range in this product?

31. What is the minimum and maximum market cap of an individual security for this product?

32. At what level would you close this product to new assets?

33. What factors differentiate this product from others with a similar style (please limit your response to 150 words)?

Trading

1. How many full-time traders does the firm employ?

2. What level of input do traders have in the investment decision-making process? How much discretion do traders enjoy when implementing a buy or sell decision?

3. Does the firm or an affiliate underwrite securities?

4. Does the firm or an affiliate purchase securities for client accounts on a principal basis?

Compliance/Risk Controls

1. Does your firm have a separate compliance department?

2. How are accounts monitored for compliance with strategy targets, model portfolios, approved list holdings, restrictions, etc.?

3. What tools are used to automate the compliance process?

Performance

1. Please provide AIMR compliant quarterly performance data in an attached Microsoft Excel spreadsheet in the following format:

	A	B
1	Date	Return
2	12/2003	3.43
3	9/2003	2.34

Also include all AIMR disclosures.

2. Please provide the following information regarding the composite.

Period Ending	Number of Accounts	Composite as a % of Total Assets	Dispersion Range	
			High	Low
12/03				
12/02				
12/01				
12/00				
12/99				
12/98				
12/97				
12/96				

3. What is the size of the smallest and largest account in the composite?

4. How is dispersion monitored and controlled?

5. Does the composite comply with AIMR performance presentation standards? If yes, since what date?

6. Are results actual or simulated? Please provide the dates from which actual results begin.

7. Does the firm monitor historical performance attribution? What system is used?

8. Do you manage or subadvise mutual funds in the same style as this product? If so, how does the fund differ from the product provided above?

Questionnaire completed by.

Name:

Title: _____

Date: _____

Sample Search:
Investment Analysis

DEFINITION OF KEY STATISTICS

- **Return**

  Time-weighted average annual returns for the time period indicated.

- **Standard Deviation**

  Standard deviation is a statistical measure of the range of performance within which the total returns of a fund fall. When a fund has a high standard deviation, the range of performance is very wide, meaning that there is a greater volatility. Approximately 68% of the time, the total return of any given fund will differ from the average total return by no more than plus or minus the standard deviation figure. Ninety-five percent of the time, a fund's total return will be within a range of plus or minus two times the standard deviation from the average total return. If the quarterly or monthly returns are all the same, the standard deviation will be zero. The more they vary from one another, the higher the standard deviation. Standard deviation can be misleading as a risk indicator for funds with high total returns because large positive deviations will increase the standard deviation without a corresponding increase in the risk of the fund. While positive volatility is welcome, negative is not.

- **R-Squared**

  This reflects the percentage of a fund's movements that are explained by movements in its benchmark index. An R-squared of 100 means that all movements of a fund are completely explained by movements in the index. Conversely, a low R-squared indicates that very few of the fund's movements are explained by movements in the benchmark index. R-squared can also be used to ascertain the significance of a particular beta. Generally, a higher R-squared will indicate a more reliable beta figure. If the R-squared is lower, then the beta is less relevant to the fund's performance. A measure of diversification, R-squared indicates the extent to which fluctuations in portfolio returns are explained by market. An R-squared = 0.70 implies that 70% of the fluctuation in a portfolio's return is explained by the fluctuation in the market. In this instance, overweighting or underweighting of industry groups or individual securities is responsible for 30% of the fund's movement.

- **Beta**
  This is a measure of a fund's market risk. The beta of the market is 1.00. Accordingly, a fund with a 1.10 beta is expected to perform 10% better than the market in up markets and 10% worse than the market in down markets. It is important to note, however, that a low fund beta does not imply that the fund has a low level of volatility; rather, a low beta means only that the fund's market-related risk is low. Because beta analyzes the market risk of a fund by showing how responsive the fund is to the market, its usefulness depends on the degree to which the markets determine the fund's total risk (indicated by R-squared).

- **Sharpe Ratio**
  The Sharpe ratio is the excess return per unit of total risk as measured by standard deviation. Higher numbers are better, indicating more return for the level of risk experienced. The ratio is a fund's return minus the risk-free rate of return (30-day T-Bill rate) divided by the fund's standard deviation. The *higher* the Sharpe ratio, the more reward you are receiving per unit of total risk. This measure can be used to rank the performance of mutual funds or other portfolios.

- **Alpha**
  The alpha is the nonsystematic return, or the return that can't be attributed to the market. It can be thought of as how the *manager* performed if the market's return was zero. A *positive* alpha implies the manager added value to the return of the portfolio over that of the market. A *negative* alpha implies the manager did not contribute any value over the performance of the market.

- **Information Ratio**
  The information ratio is a measure of the consistency of excess return. This value is determined by taking the annualized excess return over a bench-

mark (style benchmark by default) and dividing it by the standard deviation of excess return.

- **Tracking Error**

  Tracking error measures the volatility of the difference in annual returns between the manager and the index. This value is calculated by measuring the standard deviation of the difference between the manager and index returns. For example, a tracking error of ±5 would mean there is about a 68% chance (1 standard deviation event) that the manager's returns will fall within ±5% of the benchmark's annual return.

LARGE COMPANY VALUE SEARCH: THE SCREENING PROCESS

The search began with a database of 2,242 large capitalization funds/managers. The following screens were applied:

- Assets of greater than or equal to $50 million
- Median market capitalization of $8 billion or greater
- Foreign stock of less than 20%
- Cash holdings of less than 15%
- Bond holdings of less than 5%
- Manager tenure greater than or equal to 2 years
- Fund inception date of 3 years ago or longer (may consider funds with shorter history under special circumstances)
- Expense ratio less than the Morningstar category group average
- Consistent style emphasis
- Consistent and clearly defined investment process
- Organization: stability of personnel/infrastructure
- Ability to have loads/sales charges waived
- Manageable growth in assets
- Quantitative analysis includes ranking of the following risk/return scores: 1, 3, 5 rolling year total return; 3, 5 year standard deviation; 3, 5 year Sharpe ratio; 3 year Morningstar risk score
- Additional screens may have been applied for administrative capabilities

LARGE COMPANY VALUE INVESTMENT ANALYSIS

Fund / Manager	Manager A	Manager B	Manager C	Manager D
Objective	Management tries to select a portfolio that an investor with fiduciary responsibility might select under the prudent investor rule of the Superior Court of the District of Columbia. They insist on buying blue-chip companies that have paid dividends 9 out of the past 10 years. This factor has kept the fund overweighted in financial, energy and utility stocks. This fund cannot invest in alcohol and tobacco stocks and seldom invests in foreign stocks.	The fund seeks companies with financial strength and a sound economic background. Purchases are made with the intent to hold for a long time. Management's strategy is to purchase well established companies that have positive earnings prospects not reflected in their current price. They especially like companies well positioned for the global economic recovery.	The fund uses a bottom-up approach to identify under-valued and overlooked stocks with improving fundamentals. Valuation is compared with both industry and broad market benchmarks to identify potential investments. Fundamental research is used to assess company and industry growth opportunities and risks, and to determine whether sufficient catalysts exist to generate a positive revaluation of the stock over 6-12 months.	Management believes that stocks which sell at below-average valuation relative to future earnings, cash flow, and dividends will provide the best total return with less risk on a consistent basis. The firm's approach combines traditional value measures such as low P/E and high yield with a proprietary value ranking process based on future earnings potential. Stock selection is viewed as the most important factor in determining investment performance.
Manager	Management Team	Management Team	Lisa Nurme	Tom Dezort
Manager Tenure	11 Years	22 Years	7 Years	21 Years
Inception	07-1952	01-1965	01-1989	01-1988
Net Assets	$50.2 Billion	$6.3 Billion	$3.7 Billion	$200 Million
Medium Market Cap	$30.0 Billion	$11.1 Billion	$20.3 Billion	$12 Billion
% in top 10 holdings	23%	28%	24%	24%
% Cash	2.3%	8.8%	0–5%	3.0%
% Foreign	0.2%	4.4%	9.5%	0.0%
Portfolio P/E	21.1	21.4	20.1	14.5
Portfolio P/B	4.2	2.9	3.5	2.3
3 Yr Earnings Gr	10.9%	13.3%	8.0%	9.0%
# Stocks	166	79	102	60
% Turnover	26%	18%	83%	40%

Fund / Manager	Manager A	Manager B	Manager C	Manager D
Expense ratio	0.63 % (includes a 12b-1 fee of 0.24%)	0.55%	0.56%	0.75%
Top 5 holdings	Bank of America, Texaco, Wells Fargo, AT&T, Household Int'l	Golden West Finl, Union Pacific, Bank One, Dow Chemical, Loews, Philips Petro	ExxonMobil, St. Paul, Verizon Communications, Alcoa Inc, Novartis	USX Marathon, Avery Dennison, Illinois Tool Works, Exxon Mobil, Citigroup
Top 3 sectors	Financials (26%), Industrial Cyclicals (16%), Services (10%), Energy (10%)	Industrial Cyclicals (25%), Financials (19%), Energy (12%), Services (11%)	Financial (25%), Services (18%), Industrial Cyclicals (13%)	Financials (27%), Industries (12%), Health Care (11%)

LARGE-CAP VALUE EQUITY ANALYSIS

	Russell 1000 Value Index		Manager A		Manager B		Manager C		Manager D	
2Q 1999	11.28		9.39		16.64		10.12		10.70	
3Q 1999	(9.80)		(9.39)		(8.39)		(6.50)		(7.41)	
4Q 1999	**5.43**	**7.35**	**1.83**	**1.16**	**7.61**	**20.21**	**(5.20)**	**8.55**	**(0.43)**	**2.38**
1Q 2000	0.48		(0.82)		0.27		1.64		(2.03)	
2Q 2000	(4.69)		(3.05)		(2.22)		5.82		0.16	
3Q 2000	7.86		6.50		6.24		10.93		10.22	
4Q 2000	**3.60**	**7.02**	**6.51**	**9.06**	**11.66**	**16.31**	**9.93**	**31.16**	**6.48**	**15.16**
1Q 2001	(5.86)		(1.53)		0.95		(7.63)		(1.69)	
2Q 2001	4.88		4.17		7.30		4.34		4.47	
3Q 2001	(10.95)		(7.41)		(10.23)		(10.65)		(9.32)	
4Q 2001	**7.37**	**(5.59)**	**6.89**	**1.51**	**12.44**	**9.33**	**9.00**	**(6.14)**	**12.39**	**4.68**
1Q 2002	4.09		3.63		4.89		3.62		2.91	
2Q 2002	(8.52)		(7.36)		(6.22)		(6.62)		(11.58)	
3Q 2002	(18.77)		(17.90)		(15.84)		(15.20)		(17.94)	
4Q 2002	**9.22**	**(15.52)**	**8.04**	**(14.85)**	**8.06**	**(10.54)**	**6.02**	**(13.01)**	**8.03**	**(19.34)**
1Q 2003	(4.86)		(4.92)		(5.29)		(5.93)		(4.66)	
2Q 2003	17.27		15.94		16.59		14.83		18.29	
3Q 2003	2.06		1.25		5.24		2.28		2.13	
4Q 2003	**14.19**	**30.03**	**12.73**	**25.83**	**13.88**	**32.34**	**14.22**	**26.19**	**15.41**	**32.93**
1Q 2004	3.03		1.62		4.96		2.09		2.70	
MAX Qtr	17.27		15.94		16.64		14.83		18.29	
MIN Qtr	(18.77)		(17.90)		(15.84)		(15.20)		(17.94)	

264

LARGE-CAP VALUE EQUITY ANALYSIS (CONTINUED)

	Russell 1000 Value Index	Manager A	Manager B	Manager C	Manager D
5-Year Statistics					
Return	3.89	4.00	12.69	8.37	6.26
Std Dev	18.40	16.28	18.30	17.02	18.59
R-Squared	1.00	0.96	0.92	0.88	0.92
Beta	1.00	0.87	0.95	0.87	0.97
Sharpe	0.03	0.04	0.51	0.30	0.16
Alpha	NA	0.19	8.83	4.56	2.39
Info. Ratio	NA	(0.08)	1.58	0.61	0.40
Tracking Error	NA	+/−3.93	+/−5.29	+/−6.39	+/−5.40
3-Year Statistics					
Return	4.31	3.93	10.41	4.43	5.45
Std Dev	21.16	19.01	20.29	18.85	22.17
R-Squared	1.00	0.99	0.97	0.98	0.97
Beta	1.00	0.89	0.94	0.88	1.03
Sharpe	0.11	0.11	0.42	0.13	0.16
Alpha	NA	(0.13)	6.24	0.41	1.06
Info. Ratio	NA	(0.28)	1.50	(0.11)	0.31
Tracking Error	NA	+/−2.90	+/−3.76	+/−3.71	+/−3.92

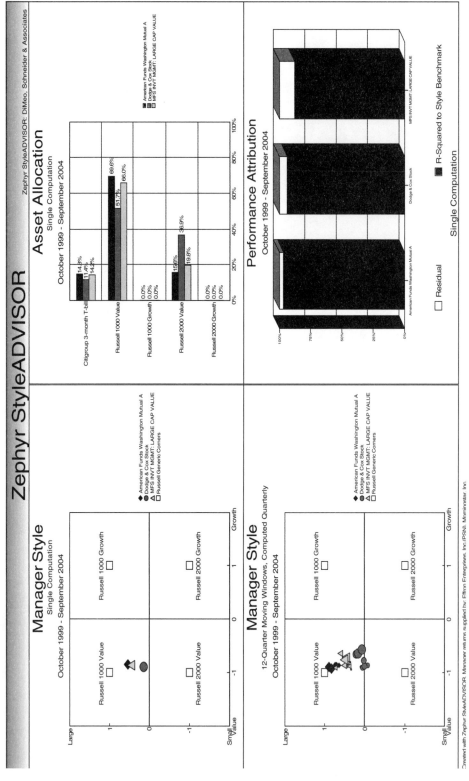

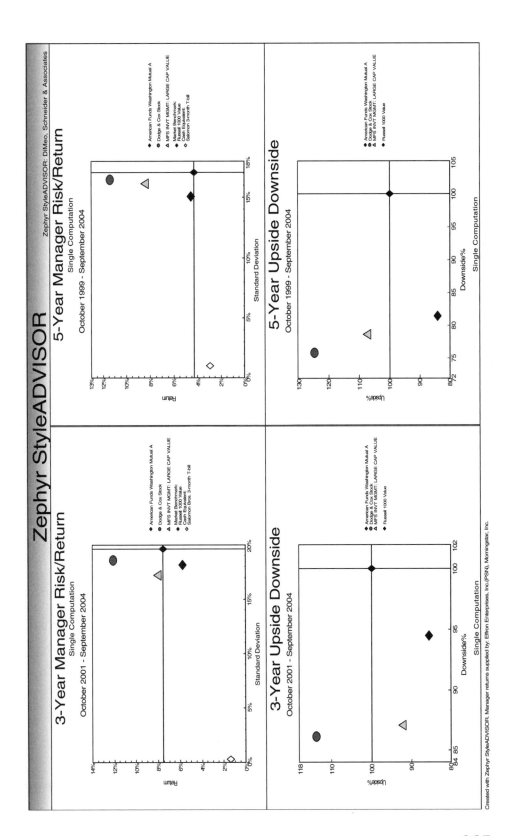

Zephyr StyleADVISOR   Zephyr StyleADVISOR: DiMeo, Schneider & Associates

Zephyr StyleADVISOR

5-Year Manager Risk/Return
Single Computation
October 1999 - September 2004

- ◆ American Funds Washington Mutual A
- ● Dodge & Cox Stock
- ▲ MFS INVT MGMT: LARGE CAP VALUE
- Market Benchmark:
  Russell 1000 Value
- ◆ Cash Equivalent:
  Salomon 3-month T-bill

5-Year Upside Downside
October 1999 - September 2004

- ◆ American Funds Washington Mutual A
- ● Dodge & Cox Stock
- ▲ MFS INVT MGMT: LARGE CAP VALUE
- ◆ Russell 1000 Value

Single Computation

3-Year Manager Risk/Return
Single Computation
October 2001 - September 2004

- ◆ American Funds Washington Mutual A
- ● Dodge & Cox Stock
- ▲ MFS INVT MGMT: LARGE CAP VALUE
- Market Benchmark:
  Russell 1000 Value
- ◆ Cash Equivalent:
  Salomon Bros. 3-month T-bill

3-Year Upside Downside
October 2001 - September 2004

- ◆ American Funds Washington Mutual A
- ● Dodge & Cox Stock
- ▲ MFS INVT MGMT: LARGE CAP VALUE
- ◆ Russell 1000 Value

Single Computation

Created with Zephyr StyleADVISOR. Manager returns supplied by: Effron Enterprises, Inc.(PSN), Morningstar, Inc.

267

Zephyr StyleADVISOR

Manager vs Universe: Return through September 2004
(not annualized if less than 1 year)

Zephyr Large Value Universe (Morningstar)

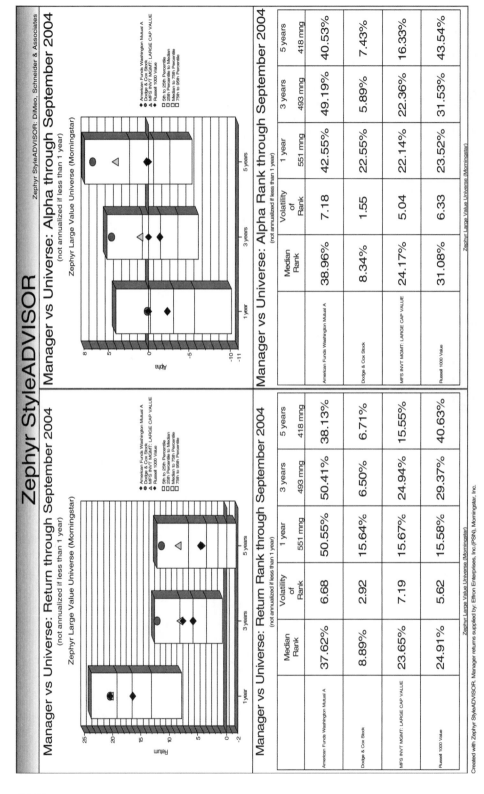

Manager vs Universe: Alpha through September 2004
(not annualized if less than 1 year)

Zephyr Large Value Universe (Morningstar)

- ◆ American Funds Washington Mutual A
- ● Dodge & Cox Stock
- ▲ MFS INV'T MGMT: LARGE CAP VALUE
- ◆ Russell 1000 Value
- □ 5th to 25th Percentile
- □ 25th Percentile to Median
- □ Median to 75th Percentile
- □ 75th to 95th Percentile

Manager vs Universe: Alpha Rank through September 2004
(not annualized if less than 1 year)

	Median Rank	Volatility of Rank	1 year 551 mng	3 years 493 mng	5 years 418 mng
American Funds Washington Mutual A	38.96%	7.18	42.55%	49.19%	40.53%
Dodge & Cox Stock	8.34%	1.55	22.55%	5.89%	7.43%
MFS INV'T MGMT: LARGE CAP VALUE	24.17%	5.04	22.14%	22.36%	16.33%
Russell 1000 Value	31.08%	6.33	23.52%	31.53%	43.54%

Zephyr Large Value Universe (Morningstar)

Manager vs Universe: Return Rank through September 2004
(not annualized if less than 1 year)

	Median Rank	Volatility of Rank	1 year 551 mng	3 years 493 mng	5 years 418 mng
American Funds Washington Mutual A	37.62%	6.68	50.55%	50.41%	38.13%
Dodge & Cox Stock	8.89%	2.92	15.64%	6.50%	6.71%
MFS INV'T MGMT: LARGE CAP VALUE	23.65%	7.19	15.67%	24.94%	15.55%
Russell 1000 Value	24.91%	5.62	15.58%	29.37%	40.63%

Zephyr Large Value Universe (Morningstar)

Created with Zephyr StyleADVISOR. Manager returns supplied by: Effron Enterprises, Inc.(PSN), Morningstar, Inc.

Zephyr StyleADVISOR

Manager vs Universe: Sharpe Ratio through September 2004
(not annualized if less than 1 year)
Zephyr Large Value Universe (Morningstar)

Manager vs Universe: Information Ratio through September 2004
(not annualized if less than 1 year)
Zephyr Large Value Universe (Morningstar)

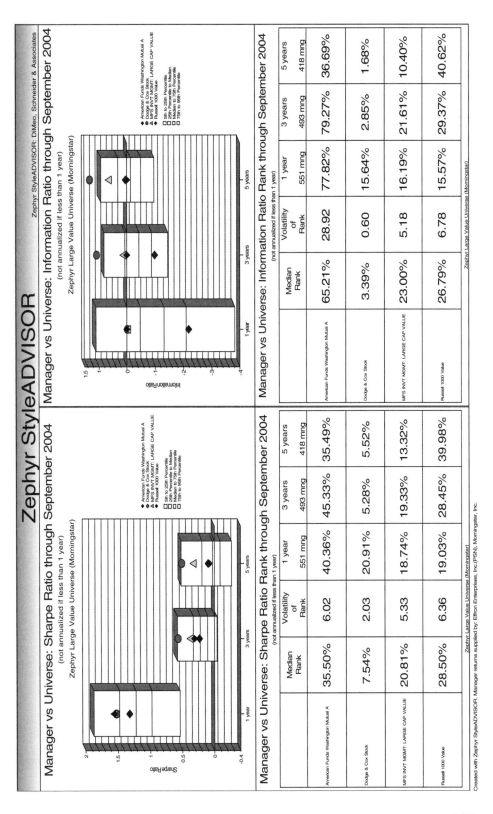

Manager vs Universe: Sharpe Ratio Rank through September 2004
(not annualized if less than 1 year)

	Median Rank	Volatility of Rank	1 year 551 mng	3 years 493 mng	5 years 418 mng
American Funds Washington Mutual A	35.50%	6.02	40.36%	45.33%	35.49%
Dodge & Cox Stock	7.54%	2.03	20.91%	5.28%	5.52%
MFS INVT MGMT: LARGE CAP VALUE	20.81%	5.33	18.74%	19.33%	13.32%
Russell 1000 Value	28.50%	6.36	19.03%	28.45%	39.98%

Zephyr Large Value Universe (Morningstar)

Manager vs Universe: Information Ratio Rank through September 2004
(not annualized if less than 1 year)

	Median Rank	Volatility of Rank	1 year 551 mng	3 years 493 mng	5 years 418 mng
American Funds Washington Mutual A	65.21%	28.92	77.82%	79.27%	36.69%
Dodge & Cox Stock	3.39%	0.60	15.64%	2.85%	1.68%
MFS INVT MGMT: LARGE CAP VALUE	23.00%	5.18	16.19%	21.61%	10.40%
Russell 1000 Value	26.79%	6.78	15.57%	29.37%	40.62%

Zephyr Large Value Universe (Morningstar)

Created with Zephyr StyleADVISOR. Manager returns supplied by: Effron Enterprises, Inc.(PSN), Morningstar, Inc.

zzz eVestment Alliance, L.L.C.: eA U.S. Equity Sample Product

Assets and Accounts by Type ($US Million)

	Total Assets	Institutional Assets	Taxable Assets	Tax-Exempt Assets	Total Accounts*	Institutional Accounts*	Taxable Accounts*	Tax-Exempt Accounts*
Total	$27,723	$26,899	$3,399	$24,324	465	327	155	310
Corporate	$5,353	$5,353	$253	$5,100	115	115	11	104
Public Fund	$7,263	$7,263	$0	$7,263	35	35	0	35
Union/Multi-Employer	$1,301	$1,301	$0	$1,301	28	28	0	28
Foundation & Endowment	$1,895	$1,895	$0	$1,895	91	91	0	91
Healthcare	$0	$0	$0	$0	0	0	0	0
High Net Worth Individuals	$434	$0	$421	$13	112	0	104	8
Wrap Accounts	$337	$0	$254	$83	5	0	4	1
Defined Contribution	$186	$186	$0	$186	6	6	0	6
Other**	$10,954	$10,901	$2,471	$8,483	73	52	36	37

*Note: Prior to 1Q04, data was reported based on number of *clients*. Effective 1Q04, eA requests that data be reported based on number of *accounts*.
**Explanation of Other Assets: Credit Union T&TE; Mutual Fund T&TE; Special T&TE

Assets by Vehicle Type ($US Million)

		% Product Assets*
Assets by Vehicle: Separate Account	$18,872	1.00%
Assets by Vehicle: Commingled Fund	$0	7.00%
Assets by Vehicle: Mutual Fund (Inst. Class)	$8,851	7.00%
Assets by Vehicle: Mutual Fund (Retail Class)	$0	1.70%

Accounts by Vehicle Type

Assets by Vehicle: Separate Account	465
Assets by Vehicle: Commingled Fund	0
Mutual Fund Accounts Not Tracked	

Account Turnover

	Accounts Gained			Accounts Lost		
	Number	Dollars ($million)	% Product Assets*	Number	Dollars ($million)	% Product Assets*
Full Year 1999	6	$259	1.00%	20	$1,059	3.00%
Full Year 2000	32	$1,975	7.00%	7	$447	2.00%
Full Year 2001	22	$1,381	7.00%	9	$872	4.00%
Full Year 2002	14	$359	1.70%	25	$4,074	19.20%
Full Year 2003	28	$619	2.91%	34	$1,731	8.14%
YTD 2004	21	$2,501	9.02%	2	$445	1.55%

*Based on beginning of year assets
Explanation of Account Turnover:

Fee Information

This Product Offered As: Separate Account, Commingled Fund, Mutual Fund: Institutional Class, Mutual Fund: Retail Class

Separate Account Fee Information

Separate Account Availability	Open
Minimum Account Size ($ Million)	$50
Minimum Annual Fee	$50,000
Fee Includes Custody:	No
Performance-based Fees Available:	Yes
"Most Favored Nation" Arrangements Available:	Yes

First $50 Million At 0.950%
Next $50 Million At 0.900%
Next $100 Million At 0.800%
Next $100 Million At 0.600%
Next $100 Million At 0.500%
Next __ Million At ___
Next __ Million At ___
Balance At 0.400%
All Assets At __

Commingled Fund Fee Information

Commingled Account Availability	Open
Minimum Account Size ($ Million)	$5
Minimum Annual Fee	$50,000
Fee Includes Custody:	Yes
Accepts ERISA Qualified Assets:	Yes
Accepts Non-ERISA Qualified Assets:	No

First $50 Million At 1.000%
Next $50 Million At 0.900%
Next $100 Million At 0.800%
Next $100 Million At 0.600%
Next __ Million At ___
Next __ Million At ___
Next __ Million At ___
Balance At 0.500%
All Assets At __

Mutual Fund Fee Information

Fund Name	eA US Equity Fund
Fee Schedule Provided Here For:	Institutional Class
Minimum Account Size ($ Million)	$1
Minimum Annual Fee	$10,000
Fee Includes Custody:	Yes
Fund Subadvised/Distributed By Another Firm:	Yes
Subadvised or Distributed By:	Firm 1
Subadvised or Distributed By:	Firm 2
Subadvised or Distributed By:	Firm 3

Ticker Symbol   EAUSX
Applicable Fee:
All Assets At   1.250%

Fee Disclosures and Calculated Fee Table

Fee Disclosure:
Most favored nation arrangements are available.
Annual Fees by Account Size ($ US)

Vehicle Type:	Account Sizes				
	$10 mm	$25 mm	$50 mm	$75 mm	$100 mm
Separate Account	$95,000	$237,500	$475,000	$700,000	$925,000
	95 bps	95 bps	95 bps	93 bps	93 bps
Commingled Fund	$100,000	$250,000	$500,000	$725,000	$950,000
	100 bps	100 bps	100 bps	97 bps	95 bps
Mutual Fund	$125,000	$312,500	$625,000	$937,500	$1,250,000
	125 bps	125 bps	125 bps	125 bps	125 bps

*Please note that the fees calculated are based upon the published fee schedules provided and do not incorporate minimum account sizes, minimum annual fees, product availability or negotiated fee rates. In addition, the last fee rate provided is applied in instances where no "Balance at" rate is given.

Product Team Description

	Portfolio Managers	Research Analysts	Traders	Economists	Client Service	Marketing	CFA Charterholders	MBAs	PhDs
Total Number	14	5	3	0	15	4	20	10	—
Avg. Yrs. Of Experience	25	15	19	19	19	23			
Avg. Yrs. At Firm	15	10	8	—	4	4			

Explanation of How Professionals are Categorized:
Sample Firm applies a team approach to decision making.

Professional Turnover

	Professional Gained				Professional Lost			
	Portfolio Managers	Analysts	Traders	Marketing/ Client Service	Portfolio Managers	Analysts	Traders	Marketing/ Client Service
Full Year 1999	2	0	0	1	0	0	0	0
Full Year 2000	1	0	0	2	0	0	0	0
Full Year 2001	3	1	0	0	0	0	0	0
Full Year 2002	1	2	3	0	0	0	0	0
Full Year 2003	1	1	1	1	0	0	0	0
YTD 2004	1	1	1	1	1	1	1	1

Explanation of Professional Departures:

Investment Professionals Managing This Strategy

James E. Minnick,
Primary Role: _____ Percentage Ownership: _____
Start Year: _____ Industry: _____ Firm: _____
Biography: None provided.

Heath Wilson,
Primary Role: _____ Percentage Ownership: _____
Start Year: _____ Industry: _____ Firm: _____
Biography: None provided.

Matt Robison,
Primary Role: _____ Percentage Ownership: _____
Start Year: _____ Industry: _____ Firm: _____
Biography: None provided.

Investment Strategy

eVestment Alliance's (eA's) process is primarily bottom up in which they interrelate price with earnings momentum. Their strategy uses a present valuation model in which the current price of the stock is related to the risk-adjusted present value of the company's future earnings stream.

Screening Process

The Investment Policy Group works as a team by using a bottom-up selection process.

The identification of appropriate stocks for consideration begins with screening a database of 9,000 common equity securities for market capitalization of at least $3 billion, a minimum 10% historical earnings growth rate, and a proprietary quality evaluation. The resultant universe of approximately 500 common stocks is then subject to our proprietary earnings and valuation models. Analyst judgment based on qualitative factors and strong financial characteristics further narrow the universe to a select list of approximately 150 names.

Analysts follow these stocks closely, regularly evaluating their valuation and relative earnings growth. We typically initiate a position in a stock that is trading at a discount (normally 10%–25%) to our estimate of its intrinsic value. This value is computed using a modified present value model that incorporates our analysts' assumptions for normalized earnings, secular earnings growth rate (minimum 10%, maximum 20%), dividend payout ratio, and a stock-specific risk-adjusted discount rate.

The discount rate is determined by our proprietary 11 factor financial scoring process, which reflects a company's historical long-term growth, earnings quality, balance sheet strength, and profitability. This score, combined with earnings variability, net worth, and trading volume, determines a company's relative place within a range of discount rates. The base rate is the current 10-year Treasury yield. We then assign a suitable equity risk premium that may range from 0.50% up to 4.00% above the 10-year Treasury yield, depending upon the quality of the company. The valuation model is a dynamic process in which the earnings base is adjusted each quarter. In addition, the fundamental attributes that contribute to the risk-adjusted discount rate are reevaluated annually for each security and more frequently if market, industry, or specific company issues so demand. Our valuation model is updated daily and published every two weeks.

We consider above median relative earnings growth to be the catalyst driving share price appreciation. This measure is determined by comparing estimated and historical six-month annualized earnings growth to a benchmark and subsequently ranking companies by decile.

Analyst judgment based on fundamental analysis that includes thorough due diligence of company and industry fundamentals is the final arbiter in determining candidates to be presented to the IPG for investment consideration and potential inclusion in the growth model portfolio of 30 to 40 issues.

Portfolio Construction Methodology

Portfolio risk is primarily controlled by: eA's purchase of high-quality companies with strong balance sheets, management, and earnings momentum; the Firm's emphasis on price; their diversification guidelines; the conservative growth assumptions used when valuing companies and their sell discipline. Risk is controlled through the continuous evaluation of the Model Portfolio, which is implemented across all fully discretionary accounts, and by monitoring the dispersion of portfolio characteristics relative to the target benchmark. eA does not use derivatives to control portfolio or security risk.

The Firm's diversification guidelines include a maximum 7% exposure to any one security, although a position will rarely exceed 5%. Their sector allocation may range from 0% up to no more than 2.5× the weighting of any given sector in the S&P 500, subject to a 40% cap. Typically, initial security purchases will be 2% to 3% of the market value of the portfolio. Some holdings may comprise as little as 1%. They buy U.S. domiciled companies, U.S. registered ADRs, and foreign companies listed on U.S. stock exchanges.

(For client and consultant relationships comparing eA to the Russell 1000 Growth index, eA utilizes the S&P 500 index in sector allocation because they believe it to be a better indication of the broad market, whereas the R1000G index can become overweighted at times in individual sectors. This helps to insure that eA's guidelines monitor the diversification of their portfolio at the broadest level possible.)

Buy/Sell Discipline

eA's IPG is the catalyst in their decision-making process. Portfolio policy and stock selection are reviewed at IPG meetings held at least twice weekly. Specific decisions, regarding purchases and sales and the percentage of the portfolio any security is to represent, are based on consensus resulting from these meetings and are implemented across all accounts unless there are specific client restrictions. In fully discretionary accounts with no client restrictions, the portfolio managers have no discretion to enact trades that are not approved by the IPG.

Sell Discipline: If a company's results remain consistent with eA's forecast, they could hold the position for a number of years. On average, their holdings tend to make the maximum move in price with a two-year period. However, if a security becomes excessively valued before that time or if they foresee a slowdown in earnings momentum, they would take profits. eA would also reduce a position when it exceeds 5% of the equity portion of a portfolio. Their average annual turnover is normally 30% to 40%.

A holding will be reviewed for probable sale when it reaches eA's target price ratio, which is normally 120% of their determination of its fair value. Trimming the position, rather than total sale, might be the decision in the case of a big-growth company with rapidly compounding earnings. Stocks are also sold when experiencing weakening earnings momentum, or underperforming the market.

Any significant earnings disappointment will trigger an immediate review of the holdings and a decision to "add or sell." Since eA's investment policy centers on positive earnings momentum within a six-month period, "add or sell" decisions are made within that framework. This time frame may be extended for one quarter out to nine months, in order to capture exceptionally good value occurring just prior to restored earnings momentum. Unless they discern visible earnings growth for the next six to nine months and the valuation is attractive enough to justify adding positions, they will sell on earnings disappointments.

Trading/Execution Strategy

Once the decision to buy or sell a security is approved, eA's trading department determines (based on the percent position of a portfolio and the security's price) the total number of shares to be allocated a group of larger fully discretionary institutional portfolios that have no restrictions. Trading then forwards via e-mail the optimization sheet for the security to all portfolio managers and portfolio assistants. Trading is able to begin the execution process with the group of accounts for which it has optimized and then merges orders submitted by the managers as they come into trading for which the block execution process has begun. The trade orders are prepared by the assistants and checked by the portfolio managers for compliance with the directives of the

IPG and the client's guidelines. Orders are imported into the Longview 2000 Order Management System from the AXYS Portfolio Accounting System.

The broker selection for a trade is of paramount importance. The traders take the actual execution reports from brokers and compare those with time and sales monitored from the quote system.

eA focuses on getting total participation across all portfolios in order to avoid opportunity costs. In the process they try to limit price variation as much as possible. Their traders maintain close communication with the chief investment officer, the portfolio managers, and analysts, relaying trends in the market that may affect the buy or sell program.

Normally, fully discretionary accounts are traded before directed trades. Generally, eA will execute nondirected brokerage orders in securities before directed orders in order to minimize market movement in the substantial positions of securities held in client accounts. The sequence of trades of securities with directed brokers is varied so that all directed brokerage accounts over time are treated fairly. Because of the length of time required for numerous brokers to complete the trades, some directed brokerage accounts for securities may obtain either higher or lower prices that were obtained for the completed nondirected trades.

Although eA will follow its clients' instructions regarding directed trades, they strongly suggest that clients direct no more than 25% to 30% of the commission business. They recommend that in directed accounts, the directed trades be used in an initial buy-in or in cash flows. They do not recommend directed brokerage when they are executing programs across all accounts.

Additional Comments

This is test language.

Characteristics

Product Profile Fields:

Portfolio Management Strategy	Active
Preferred Benchmark	Russell 1000 Growth
Primary Equity Capitalization	Large Cap
Primary Equity Style Emphasis	
Product Sub Type	Core

Strategy Snapshot:

Secondary Equity Style Emphasis*	Pure Growth
Current Number of Holdings	35
Historical Range in Holdings*	30–40
Annual Turnover (By weight)	53%
Current Cash Position	2.1%
Historical Range in Cash*	0–5

Market Capitalization:

Weighted Avg. Mkt. Cap ($Mil)	$84169
Median Market Cap ($Mil)	$59058
Cap Range at Purchase ($Mil)*	3000+

% of Portfolio In Cap Range:

> $50 Billion	59.4%
$15–50 Billion	30.5%
$7.5–15 Billion	10.1%
$1.5–7.5 Billion	0.0%
$750–1.5 Billion	0.0%
$400–750 Million	0.0%
< $400 Million	0.0%
Total	100.0%

Fundamental Characteristics:

Data Source for Characteristics*	Vestek
Current Dividend Yield	1.2%
Current P/E (12-mo Trailing)	28.35×
Current P/E (12-mo Forward)	23.34×
Current P/B (12-mo Trailing)	6.99×
Current P/S (12-mo Trailing)	5.59×
Current P/CF (12-mo Trailing)	26.23×
5 Year ROE	29.9%
Earnings Growth (Past 5 Yrs)	14.2%
Earnings Growth (Next 5 Yrs)	17.2%

Non-US Security Utilization:

Intl. Securities Utilized?*	No
% in ADRs	10.0%
% in Ordinary Shares	—

Policy Limits: (Enter As Absolute % or Index)

Max Sector Exposure*	40
Max Industry Exposure*	—
Max Position Size*	7
Max Cash Position*	15
Security Cap Limits ($Min-$Max)*	—

Allocations

S&P/MSCI Global Industry Classification Standard

Exclude Cash (Invested Portfolio Only)	
Consumer Discretionary	15.3%
Consumer Staples	19.4%
Energy	4.8%
Financials	9.3%
Healthcare	20.4%
Industrials	15.9%
Information Technology	14.9%
Materials	0.0%
Telecom Services	0.0%
Utilities	0.0%
Total:	100.0%

Russell/FTSE Sectors (Global Definitions)

Exclude Cash (Invested Portfolio Only)	
Resources	—
Basic Industries	—
General Industrials	—
Cyclical Consumer Goods	—
Non-cyclical Consumer Goods	—
Cyclical Services	—
Non-cyclical Services	—
Utilities	—
Financials	—
Information Technology	—
Total	0.0%

Use of Derivatives

Derivatives Used in Managing This Product:

Explanation of How Derivatives Are Utilized in Managing This Product:
We utilize S&P 500 futures to equitize any cash held in the portfolios.

Social Screening

Product Available Under Socially Responsible Investing Guidelines: Yes

List of Social Screens That Are Applied:
Alcohol, Tobacco, Firearms/Weaponry, Pornography, Gambling

Further Explanation of Social Screening Process:
We screen for stocks that participate in the distribution of high-content alcohol, the sale and distribution of weapons and the promotion of pornography.

Risk Benchmark: Russell 1000 Growth
Risk-Free Benchmark: Citigroup 3-Month T-Bill
Data Frequency: Quarterly
As Of Date: 6/2004

Separate Account Composite—Gross of Fees

	Trailing Periods								Calendar Years				
	MRQ	YTD	1 Year	3 Year	5 Year	7 Year	10 Year	Since Incp	2003	2002	2001	2000	1999
Returns	-7.72	-9.81	-23.26	-9.95	-5.61	-1.07	—	6.60	-19.66	12.45	-11.45	-2.20	9.86
Bmk	1.94	2.75	17.88	-3.74	-6.48	2.60	—	9.55	29.74	-27.89	-20.42	-22.43	33.16
Excess Returns	-9.66	-12.55	-41.14	-6.21	0.87	-3.67	—	-2.95	-49.40	40.33	8.97	20.23	-23.30
Standard Deviation	—	—	—	17.88	14.58	17.39	—		—	—	—	—	—
Annualized Alpha	—	—	—	-8.70	-4.73	0.31	—		—	—	—	—	—
Tracking Error	—	—	—	31.91	30.63	30.63	—		—	—	—	—	—
Information Ratio	—	—	—	-0.19	0.03	-0.12	—		—	—	—	—	—
Sharpe Ratio	—	—	—	-0.65	-0.60	-0.27	—		—	—	—	—	—

First Return Observation:	Q4/1994		Last Return Observation:	Q3/2004
Total # of Quarters Above Benchmark:	17		Longest # of Consecutive Quarters Above Benchmark:	4
Total # of Quarters Below Benchmark:	22		Longest # of Consecutive Quarters Below Benchmark:	7

CF ERISA—Gross of Fees

| | Trailing Periods | | | | | | | Since | Calendar Years | | | | |
	MRQ	YTD	1 Year	3 Year	5 Year	7 Year	10 Year	Incp	2003	2002	2001	2000	1999
Returns	—	—	—	—	—	—	—	—	—	29.26	-1.87	10.10	1.87
Bmk	—	—	—	—	—	—	—	—	—	-27.89	-20.42	-22.43	33.16
Excess Returns	—	—	—	—	—	—	—	—	—	57.14	18.55	32.52	-31.29
Standard Deviation	—	—	—	—	—	—	—	—	—	—	—	—	—
Annualized Alpha	—	—	—	—	—	—	—	—	—	—	—	—	—
Tracking Error	—	—	—	—	—	—	—	—	—	—	—	—	—
Information Ratio	—	—	—	—	—	—	—	—	—	—	—	—	—
Sharpe Ratio	—	—	—	—	—	—	—	—	—	—	—	—	—

First Return Observation: Q1/1988
Total # of Quarters Above Benchmark: 29
Total # of Quarters Below Benchmark: 33

Last Return Observation: Q4/2003
Longest # of Consecutive Quarters Above Benchmark: 6
Longest # of Consecutive Quarters Below Benchmark: 6

CF Non-ERISA—Gross of Fees

| | Trailing Periods | | | | | | | | Calendar Years | | | | |
	MRQ	YTD	1 Year	3 Year	5 Year	7 Year	10 Year	Since Incp	2003	2002	2001	2000	1999
Returns	—	—	—	—	—	—	—	—	—	—	-2.56	9.38	—
Bmk	—	—	—	—	—	—	—	—	—	—	-20.42	-22.43	—
Excess Returns	—	—	—	—	—	—	—	—	—	—	17.86	31.81	—
Standard Deviation	—	—	—	—	—	—	—	—	—	—	—	—	—
Annualized Alpha	—	—	—	—	—	—	—	—	—	—	—	—	—
Tracking Error	—	—	—	—	—	—	—	—	—	—	—	—	—
Information Ratio	—	—	—	—	—	—	—	—	—	—	—	—	—
Sharpe Ratio	—	—	—	—	—	—	—	—	—	—	—	—	—

First Return Observation:	Q1/1988	Last Return Observation:	Q2/2003
Total # of Quarters Above Benchmark:	26	Longest # of Consecutive Quarters Above Benchmark:	6
Total # of Quarters Below Benchmark:	32	Longest # of Consecutive Quarters Below Benchmark:	9

Institutional Mutual Fund—Net of Fees

	\<Trailing Periods\>								\<Calendar Years\>				
	MRQ	YTD	1 Year	3 Year	5 Year	7 Year	10 Year	Since Incp	2003	2002	2001	2000	1999
Returns	—	—	—	—	—	—	—	—	—	122.27	−12.78	−14.98	22.40
Bmk	—	—	—	—	—	—	—	—	—	−27.89	−20.42	−22.43	33.16
Excess Returns	—	—	—	—	—	—	—	—	—	150.16	7.65	7.45	−10.76
Standard Deviation	—	—	—	—	—	—	—	—	—	—	—	—	—
Annualized Alpha	—	—	—	—	—	—	—	—	—	—	—	—	—
Tracking Error	—	—	—	—	—	—	—	—	—	—	—	—	—
Information Ratio	—	—	—	—	—	—	—	—	—	—	—	—	—
Sharpe Ratio	—	—	—	—	—	—	—	—	—	—	—	—	—

First Return Observation: Q1/1988

Total # of Quarters Above Benchmark: 31

Total # of Quarters Below Benchmark: 31

Last Return Observation: Q2/2003

Longest # of Consecutive Quarters Above Benchmark: 5

Longest # of Consecutive Quarters Below Benchmark: 5

Composite Information for eA US Equity—Separate Account Composite

Assets in Composite	—
# of Accounts in Composite	—

Composite Represents 99.00% of actively managed assets in this investment approach

AIMR Performance Disclosures

Product Inception Date	1/1/1986
Composite Includes Terminated Accounts	Yes
Composite Includes Performance from Prior Firm	No
Composite Includes Simulated Results	No
# of Months Managed Before Eligible for Inclusion	3 months
Portfolio Weighting Method	Asset-Weighted
Rate of Return Weighting Method	Dollar-Weighted
Valuation Frequency	Monthly
Equity Accounting Method	Accrual
Fixed Income Accounting Method	Accrual
Composite Includes	Asset-Plus-Cash-Returns

Composite Dispersion	2003	2002	2001	2000	1999
Highest Return %	—	12.00%	11.00%	10.00%	9.00%
Median Return %	—	5.00%	5.00%	5.00%	5.00%
Lowest Return %	—	6.00%	5.00%	4.00%	3.00%

Dispersion Comments

Separate account dispersion disclosure.

Additional Performance Disclosure

Separate account, gross of fees additional performance disclosure text.

MPI Stylus Charts for zzz eVestment Alliance, LLC: eA US Equity Sample Product

Analysis As of Date: 06/2004
Data frequency: Quarterly

Style Map: Total Period	Asset Allocation: Total Period
Return Index Total Period Jan 86–Jun 04	Total Period Jan 86–Jun 04

Cumulative Performance: Total Period	Batting Average (Annualized Periods)
Total Period Jan 86–Jun 04	Total Period Jan 86–Jun 04

This analysis is created using MPI Stylus performance-based style regression software and draws upon information sources believed to be reliable. eA does not guarantee or warrant the accuracy, timeliness, or completeness of the information provided or the analysis generated and is not responsible for any errors or omissions. Performance and subsequent performance analysis may be provided with additional disclosures available on eA systems and other important considerations, such as appropriateness of the style regression parameters, may be applicable.

General Firm Information

Firm Legal Name — zzz eVestment Alliance, LLC
Firm Headquarters — 501 E-Johnson Ferry Road
Suite 250
Marietta, Georgia 30068
United States

Secondary Office Locations:
City, State, Purpose:

Main Phone/Main Fax — Phone: 678.560.8095, Fax: 678.560.3036
Year Firm Founded — 2000
Registered Inv. Advisor — No
Firm Website Address — www.eVestmentAlliance.com

Marketing Contact

Heath Wilson, Principal
501-E Johnson Ferry Road, NE, Suite 250
Marietta, Georgia 30068
Phone: 678.560.8075, Fax: 678.560.3036
E-mail: heath@evestmentalliance.com

Database Contact

Ottis Crisp, Principal & Chief Operating Officer
2377 Litchfield Way
Virginia Beach, Virginia 23453
Phone: 757.301.9951, Fax: 678.560.3036
E-mail: Matt@evestmentalliance.com

Assets and Accounts by Type ($C Million)

	Total Assets	Institutional Assets	Taxable Assets	Tax-Exempt Assets	Total Accounts*	Institutional Accounts*	Taxable Accounts*	Tax-Exempt Accounts*
Total	$29,465	$28,281	$3,758	$25,707	617	408	212	405
Corporate	$5,952	$5,952	$264	$5,688	144	144	13	131
Public Fund	$7,430	$7,430	$0	$7,430	47	47	0	47
Union/Multi-Employer	$1,308	$1,308	$0	$1,308	29	29	0	29
Foundation & Endowment	$2,097	$2,097	$0	$2,097	118	118	0	118
Healthcare	$0	$0	$0	$0	0	0	0	0
High Net Worth Individuals	$755	$0	$715	$40	181	181	158	23
Wrap Accounts	$356	$0	$261	$95	5	5	4	1
Defined Contribution	$302	$302	$0	$302	15	15	0	15
Other**	$11,265	$11,192	$2,518	$8,747	78	78	37	41

*Note: Prior to 1Q04, data was reported based on number of *clients*. Effective 1Q04, eA requests that data be reported based on number of *accounts*.
**Explanation of Other Assets:

287

Assets by Account Size ($US Million) | | **Accounts by Size** |
---|---|---|---
Assets by Account Size: < $1 million | $43 | Accounts by Size: < $1 million | 84
Assets by Account Size: 1–10 million | $984 | Accounts by Size: 1–10 million | 229
Assets by Account Size: 10–100 million | $8,582 | Accounts by Size: 10–100 million | 260
Assets by Account Size: 100–500 million | $7,642 | Accounts by Size: 100–500 million | 36
Assets by Account Size: > $500 million | $12,214 | Accounts by Size: > $500 million | 8

Assets by Vehicle Type ($US Million) | | **Accounts by Vehicle Type** |
---|---|---|---
Assets by Vehicle: Separate Account | $20,376 | Accounts by Vehicle: Separate Account | 586
Assets by Vehicle: Commingled Fund | $0 | Accounts by Vehicle: Commingled Fund | —
Assets by Vehicle: Mutual Fund (Inst. Class) | $9,089 | *Mutual Fund Clients Not Tracked* |
Assets by Vehicle: Mutual Fund (Retail Class) | $0 | |

U.S. Assets by Category ($US Million) | | |
---|---|---|---
Assets in U.S. Equity | $27,723 | Assets in Non-U.S. Equity | $0
Assets in U.S. Fixed Income | $143 | Assets in Non-U.S. Fixed Income | $0
Assets in U.S. Balanced | $1,559 | Assets in Non-U.S. Balanced | $0
Alternatives | $0 | *Includes Non-U.S. Global and Emerging Markets* |
Other | $0 | |

Largest Accounts by Size

Rank	Aggregate Account Size	Account Type
1	$3,458	Other
2	$3,190	Public Fund
3	$1,734	Other

Historical Assets ($US Million)

Assets As Of	Total	Institutional	Taxable	Tax-Exempt
Year-End 1999	$20	$20	$10	$10
Year-End 2000	$2,500	$1,500	$1,000	$1,500
Year-End 2001	$10,000	$5,000	$5,000	$5,000
Year-End 2002	$760,000	$2,500	$500	$2,000
Year-End 2003	—	—	—	—

Assets by Region ($US Million)

	United States	Asia ex-Japan	Japan	United Kingdom	Continental Europe	Canada	Emerging Markets	Other
By Domicile of Account	$0	$0	$0	$0	$0	$0	$0	$0
Invested in Each Region	$0	$0	$0	$0	$0	$0	$0	$0

Account Turnover

	Accounts Gained Dollars ($million)	% Firm Assets*	Number	Accounts Lost Dollars ($million)	% Firm Assets
Number					
Full Year 1999	0	$1	0.0%	1	$0	1.0%
Full Year 2000	0	$1	0.0%	1	$0	1.0%
Full Year 2001	1	$0	1.0%	1	$0	1.0%
Full Year 2002	3	$1	0.0%	0	$1	0.0%
Full Year 2003	0	$1	0.0%	1	$0	1.0%
YTD 2004	1	$0	1.0%	1	$1	0.0%

*Based on beginning of year assets
Explanation of Account Turnover: —

AIMR Information

AIMR Compliance

		Amount
Firm AIMR Compliant:	Yes	
Date Compliance Began:	01/01/2000	
Performance Audited:	Yes	
Effective Date:	01/01/2002	
Attestation Firm:	—	
Explanation if not AIMR Compliant:	—	

Insurance Coverage

		Amount
Errors & Omissions Insurance:	Yes	$250 Million
Fiduciary Liability Insurance:	Yes	$250 Million
Firm Bonded:	Yes	$500 Million

Firm Ownership Structure

General Ownership Structure

% Employee Owned	35.0%
% Parent Owned	0.0%
% Publicly Held	60.0%
% Other Ownership	5.0%
# of Employee Owners	—
Parent Company Name	—
Description of Other Owners:	—

Minority/Female Ownership Structure

% African American Owned	0.0%
% Asian Owned	0.0%
% Hispanic Owned	0.0%
% Female Owned	0.0%
% Other Owned	0.0%
Total % Minority/Female Owned	—

Team Description

	Portfolio Managers	Research Analysts	Traders	Economists	Client Service	Marketing	Other Staff	CFA Charterholders	PhDs
Total Number	14	25	3	0	15	4	20	20	20
Avg. Yrs. Experience	25	15	19	—	—	19	—	20	20
Compensation Structure for Portfolio Managers:	Salary, Bonus, Equity, Profit Sharing								
Compensation Structure for Analysts:	Salary, Bonus								
Explanation of How Professionals are Categorized:									

Professional Turnover

	Professionals Gained				Professionals Lost			
	Portfolio Managers	Analysts	Traders	Marketing/ Client Service	Portfolio Managers	Analysts	Traders	Marketing/ Client Service
Full Year 1999	0	1	1	1	2	1	1	1
Full Year 2000	1	1	1	1	1	1	1	1
Full Year 2001	1	1	1	1	1	0	1	—
Full Year 2002	1	2	1	1	1	1	1	1
Full Year 2003	1	1	1	1	1	1	1	1
YTD 2004	1	1	1	1	1	1	3	1

Explanation of Professional Departures: —

Investment Professional Departures or Changes Within Firm:

Name:	Brad Hammond	**Title:**	Senior Advisor
Explanation:	Terminated	**Effective Date:**	02/02/2002
Name:	Robert Jetmundsen	**Title:**	Senior Advisor
Explanation:	New Role w/in Firm	**Effective Date:**	04/11/2002
Name:	Evelyn Leyva	**Title:**	Assistant Vice President
Explanation:	New Role w/in Firm	**Effective Date:**	03/19/2003
Name:	Karen W. Minnick	**Title:**	CFO
Explanation:	New Role w/in Firm	**Effective Date:**	01/24/2003
Name:	Chris Paino	**Title:**	Chief Technology Officer
Explanation:	New Role w/in Firm	**Effective Date:**	08/02/2002
Name:	Heath E. Wilson	**Title:**	Principal & Chief Marketing Officer
Explanation:	New Role w/in Firm	**Effective Date:**	02/01/2003

Investment Professionals

Matt Crisp,
Primary Role: ___ Percentage Ownership: ___
Start Year: ___ Industry: ___ Firm: ___

Karen Minnick,
Primary Role: ___ Percentage Ownership: ___
Start Year: ___ Industry: ___ Firm: ___

Heath Wilson,
Primary Role: ___ Percentage Ownership: ___
Start Year: ___ Industry: ___ Firm: ___

James E. Minnick,
Primary Role: ___ Percentage Ownership: ___
Start Year: ___ Industry: ___ Firm: ___

Matt Robison,
Primary Role: ___ Percentage Ownership: ___
Start Year: ___ Industry: ___ Firm: ___

Firm Background

eVestment Alliance was founded 4 years ago by the following individuals: Matt Crisp, Heath Wilson, Jim Minnick, and Karen Minnick. They later made an outstanding acquisition of Matt Robison. eA continues to build clients and enhance products.

Joint Ventures/Affiliations

Sample Capital is affiliated with ZZZ capital.

Prior or Pending Ownership Changes

In April 1994, Montag & Caldwell signed a merger agreement with Alleghany Corporation of New York, a New York Stock Exchange–listed company, to become a member of the Alleghany family of companies. The merger was completed July 29, 1994. On October 19, 2000, Montag & Caldwell entered into an intent agreement whereby Alleghany Asset Management—including Montag & Caldwell, Inc.—would be acquired by a subsidiary of ABN AMRO. ABN AMRO Bank is headquartered in the Netherlands and has operations in over 50 countries. The parent company's shares (ADRs) are listed on the New York Stock Exchange (Symbol: ABN). On February 1, 2001, the merger was consummated.

ABN AMRO fully understands the investment management business, providing an excellent fit with Montag & Caldwell. As a separate subsidiary of ABN AMRO, we operate under our own name and with our own corporate officers and staff. Montag & Caldwell will continue to exercise complete independence in its investment counseling activities.

None

Prior or Pending Litigation

No.

Additional Comments

No additional comments.

Request for Proposal for Hedge Fund-of-Funds Management

A. Organizational and Regulatory Considerations

1. Please provide the name, title, address, e-mail address, and phone number of the person completing this RFP and the date of its completion.

2. Provide the name and address of your firm.

3. Is your firm a registered investment adviser? If so, e-mail a PDF copy of the firm's Form ADV Parts I and II.

4. What regulatory authority(s) is your firm registered with and what was the date of the last inspection?

5. Does your firm have a compliance officer on staff? If so, please provide their name, contact information, and CV.

6. E-mail a copy of the offering memorandum in a PDF.

7. Does your firm serve as a stated "ERISA fiduciary" and do you possess an ERISA bond?

8. Does the firm have errors and omissions and fiduciary liability insurance?

9. Please describe any litigation that your firm has ever been a party to. Also, is there any pending or imminent litigation?

10. Has there ever been a criminal, civil, or administrative proceeding against your firm's principals? If so, please summarize the situation(s).

11. Provide a short history of your firm with important milestones.

12. Please describe your firm's growth objectives.

13. Does your firm have business activities outside of asset management in alternative strategies? If so, please explain them.

14. Discuss the firm's capacity constraints.

15. Please provide the name and contact information of the named fund(s)'s external legal counsel, audit firm, custodian, and administrator.

16. Discuss the due diligence process you employed to select a custodian and administrator.

17. What disaster recovery plans or other emergency procedures are in place?

18. Describe the ownership structure of your firm. Please summarize any ownership changes that have occurred over the past 10 years or are anticipated to occur in the future.

19. What percentage of the firm is owned by active employees? Please summarize the ownership stake of each employee-owner.

20. How many people are currently employed with your firm? Please break them down into the following categories:
    - Key decision makers/investment committee members
    - Additional investment professionals
    - Sales staff
    - Administrative staff

21. Clearly summarize the decision-making authority for the firm from an operating standpoint. For example, does a single person, a board of directors, a committee of people, etc. make decisions? Please provide the names and titles of applicable people.

22. Provide an organization chart for your firm in a Word or PDF file as an attachment to the response of this RFP.

B. Product Summary

23. What are the legal structures of all of your products? For all products, clearly state where the product is domiciled.

Product Legal Structure

Product Name	Legal Structure	Where Domiciled
XYZ Fund	Offshore	Bermuda

24. Summarize the allowable contribution and distribution (and required notice) frequency for all named product(s)?

25. Summarize any initial lock-up period if applicable for all named product(s).

C. Assets Under Management

26.   What are your firm's total assets under management as of the RFP date?

27.   Summarize how your total firm assets are divided by investor type according to number of clients and assets by filling in the following tables.

	Number of Clients				
Investor	**2004**	**2003**	**2002**	**2001**	**2000**
All clients					
Firm employees					
Corporate pension (ERISA)					
Public pension funds					
Taft Hartley					
Endowment/foundations					
Taxable institutions					
Tax-exempt high-net-worth investors					
Taxable high-net-worth investors					
Non-U.S. institutional					
Non-U.S. high-net-worth					
Other investors					

	Number of Clients				
Investor	**2004**	**2003**	**2002**	**2001**	**2000**
All clients					
Firm employees					
Corporate pension (ERISA)					
Public pension funds					
Taft Hartley					
Endowment/foundations					
Taxable institutions					
Tax-exempt high-net-worth investors					
Taxable high-net-worth investors					
Non-U.S. institutional					
Non-U.S. high-net-worth					
Other investors					

28.   Summarize the investor type for your *largest five clients*, what percentage of your total firm assets they represent individually, and which products they are invested in, respectively.

29.   Summarize the growth history of the *firm's assets under management* for the last ten years (or since inception).

	1995	1996	1997	1998	1999	2000	2001	2002	2003	2004

Assets
(in millions)

D. Allocation of Assets Among Strategies

30. Outline your product allocation as of the RFP date, and product inception dates for the named and non-named products. Please use the following template as your guide.

Product Name	Allocation ($)	Allocation (%)	Inception Date
All Named Products:			
Named Product #1	$X	X%	X/XX/19XX
All Non-Named Products:			
Non-Named Product A	$A	A%	X/XX/19XX

31. What type of investor is each product above designed to serve based on its legal structure? For example, pensions, endowments, wealthy individuals, etc.? Also, are there any restrictions regarding ERISA assets for any of the above products?

32. Provide the growth history of the *named product's assets under management* for the past 10 years (or since inception). Please use the following template as your guide.

Named Product #1—Name:

	1995	1996	1997	1998	1999	2000	2001	2002	2003	2004

Assets
(in millions)

33. Provide the growth history of the *non-named product's assets under management* for the past 10 years (or since inception). Please use the following template as your guide.

Named Product #1—Name:

	1995	1996	1997	1998	1999	2000	2001	2002	2003	2004

Assets
(in millions)

(Other non-named products if applicable)

E. Product Investment Strategies

34. What are the named product(s)'s targeted return, volatility, and correlation (to S&P 500 & Lehman Aggregate Bond index).

35. List all of the underlying investment strategies employed by managers in the named product(s).

36. Clearly summarize the *source of investment returns* for each underlying strategy used in the named fund(s) and use examples if necessary.

     Strategy

     (e.g.) *Merger Arbitrage*: Merger arbitrage, sometimes called risk arbitrage, involves investment in corporate events, mergers, and hostile takeovers. Managers typically purchase stocks of the company being acquired and sell short the stocks of the acquiring company in order to profit off the inevitable decline in spread. *Example:* Long People Soft & Short Oracle.

37. Clearly summarize the *sources of risk* (and uses of leverage) for each of the above strategies (feel free to use examples).

     Strategy

     (e.g.) *Merger Arbitrage*: The main risk of this strategy is that the merger will fall through or the spread between the long and short positions widens (hurting the long and short positions). Leverage, which is frequently employed, can magnify the magnitude of losses.

38. Summarize the number of managers being used in the named product(s) as of the date of this RFP. Also, what is the current largest allocation to a single manager?

F. Investment Philosophy

39. Describe your overall investment philosophy (core investment beliefs) and principles.

40. What investment strategies, if any, do you avoid and why?

41. Have there been any changes in the investment philosophy adopted by your firm over the past five years? If yes, please specify.

42. What percentage of the named fund(s) will be held in cash at any time?

G. Investment Process

43. Summarize your overall investment process for the named product(s).

H. Key Investment Professionals

44. List all of your key investment professionals (e.g. investment committee members or decision-makers) and their tenure with the firm and their job function. Also, list all key investment professionals that have departed the firm in the past 10 years and the date they departed and their job function.

45. For each of the people listed (both current and departed), supply a CV showing their qualifications and what they did prior to their current responsibilities.

46. Please list all of your research professionals (not designated above as key investment professionals) and their tenures with the firm. Also, list all research professionals that have departed the firm in the past five years, the date they departed, and a description of their job function.

47. Are your investment professionals required to invest in your funds? If so, to what extent? List the total amount of assets invested in the firm's funds by employees.

48. Are investment professionals allowed to invest in the underlying managers outside the firm's funds? If so, describe to what extent? How much of employee assets are invested in the underlying firms outside the firm's funds.

49. Please disclose any potential conflicts of interest (real or perceived) that may exist for the firm or any of the firm's key investment professionals.

50. Please describe the compensation structure for all of the firm's professionals.

I. Asset/Strategy Allocation Process

51. Describe the firm's asset/strategy allocation process for the named product(s).

52. What percentage of your value added as a manager would you say is asset/strategy allocation vs. manager selection?

53. Discuss how you go about defining and changing the asset/strategy allocation for your funds. Does traditional Markowitz optimization guide your diversification principles or are there other competing models or methodologies that drive the portfolio optimization process?

54. Define your firm's main competitive advantage(s) in the asset/strategy allocation of your hedge fund of funds.

55. What aspect of your asset allocation approach do you think distinguishes your firm from other hedge fund of fund managers?

56. Do you employ a tactical asset/strategy allocation strategy or a strategic asset/strategy allocation policy?

57. If you employ a strategic long-term asset/strategy allocation policy, how often do you review the policy and how often have you made changes?

58. If you employ a tactical asset/strategy allocation, how frequently and to what extent have you made tactical shifts to the allocation? Please feel free to provide specific examples.

59. Clearly summarize the investment decision-making authority for the firm from an asset/strategy allocation perspective:
    - Does a single person, a group of people, a committee of people, etc. make decisions?
    - Does a committee of people vote decisions with certain committee members getting double votes?
    - Do decisions have to be unanimous?
    - Does any committee member have veto power?

J. Manager Evaluation and Due Diligence

60. What process do you have in place to identify potential new managers? Do you employ the services of any external agents?

61. Do you have any guidelines regarding when in the life cycle of the hedge fund you will invest (i.e., new talent vs. more established hedge fund managers)?

62. Describe in detail the firm's due diligence process, clearly stating who is responsible for carrying out each stage and for decision making. Please outline the qualitative and quantitative selection criteria used in this process including any screens on managers you will invest with. E-mail a PDF version of a manager report you generated internally.

63. How do you gather, assess, and utilize the following information on hedge funds:
    - Background and integrity of personnel
    - Legal structure
    - Incentive structure
    - Investment decision and portfolio management process
    - Internal controls
    - Risk management
    - Managers' personal investments in fund
    - Security of credit
    - Custody arrangements

64. Do you have any absolute standards regarding liquidity, use of prime brokers, transparency, or the fee structure of hedge funds that you would invest in?

65. How do you measure risk at the individual hedge fund level (include review of any analytical tools, software, and quantitative methods used and state the specific measures used)?

66. What attribution software (or processes) do you employ to determine the source of manager performance and whether it is as a result of skill (active component of management process) or luck (returns result from external factors not inherent in manager's stated objective).

67. In assessing risk at the individual manager level, what tools do you use to detect changes in the manager's behavior (e.g., style drifts, increase in leverage, fraud, increase in risk)?

68. How long do you expect due diligence to take and how much time would you expect to spend with each manager during the due diligence process?

69. On average, how many new managers do you research per year?

70. Do you have an approved list of managers? If so, how many managers are currently on it and what is their aggregate capacity? What is the capacity by investment strategy?

71. Describe the ongoing monitoring process.

72. Describe your manager termination discipline/process.

73. How has the number of managers in your portfolio(s) changed over time? Complete the following table for the named product(s):

	1995	1996	1997	1998	1999	2000	2001	2002	2003	2004
# Managers										

74. How many managers have been terminated per year over the past 10 years? Complete the following table for the named product(s):

	1995	1996	1997	1998	1999	2000	2001	2002	2003	2004
# Managers										

75. How many new managers have been hired per year over the past 10 years? Complete the following table for the named product(s):

	1995	1996	1997	1998	1999	2000	2001	2002	2003	2004
# Managers										

76. What is the reason for the growth or decline in the number of managers over the past few years?

77. How does your process deal with multistrategy managers? What is the most you would allocate to multistrategy managers? How much do you currently have allocated to multistrategy managers?

78. Does your firm currently possess an ownership stake in any of the underlying managers in any of your portfolios? If so, please provide the number of current managers in your portfolios that your firm has an ownership interest in.

79. Has your firm ever possessed an ownership stake in any underlying managers in your portfolio. If so, please explain when and how they were divested or to what extent any ownership position still exists. Disclose the number of current managers in your portfolios that your firm has ever had an ownership interest in.

80. Have you ever received finder's fees or "kick-backs" for investing with a manager? If so, please explain how you used or allocated this finder fee(s).

81. What is the aggregate additional capacity of your managers? What is the additional capacity of your managers by investment category?

82. Have you ever told a manager that you were going to terminate them if they refused to provide you with additional capacity? If so, how frequently have such things occurred?

83. Does your firm have unique access to certain managers that might be closed to new investors, but have reserved capacity for your firm? If so, please explain.

K. Level of Transparency

84. Describe the level of transparency *you receive from your underlying managers*. Please include a discussion of (at least) following issues:
    - Ownership structure
    - Funds managed and strategies employed
    - Accounting leverage
    - Implied (use of derivatives) leverage
    - Individual holdings
    - Firm assets under management
    - Staffing
    - Investment decision making process
    - Division of responsibility of investment professionals and key operational professionals
    - Detailed biographies of key investment and operational professionals

85. Please describe the level of transparency *you are willing to provide your*

clients about the underlying managers. Please include a discussion of (at least) the following issues:

- Manager name, location, and strategy
- Ownership structure
- Funds managed and strategies employed
- Accounting leverage
- Implied (use of derivatives) leverage
- Individual holdings
- Firm assets under management
- Staffing
- Investment decision making process
- Division of responsibility of investment professionals and key operational professionals
- Detailed biographies of key investment and operational professionals

86. For the *named product(s)*, list the name of all your managers, their city of location, date of your first investment with their firm, and the strategy they employ. If you are unwilling to share, please explain why.

Named Product(s):

Firm Name   Firm City   Date of First Investment   Strategy

L. Leverage at the Portfolio Level

Please note any differences between the named product(s) for the following leverage questions.

87. Summarize the current level of *accounting* leverage for the *named products* (accounting leverage defined as: [long + shorts] / [equity capital]).

88. Summarize the current level of *implicit* leverage for the *named products* (implicit leverage defined as leverage caused by use of options, swaps, futures, and/or other derivative instruments).

89. Summarize the *total* (accounting + implicit) leverage for the named *products.*

90. What limits or caps to portfolio leverage (accounting + implicit) would you apply for the *named products*?

91. What were the aggregate long/short positions over the past five years for the named product(s)? Please use the following template.

	1999	2000	2001	2002	2003	2004
Gross Long						
Gross Short						
Net Long						

M. Leverage at the Manager Level

92. What limits to leverage (accounting + implicit) do you allow at the manager level? If this leverage limit (or cap) varies based on the investment strategy, summarize how for each underlying strategy.

93. Do you periodically employ additional leverage at the portfolio level to enhance returns or reduce risk? If so, explain how and why.

N. Risk Management

94. Describe your risk management procedures and philosophy both at the FOF level and at the manager level. Feel free to include discussions of the following in your response:
    - Organizational risk
    - Model risk
    - Liquidity risk
    - Value-at-risk (VaR)
    - Sensitivity analysis
    - Factor push analysis
    - Scenario analysis
    - Event risk
    - Herd risk
    - Equity risk
    - Exchange rate risk
    - Interest rate risk
    - Yield spread risk
    - Commodity risk

95. Do you have a written risk management policy? If so, would you be willing to provide it if asked?

96. What internal VaR target (95% and/or 99%) have you set for each of the named portfolios (please express in % terms instead of dollar terms)? Please summarize your methodology for calculating VaR (Variance-Covariance Method, Monte Carlo Simulation, Scenario Analysis, etc.).

97. How do you manage any liquidity mismatch between the hedge funds in which you invest and the level of liquidity you offer to your clients? Would you be willing to borrow funds to pay out redeeming investors (causing leverage)?

O. Fees

98. Summarize your fee schedule for each named product(s).

99. What fees, if any, are not fully covered by the above fee schedule (other

than underlying manager fee structures and trading costs by each of the underlying managers). For example, do you charge travel expenses, research expenses, audit expenses, trust-custody expenses, etc. to the portfolio. If so, summarize (in basis point terms) how much these fees have averaged on an annual basis over the past 5 years and whether they are reflected in your performance numbers.

P. Investment Performance

100. Provide the monthly returns for the *named products* dating back to product inception in an Excel spreadsheet. If linked performance is used between products, clearly state how?

101. Describe the benchmark that you think is the best proxy for evaluating your portfolio and why.

102. Provide the monthly returns of this benchmark (specified above) in an Excel spreadsheet.

103. Provide monthly returns of each of your strategies (e.g. event driven, convertible arbitrage, distressed debt, etc.) in an Excel spreadsheet. In other words, provide the underlying strategy returns that can be combined to generate the named product's total return.

104. Are these performance numbers gross or net of all fees? Please specify any fee that is not factored into the monthly performance numbers.

105. With what frequency are the asset management, performance based, and/or additional fees charge to the portfolios?

106. How often is NAV calculated for each named product?

107. What entity is responsible for calculating returns? If returns are calculated internally, what external entity is responsible for auditing the returns?

108. How often are performance reports provided to clients? How long after the month or quarter does it take for the performance reports to go out?

109. Provide an electronic version of a periodic (monthly or quarterly) performance report.

Request for Proposal: Record-Keeping Services Firm Background

1. Please state the name, title, address, telephone number, and e-mail address of the person we may contact with questions about the responses to this request for proposal.

2. Please provide the following information about your firm:
   - Date founded
   - Total employees in the organization
   - Total employees in the defined contribution services segment
   - Number of firm locations
   - Number of defined contribution services locations (specify the locations and what functions are performed at each site)
   - Describe any parent/subsidiary/affiliate relationships
   - Firm's financial condition

3. Please provide the following information about your defined contribution business:
   - Number of years providing defined contribution record-keeping services
   - Number of years providing daily valuation defined contribution record-keeping services
   - Total number of defined contribution participants for which you record-keep
   - Number of daily valued defined contribution plans your company currently provides full-service capabilities for in the following size groups:

Plan Size (by participants)	Number of Daily Value Defined Contribution Plans	Total Assets	Total Number of Participants
Under 100			
100–999			
1,000–4,999			
5,000–9,999			
Over 10,000			

4. Please state the total number of full-service defined contribution relationships for your firm during the following periods:

	2001	2002	2003	2004
Total Full Service DC Plans				

5. How many new full-service defined contribution relationships were *added* over the following periods (based on plan size):

Plan Size (by participants)	2001	2002	2003	2004
Under 100				
100–999				
1,000–4,999				
5,000–9,999				
Over 10,000				

6. What is the size of your largest and smallest record-keeping account by number of participants and assets?

7. Please provide the following as of the most recent period available:
   - Total assets under management
   - Defined contribution assets under management
   - Defined contribution assets under your firm's administration, but managed by alliance/outside firms

8. What are your firm's various sources of revenue? What percentage does record-keeping services provide? What source produces the greatest percentage of revenues?

9. Please state your firm's target market for defined contribution services by participant size, total assets, and/or average balance per participant.

10. What was your firm's capital investment made to the defined contribution business in 2003 and 2004? What capital investments are budgeted for 2005?

11. Describe your firm's organizational structure.

12. What benefit outsourcing services does your firm provide other than defined contribution services?

PLAN SPONSOR SERVICES

1. Describe your organizational philosophy/approach to client services.

2. From what geographic location will this account be serviced?

3. What is the ratio of clients to client service managers? If this differs based on plan size, what is the ratio of clients to client service managers for a plan of this size?

4. What is the average annual personnel turnover in your defined contribution unit?

5. How are client service managers compensated? What is their performance based on?

6. Describe the typical employment and educational background of a client service manager?

7. What is the average firm tenure for client service managers?

8. How many new employees were added to the defined contribution unit in 2002, 2003, and 2004?

9. Please specify the methods used by your organization to monitor client satisfaction and with what frequency?

10. Do you conduct client conferences or organize client advisory councils? If so, please describe.

11. Identify the client service structure/team responsible for this relationship and their primary roles/functions.

12. Are your service levels audited or surveyed by any outside firms? Please describe.

13. Can your firm provide the client Internet access to plan level information? If yes, do they have the ability to generate customized reports? Does this include the ability to make correction changes?

14. How often will your firm conduct on-site meetings with the client to review your services and the plan?

15. How many daily valued record-keeping clients has your firm lost in the past three years for reasons other than a merger or acquisition? Please provide the name of three former clients that can be contacted (Please note: while we require you to provide references, they will not be contacted unless your firm is selected as a finalist).

16. *Important*: Please provide three references for current clients with similar demographics (contact name, title, telephone number, company name, company size, length of record-keeping relationship, types of services provided, any other relevant information) (please note: while we require you to provide references, they will not be contacted unless your firm is selected as a finalist).

ADMINISTRATION/RECORD KEEPING

1. Is record-keeping/administration performed internally? If not, please provide details on the organization providing these services.

2. What software/system is used to provide record-keeping services?

3. Please describe your disaster recovery systems and insurance for your record-keeping and 800 number systems.

4. How often are your disaster recovery systems tested?

5. What is the "cutoff" time for investment transfers to be made the same day? Does this differ for proprietary, alliance, and nonalliance/outside funds? If so, please describe.

6. What is the "cutoff" time for contribution wires to post to participants' accounts the same day?

7. Please specify which of the following transactions *cannot* be performed paperless?
    - Enrollment
    - Designation of beneficiary
    - Deferrals
    - Fund transfers
    - Fund elections
    - Loans
    - Contribution changes
    - Distributions
    - Hardship withdrawals
    - Address changes

8. If paperwork is required, can it be returned to your firm for processing?

9. With what transactions will the plan sponsor need to remain involved?

10. Once proper information is received, how much time is required to issue a distribution or withdrawal check for payment?

11. Please indicate which of the following compliance testing you will provide and at what costs? Please specify frequency of tests (annual, semi-annual, etc.).
    - ADP/ACP
    - Annual addition limitation - 415(c)
    - HCE determination

12. Will your firm supply a signature-ready 5500 form? At what cost?

PARTICIPANT SERVICES

1. How soon after the end of a quarter will you provide participant statements? Is this guaranteed? Can they be sent to participants' homes? *Please supply a sample statement.*

2. Is your firm able to supply statements on demand for periods other than quarter end?

3. Does your firm calculate a "personalized rate of return" for each participant? Is this information available on the statement? On the Internet?

4. Do you offer 24-hour voice response service? Please provide the 800 number and a sample ID for demonstration purposes (if available).

5. Is your interactive voice response system fully integrated with your record-keeping system?

6. How often and for how long has the voice response system been down in the past 24 months?

7. Are live representatives available? What times/days?

8. Please describe the typical experience and training of telephone representatives? Are they required to be licensed (Series 6, 7, etc.)?

9. Do you offer Internet access to participants? Inquiries only or transactions? Please describe.

10. Please provide your retirement plan services Internet address, for both participants and Plan Sponsors, along with a sample ID for demonstration purposes.

11. Is your Internet site fully integrated with your record-keeping system?

12. Can the Internet site be customized? Briefly describe.

13. What services are available through your voice response system and Internet?

	Voice Response	**Internet**
Enrollment		
On-demand statements		
Up-to-date statements		
Most recent quarter-end statement		
Balance inquiries		
Rebalancing feature		
Contribution changes, stops, restarts		
Contribution inquiries		
Change future and existing contributions		
Loan modeling		
Loan payoff balances		
Termination options		
Fund objectives		
Investment performance		
Initiate and request paperwork for:		
Withdrawals		
Termination distributions		
Loans		
Change in beneficiary		

14. Please provide the following statistics for 2004:
    - Average total number of voice response system calls per day
    - Average total number of retirement service site Internet contacts per day
    - Average number of rep-assisted calls per day
    - Average speed of answer for rep-assisted calls
    - Average call-handling time

15. Would the client have an exclusive 800 number or dedicated telephone representatives?

16. Do telephone representatives have electronic access to plan provisions when a participant calls?

17. Do telephone representatives have electronic access that allows them to track forms/documents mailed to and from participants?

COMMUNICATION AND EDUCATION SERVICES

1. Identify the standard education meetings and materials included in your pricing.
2. How many initial enrollment meetings are included in your pricing? If additional meetings are needed, what are the costs? Are travel expenses included?
3. How many annual ongoing education meetings are included in your pricing? If additional meetings are needed, what are the costs? Are travel expenses included?
4. Which of the following education/communication materials will you provide and at what cost?

	Service Provided (Yes or No)	Cost
Enrollment meetings		
Ongoing meetings		
Enrollment kits		
Videotapes (off-the-shelf)		
Videotapes (customized)		
Retirement planning software (Internet-based)		
Retirement planning software (customized)		
Payroll stuffers		
Posters		
Quarterly newsletters		
Personal projection letters		
Internet access		

5. Can education materials be customized? To what extent and at what cost?
6. Please provide details of *any* work that is outsourced. This includes mailings, education meetings, materials, etc.

7. Does your firm allocate an annual education budget to clients? If so, how much would be allocated annually to this client?

8. Do you provide basic and advanced level meetings for different participant groups? If so, please describe.

9. Do you have a dedicated education meeting team? If so, how many individuals make up that department?

10. Does your organization provide financial planning services? If so, please describe? At what cost?

11. Does your organization provide retirement planning software? If so, please describe? At what cost?

12. Describe in detail how your firm would provide education meetings at various client locations throughout the country?

13. Please provide a sample calendar demonstrating education efforts for a similar client.

14. What quarterly education/communication material will you provide? Please describe. Are there extra costs?

INVESTMENTS

1. Which of the existing funds, if any, can you accommodate?

2. How many proprietary funds do you offer for defined contribution plans?

3. Do you require clients to use your proprietary funds? If so, to what extent? Please be precise as to the percentage of assets or number of funds that must be with proprietary funds.

4. Do you offer alliance (nonproprietary) funds within your program? If so, how many? *Please provide a complete listing of the alliance funds available.*

5. Do you limit the number of alliance funds that can be used?

6. Are there any additional asset-based fees on alliance funds?

7. Can you accommodate nonproprietary funds outside of your alliance fund offerings?

8. If you permit outside (nonalliance) funds are there any additional asset-based fees?

9. Are all trades processed on a *true daily* basis, including the use of nonproprietary/alliance funds (e.g., buy and sell on the same day)? If not, please describe.

10. How many investment options are included in your pricing? What are the costs for additional investment options beyond this number?

11. *Please complete the request for information in Appendix I* by identifying one proprietary and one alliance/outside fund you propose to offer within each of the following categories:
    - Money market
    - Stable value
    - Intermediate-term bond
    - Balanced
    - Large company value
    - S&P 500 index
    - Large cap growth
    - Small company value
    - Small company growth
    - International
    - Real estate
    - Lifestyle/asset allocation funds

TRUSTEE SERVICES

1. Will you act as, or provide, trustee services? If not, who will provide trust services?
2. Please indicate where your trust company or trust alliance partner is located.
3. Will you act as trustee on outside funds?
4. Is your trust accounting system integrated with your record-keeping system?
5. How often are trust statements reconciled with the record-keeping statements?
6. Describe the controls and lines of communications between the record-keeping function and the trustee function.

MUTUAL FUND TRADING PRACTICES

1. Has your firm or any of its affiliates received a subpoena or similar request from any governmental entity seeking information regarding its mutual fund trading practices?
2. If the answer to the above question is "yes," please detail the scope of the examination and any specific funds and professionals (current or former) named in the request for information.
3. Please provide all press releases or other public statements in response to the allegations.

4. Provide a copy of the firm's policies and procedures regarding trading in its mutual funds by clients and employees.

5. Has the firm's system of internal controls detected any violations of the policies and procedures? If so, detail the nature of the violation and the action taken to rectify the situation.

6. Has the firm launched an internal inquiry into market timing or late day trading? Detail the scope of the examination and the results thus far. Also list the beginning and end date of the inquiry?

7. Has the firm terminated any employee in connection with the trading practice investigations? Please provide information.

8. What is the firm's policy regarding after hours trading? Are there any situation where an investor can purchase shares after 4 P.M. Eastern Time, or after the fund's shares have priced, and receive that day's closing price?

9. Are brokers and retirement plan record keeps permitted to place order after 4 P.M. Eastern Time, provided those orders are received before 4 P.M. Eastern Time? How does the firm verify the original order was received before 4 P.M. Eastern Time?

10. Does the firm employ fair market value pricing? Please describe.

11. Does the firm permit hedge funds to invest in the mutual funds? Please describe how hedge fund investors may be treated differently from other investors. How is the firm compensated for working with hedge funds?

12. Please list the Board of Directors that oversees the firm's mutual funds. Please provide biographical information. Are any changes to the structure of the Board of Directors forthcoming or anticipated?

FEES

1. Are you willing to offer service guarantees and to put your fees at risk?

2. How long will you guarantee fees?

3. What has been the average increase in your organizations fees over the past three years?

4. What would cause any of the fee quotes provided to change significantly?

5. Please describe any costs or penalties incurred for terminating the agreement at contract expiration? Prior to contract expiration?

6. What is the minimum term of agreement required to avoid any plan termination/conversion penalties or fees?

7. Clearly describe how investment management fees can offset record-keeping and other administrative fees?

8. Will you provide an accounting of 12b-1, subaccounting, revenue sharing, or other fees received from fund companies and provide any credit or reimbursement of such fees?

9. Can a decrease in fees as assets increase clause be built into the contract?

10. Please provide an estimate of overall first year fees, including any conversion and/or set-up fees.

11. Please provide an estimate of overall ongoing fees (after first year).

12. Provide a detailed estimate of fees and please include all assumptions:

One-Time Plan Sponsor Fees

Conversion

   Flat fee

   Per employee

Loan conversion

Rollout communication/education

   Number of on-site meeting days

   Travel expenses

Annual Ongoing Plan Sponsor Fees

Record-keeping/administration

Trustee

Compliance testing

Contribution processing

Signature-ready 5500 form

Employee education services

   Number of on-site meeting days

   Cost per additional day

   Travel expenses

Internet services

Voice response system

Quarterly statements

Mailing, postage, and handling

Miscellaneous Plan Sponsor Fees

QDRO processing (each)

   Additional fee

Subsequent changes to VRU/Internet

Subsequent changes to investments

New fund agreement set-up charge

Additional fund options

Quarterly newsletter

Self-directed brokerage costs

   Plan sponsor fee (annual)

Miscellaneous Participant Fees

Self-directed brokerage costs

   Participant fee (annual)

   Asset-based fee

   Commissions

   Miscellaneous fee

Loans

   Initiation fee

   Annual maintenance fee

Distributions (per check)

Periodic distributions

   Initial

   Processing fee (per check)

13. Other (please include and explain all other relevant costs omitted from this matrix here):

CONVERSIONS

1. When would your firm need to be notified by for a January 1, 2006 conversion?

2. Please briefly describe the conversion process.

3. Are the individuals who oversee the conversion process the same for ongoing administration or are separate teams utilized?

4. What is a reasonable blackout period for a plan this size and structure?

5. How much advance warning will participants receive regarding the blackout period?

Please respond as requested in order to receive full consideration. Feel free to contact John Smith at (555) 555-5555 should you have any questions. Thank you.

Proposed Investment Menu

Fund Name	Objective	Averaged Annualized Returns as of 12/31/04			3-year SD	5-year SD	Manager Tenure (yrs)	Expense Ratio	Revenue Sharing* (bps)
		1-year	3-year	5-year					
Money market									
Stable value									
Intermediate-term bond									
Balanced									
Large-cap value									
Large-cap index									
Large-cap growth									
Small-cap value									
Small-cap growth									
International									
Real estate									
Asset allocation/lifestyle									

*Please specify amount of revenue sharing received by each fund.

Resources

DATA

Morningstar, Inc.
225 West Wacker Drive
Chicago, IL 60606
Tel: (312) 696-6000
www.morningstar.com
Morningstar, Inc. is a leading provider of independent investment research. The company offers an extensive line of Internet, software, and print-based products for individual investors, financial advisors, and institutional clients.

InvestorForce, Inc.
1400 Liberty Ridge Drive, Suite 107
Wayne, PA 19087
Tel: (877) 417-1240
Tel: (610) 408-3700
Fax: (610) 408-3710
www.investorforce.com
InvestorForce provides technology solutions to the institutional investment community. They offer an integrated platform of traditional asset class products and hedge fund products. InvestorForce also offers an online database of active hedge fund products and active traditional investment managers.

eVestment Alliance
501-E Johnson Ferry Road, NE
Suite 250
Marietta, GA 30068

Tel: (678) 560-3036

www.evestmentalliance.com

eVestment Alliance is an investment manager database and analytics provider servicing the institutional investment industry.

Plan Sponsor Network/Informa Investment Solutions, Inc.
4 Gannett Drive
White Plains, NY 10604
Tel: (914) 640-0200
Fax: (914) 694-6728
www.informais.com

Informa Investment Solutions provides separate account information, portfolio accounting and performance measurement systems, analytical tools, and consulting support to pension funds, investment consultants, brokerage firms, and money managers.

ANALYTICAL SOFTWARE

PPCA—StokTrib
Ron Surz
78 Marbella
San Clemente, CA 92673
Tel: (949) 488-8339
www.ppca-inc.com

PPCA is an investment consulting firm specializing in innovative analytical tools for the discriminating investor. StokTrib is a holdings-based style analysis and performance attribution software system.

Vestek
Thomson Financial
195 Broadway, 6th Floor
New York, NY 10007
Tel: (646) 822-3000
Fax: (646) 822-6450
www.vestek.com

Vestek provides software to help investment professionals make more informed decisions. Vestek offers an array of products for portfolio analysis and construction, and holdings-based attribution analysis.

Baseline
Thomson Financial
195 Broadway, 6th Floor
New York, NY 10007
Tel: (646) 822-2130
www.baseline.com
Baseline is a provider of information products and services to the investment community. Their products include an equity analytic tool for the institutional investors that aids in stock selection, portfolio evaluation, and communication.

Ibbotson Associates
225 North Michigan Avenue
Suite 700
Chicago, IL 60601
Tel: (312) 616-1620
Fax: (312) 616-0404
www.ibbotson.com
Ibbotson sells historical financial data as well as a number of analytical software packages including both mean—variance and probabilistic asset allocation models. Descriptions of several products include:

- "Ibbotson EnCorr® software combines the latest in financial theory and practice for robust performance and analytics. Utilizing the multiple components of the EnCorr Investment Analysis software program you can build optimal asset allocation recommendations. Our flexible investment analysis tools enable you to analyze historical performance data, develop and implement your asset allocation policy with managers or mutual funds and evaluate and monitor manager/fund style and performance."

- "Portfolio Strategist®, Ibbotson's Investment Planning software, helps you create better portfolios for your clients and determine the asset mix that offers the best chance of achieving the highest return for a given level of risk. Changing client needs and objectives, unique constraints, and a variety of risk tolerances—all these factors must be considered when you are designing, implementing, and monitoring asset allocation strategies for your clients. Portfolio Strategist can help you face the ongoing challenge of tailoring asset allocation recommendations to fit your clients' needs."

- "Ibbotson's Presentation Materials allow you to illustrate the benefits of long-term investing and effectively demonstrate time-tested investment concepts. All of our NASD-reviewed materials will assist you in educating your clients on the importance of asset allocation. Charts and graphs can be personalized with your firm's logo to increase visibility or we can work with you to customize any existing graph to your specification, or create an entirely new one."

CheckFree Investment Services / Mobius
4819 Emperor Boulevard, Suite 300
Durham, NC 27703
Tel: (914) 941-2600
Fax: (919) 9417018
www.checkfreeinvsvcs.com
CheckFree Investment Services (CIS) provides a broad range of investment management services to thousands of financial institutions through M-Solutions software applications. They are particularly known for their performance analysis software and data.

Zephyr Associates, Inc.
P.O. Box 12368
Zephyr Cove, NV 89448
Tel: (755) 588-0654
Tel: (800) 789-8423
Fax: (775) 588-8423
www.styleadvisor.com
Zephyr Associates is a leader in performance and returns-based style analysis software. Zephyr's StyleADVISOR® and AllocationADVISOR™ are used by investment professionals throughout the world to analyze investment managers, mutual funds, financial markets, and investment portfolios.

New Frontier Advisors, LLC
184 High Street, Floor 5
Boston, MA 02110
Tel: (617) 482-1433
Fax: (617) 482-1434
www.newfrontieradvisors.com
New Frontier Advisors is a developer and seller of patented probabilistic portfolio optimization and rebalancing applications.

OTHER RESOURCES

The Investment Management Consultants' Association (IMCA)
5619 DTC Parkway, Suite 500
Greenwood Village, CO 80111
Tel: (303) 770-3377
Fax: (303) 770-1812
www.imca.org
IMCA is an important resource for the investment consulting world on developments in investment strategies, legal and regulatory issues, economic news, and marketing techniques. The mission at IMCA is to ensure quality service to the public by developing and encouraging high standards in the investment consulting profession.

CFA Institute
560 Ray C. Hunt Dr.
Charlottesville, VA 22903-2981
Tel: 1-800-247-8132 (U.S. & Canada)
Tel: 1-434-951-5499 (Outside U.S. & Canada)
www.cfainstitute.org
CFA Institute is an international, nonprofit organization, which includes the sponsorship of the Chartered Financial Analyst (CFA) designation. They established the widely accepted AIMR-PPS ethical standards used primarily by investment managers in the United States and Canada for creating performance presentations that ensure fair representation and full disclosure.

Commonfund
15 Old Danbury Road
P.O. Box 812
Wilton, CT 06897-0812
Tel: 888-TCF-MAIN
Tel: (203) 563-5000
www.commonfund.org
The Commonfund is an investment firm that understands the specific needs of non-profit institutions.

Glossary

12b-1 Fees   A fee used to defray distribution and marketing costs. 12b-1 fee information is disclosed in a fund's prospectus and is included in the stated expense ratio.

3(c)1 Fund   Fund limited to no more than 99 accredited investors.

3(c)7 Fund   Fund limited to 499 qualified purchasers who have a minimum of $5 million in investment assets.

401(k)   Employer-sponsored retirement plan in which eligible employees may make salary deferral contributions on a pre-tax basis. Earnings accrue on a tax-deferred basis.

403(b)   Retirement plan for certain employees of public schools, churches and other tax-exempt organizations. Very similar in structure to a 401(k) plan.

Absolute Return Strategies   Strategies that seek positive returns regardless of market directions.

Arbitrage Pricing Theory (APT)   An alternative asset pricing model to the Capital Asset Pricing Model. Unlike the Capital Asset Pricing Model, which specifies returns as a linear function of only systematic risk, Arbitrage Pricing Theory may specify returns as a linear function of more than a single factor.

Accredited Investor   Securities and Exchange Commission criteria consists of the following:

"-Any natural person whose individual net worth or joint net worth with spouse exceeds $1,000,000 at time of purchase of 325 with spouse of $300,000 for the last 2 years and has reasonable expectations of reaching the same income in current year.

-A trust with total assets of $5,000,000, not formed specifically for the purpose of acquiring assets offered. Directed by a person with the knowledge and experience to make such investment."

Accrued Income   Refers to interest that is owed by the issuer but has not been paid.

Active Management   Is an investment approach that uses available information and forecasting techniques to seek better performance than a specified index.

Alpha   A coefficient measuring the risk-adjusted performance, considering the risk due to the specific security, rather than the overall market.

Alternative Investments   Category of investments outside of traditional stocks, bonds and cash instruments. This category includes hedge funds, real estate, timberland, private equity, structured products, and commodities.

Arbitrage   Attempting to profit by exploiting price differences in identical or similar financial investments.

Arithmetic Average Returns   Average returns that do not factor in the effects of compounding. For example, a return in year one is +50% and in year two is -50%. Annual Arithmetic Average Return = (+50% + (-50%)) / 2 = 0%

Asset Allocation The strategic diversification of a portfolio.

Basis Point One hundredth of a percentage point (.01%). One hundred basis points equal 1%.

Behavioral Finance A theory stating that important psychological and behavioral variables effect investors' actions.

Beta A quantitative measure of the volatility of a given stock, mutual fund, or portfolio, relative to a market proxy. A beta above 1 is more volatile than the market proxy, while a beta below 1 is less volatile.

Biased Expectations The tendency of investors to discount any information that doesn't support their opinions.

Bottom-up Investment strategy in which companies are considered on their own merit without regard for sector or economic conditions.

Breakpoint (fees) Asset-based fees that decline (on a percentage basis) above certain asset levels.

Broker/Dealer A firm in the business of buying and selling securities as an agent for clients as well as for their own account. Broker/Dealers are regulated by The National Association of Securities Dealers (NASD) and the SEC.

Bundled Recordkeeper Provides recordkeeping, compliance and regulatory reporting, servicing and investment management all in one product.

Call Option An option contract that gives the holder the right to buy a certain quantity of an underlying security, at a specified price (the strike price) up to a specified date (the expiration date).

Capital Asset Pricing Model (CAPM) An economic model for valuing investments by relating risk (beta) and expected return, based on the idea that investors demand additional expected return if asked to accept additional risk.

Capital Gain The amount by which an asset's selling price exceeds its initial purchase price.

Carve Out Investment strategy of considering a particular investment on its own merit or apart from the total portfolio asset allocation.

Central Bank The generic name given to a country's primary monetary authority, such as the Federal Reserve System in the U.S. Usually has responsibility for issuing currency, administering monetary policy, holding member banks' deposits, and facilitating the nation's banking industry.

Certificate of Deposit Financial instrument with a stated interest rate and maturity issued by a bank.

Commingled Trusts Unregistered investment products that combine some of the benefits of mutual funds with the cost efficiencies of separate accounts. Similar to a mutual fund, investors in a commingled trust pool their assets with other investors and the holdings are "unitized" into individual shares.

Commodity Physical substances, such as foods, grains, and metals, that are interchangeable with other products of the same type, and that investors buy or sell, usually through futures contracts.

Commodity Trading Advisors (CTAs) An individual or firm that advises others about buying and selling futures and/or futures options.

Community Development Bank Federally insured banks that provide loans as well as savings and checking accounts in low-income areas.

Community Development Credit Union Federally-insured institutions that offer many of the same services as traditional credit unions, but serve low-income areas.

Community Development Loan Fund Pooled capital provided by individuals and institutions to provide loans at below market rates to fund small business, affordable housing and community services.

Community Development Venture Capital Fund Pooled funds that invest in small businesses with strong growth potential in low-income areas.

Community Investing Directing capital to disadvantaged communities.

Consumer Price Index (CPI) An inflation indicator that measures the change in the cost of a fixed basket of products and services, including housing, electricity, food, and transportation.

Contrarian Rebalancing Rebalances a portfolio in opposition to the prevailing wisdom; for example, rebalancing back to stocks during a bear market when others are pessimistic and rebalancing back to bonds during bull markets when they're optimistic.

Corporate Dialogue Correspondence to effect change in corporate policies and practices.

Correlation The degree to which the price or market value of two assets moves together.

Counterparty Risk The risk that the other party in a financial agreement will default.

Credit Analysis The process of evaluating any entity's debt issue in order to determine the likelihood that the borrower will live up to its obligations.

Credit Risk The possibility that a bond issuer will default, by failing to repay principal and interest in a timely manner.

Credit Spreads The difference in yield between a low quality and high quality fixed income instrument.

Currency Risk The risk that an asset denominated in a foreign currency decreases relative to the local currency because of exchange rate fluctuations.

Currency Swaps An arrangement in which two parties exchange a series of cash flows denominated in one currency for a series of cash flows in another currency, at agreed intervals over an agreed period.

Custodian A financial institution that has the legal responsibility for a customer's securities.

Custody Costs The fee a bank charges to hold assets. These may include asset-based fees, transaction fees, income collection fees, foreign exchange fees, etc.

Daily Valuation Process by which investments in a retirement plan are priced on a daily basis.

Default Risk The possibility that a bond issuer will default or fail to pay interest and principal in a timely manner.

Defined Benefit Pension Plan Employer-sponsored retirement plan in which a formula determines the exact benefits each retiree is entitled to. Payouts are typically determined by salary history and employment tenure.

Defined Contribution Retirement Plan A retirement plan in which a certain amount of money is set aside each year for the benefit of the employee. The actual benefit is dependent on the amount contributed and the investment return on those contributions.

Derivative Instruments A collective term for securities whose prices are based on the prices of another (underlying) investment. The most common of these are futures, options and swaps.

Deterministic Describes an algorithm in which the correct next step depends only on the current state. This contrasts with an algorithm where at each point there may be several possible actions and no way to choose among them except by trying each and backtracking if it fails.

Directional Strategy A strategy which is dependent on market movement to generate positive returns. For example, a long strategy is dependent on a rising market.

Dispersion Range of returns.

Dividend Yield Ratio of annual income paid as dividends to share price.

Dollar-Weighted Return This method measures rate of growth of initial capital and subsequent cash flows. Size and timing of cash flows have an impact. Also known as internal rate of return (IRR).

Efficient Frontier The curve on a risk-reward graph comprising all efficient portfolios.

Efficient Market Hypothesis The theory that all market participants receive and act on all of the relevant information as soon as it becomes available causing all securities to be fairly priced at any given moment in time. Under this theory, superior investment performance is a result of luck rather than skill.

Emerging Market Debt Sovereign and corporate debt of a developing country.

Equity-Linked Notes A debt instrument whose return on investment is tied to the equity markets. The return on equity-linked notes may be determined by a stock index, a basket of stocks, or a single stock.

ERISA Employee Retirement Income Security Act of 1974. The federal law which established legal guidelines for private pension plan administration and investment practices.

Euro The name for the composite monetary unit that has replaced national currencies in several European countries.

Eurozone The collective group of countries which use the Euro as their common currency.

Expected Return Midpoint of all possible outcomes.

Expense Ratios The percentage of a fund's assets that are spent to run a mutual fund. This includes management and advisory fees, overhead costs, 12b-1 fees, administrative fees, and all other asset-based costs incurred by the fund. The expense ratio does not include brokerage costs for trading.

Fallen Angel A bond which was investment-grade when issued but which is now of lower quality.

Fiduciary An individual that has a special duty and responsibility in oversight of others' assets.

Form 5500 A form which all qualified retirement plans (excluding SEPs and SIMPLE IRAs) must file annually with the IRS.

Frontier Engineer™ A Proprietary, probabilistic optimization algorithm developed by DiMeo Schneider & Associates, LLC.

Futures Contracts A standardized, transferable, exchange-traded contract that requires delivery of a commodity, bond, currency, or stock index, at a specified price, on a specified future date. Unlike options, futures convey an obligation to buy.

General Partner A partner with unlimited legal responsibility for the debts and liabilities of a partnership.

Geometric Average Returns Average returns that factor in the effects of compounding. For example, a return in year one is +50% and in year two is -50%. Average Annualized geometric return = $[(1+0.5)\star(1-0.5)]^{(1/2)} - 1 = -13.4\%$.

Global Custody Capability Ability to hold securities traded on foreign exchanges.

Hedge Fund of Fund (HFoF) Fund that invests in several separate hedge funds with different strategies.

Hedge Funds Broad term used for private investment pools typically falling outside the regulation of the Investment Company Act. These funds typically are designed for wealthy or accredited investors. The manager has broad discretion to trade, buy, sell short, securities, options, and derivatives.

Herd Mentality "Go Along" attitude that leads investors to bypass a due diligence process and blindly follow others.

Heuristics Human mental shortcuts designed to deal with the complexities of existence.

High Water Mark Previous high value achieved by the fund prior to a loss. This defined value must be surpassed before the manager can again charge any incentive fees.

High Yield Bonds Non-investment-grade bonds, usually rated BB or lower; often referred to as "Junk Bonds".

Hurdle Rate of Return A minimum return that must be achieved before a manager can change an incentive fee.

Incentive Fees An additional fee paid to the manager or general partner of a fund based on a percentage of profits.

Incubator Fund A start-up fund seeded by the manager and that does not yet allow outside investors.

Inflation Risk Premium A risk premium

built into nominal bonds that provides the investor with compensation for the threat of unanticipated inflation.

Inflation-Adjusted Return   Real return adjusted for inflation.

Inflation-Indexed Bonds   Fixed income securities whose principal and coupon payments are adjusted for inflation.

Interest Rate Risk   The possibility of a reduction in the value of a security, especially a bond, based on changes in interest rates.

Internal Rate of Return (IRR)   Measures rate of growth of initial capital and subsequent cash flows. Size and timing of cash flows have an impact. Also known as dollar-weighted return.

Investment Company Act   A set of Federal laws that regulate the registration and activities of investment companies, enforced by the Securities and Exchange Commission.

Investment Flexibility   The ability of a retirement plan to offer a wide variety of mutual funds from different fund families.

Investment Policy Statement (IPS)   Document that outlines investment objectives, guidelines, performance measures as well as responsibilities of parties involved.

Kurtosis   A statistical term that refers to greater frequency and/or magnitude extreme observations or "fat tails" than what is expected based on the normal distribution.

Leverage   The use of borrowed money to amplify investment performance.

Limited Partners   Partners who enjoy rights to the partnership's cash flow, but are not liable for partnership obligations beyond their initial contribution.

Limited Partnership   A business organization with one or more general partners, who manage the business and assume legal liability for debts and obligations, and one or more limited partners, who are liable only to the extent of their investments.

Liquidity   The ability to sell an asset quickly and without any price discount.

Market Capitalization (Market Cap)   Market value of a company as determined by the number of shares outstanding multiplied by the current stock price.

Market Portfolio   A concept used in Modern Portfolio Theory which refers to a hypothetical portfolio containing every security available to investors in a given market in amounts proportional to its market value.

Master Trust Administration   Ability to provide recordkeeping on numerous accounts in which the investments are commingled.

Maximum Drawdown   Maximum reduction in value over any given time period.

Mean-Variance Optimization   Mathematic algorithm that generates the efficient frontier.

Mezzanine Financing   Late-stage venture capital financing, usually the final round of financing prior to an initial public offering.

Money Market Account   Investment in a pool of short-term interest-bearing securities.

Monte Carlo Simulation   A probability analysis technique in which a large number of simulations are generated using random quantities for uncertain variables. The name comes from the city of Monte Carlo, which is known for its casinos.

Most Favored Nations   A clause in the contract with an investment management firm that states that your organization's fees will be at least as low as those of any similar clients of the manager.

Mutual Funds   Registered investment products. They are pools of money that are managed by an investment company and regulated by the Investment Company Act of 1940.

NCREIF   National Council of Real Estate Investment Fiduciaries.

Nominal   Not adjusted for inflation.

Nominal Return   Return not adjusted for inflation.

Normal Distribution   A probability distribution shaped like a bell, often found in statistical samples. The distribution of the curve implies that for a large population of independent random numbers, the majority of the population often clusters near a central value, and the frequency of higher and lower values taper off smoothly.

Overconfidence   Believing one's expectations are more likely to be realized than those of others.

Pass-Through Entity   Trust established to allow the pooled income from investments to be distributed directly to shareholders of the trust.

Passive Management   An investment approach that seeks to merely replicate the performance of a specified index. This is the least expensive approach and is often used for assets classes that are efficient. A passive strategy assumes that the marketplace will reflect all available information in the price paid for securities, and therefore, does not attempt to find mis-priced securities.

Price/Earnings Ratio (P/E)   Ratio of earnings per share to share price, used to measure relative cost of shares.

Private Equity   Equity capital invested in a company that is not publicly traded.

Probabilistic   Relating to, or governed by, probability. The behavior of a probabilistic system cannot be predicted exactly but the probability of certain behaviors is known. Such systems may be simulated using pseudo-random numbers.

Probabilistic Optimization Models   Portfolio optimization models that develop their output based on the assumption that market returns cannot be predicted exactly but the probability of certain outcomes is known.

Proxy   A written authorization given by a shareholder for someone else, usually the company's management, to cast his/her vote at a shareholder meeting or at another time.

Proxy Voting   Voting on resolutions and other matters by shareholders.

Real Return   Return adjusted for inflation.

Recordkeeper   A firm that administers retirement plans and/or charitable trusts. They report on individual accounts and process transactions and distributions.

Regression Analysis   A statistical technique used to find relationships between variables for the purpose of predicting future values.

REIT   Real Estate Investment Trust. A corporation or trust that uses the pooled capital of many investors to purchase and manage income property (equity REIT) and/or mortgage loans (mortgage REIT).

Returns Decomposition Method   A method for estimating an asset's expected return that involves breaking a return stream into its various components which may include income and capital gains.

RFP   Request for Proposal. An invitation to bid.

Risk Premium   The reward for holding a risky investment rather than a risk-free one.

Risk-Free Rate   A theoretical interest rate that would be returned on an investment which was completely free of risk. The 3-month Treasury Bill is a close approximation, since it is virtually risk-free.

R-Squared   A measurement of the portion of an investment's return stream that can be explained by the market proxy or index. Values for r-squared range from 0 to 1, where 0 indicates no linear relationship and 1 indicates a perfect linear relationship (perfect positive or negative correlation).

Securities Lending   The temporary lending of securities to brokers in exchange for income.

Sell Short   Borrowing a security (or commodity futures contract) from a broker and selling it, with the understanding that it must later be bought back (hopefully at a lower price) and returned to the broker. Short selling (or "selling short") is a technique used by investors who try to profit from the falling price of a stock.

Semi-Bundled Recordkeeper Recordkeeping and some investment management may be provided, however, compliance testing, some investment management, and regulatory reporting may be outsourced to other firms.

Separate Accounts Individually managed accounts for institutions or high-networth persons or institutions. They hold a portfolio of individual stocks or bonds. These accounts are each specific to one individual or holder.

Settlement Date The day a trade settles (when the cash or securities are actually transferred). Typically this occurs 3 days after the trade date.

Shareholder Advocacy Active ownership methods to effect change in corporate policies and practices.

Shareholder Resolution A formal request made to a company seeking action on a specific issue.

Sharpe Ratio A risk-adjustment measure developed by William F. Sharpe (return minus risk-free rate divided by standard deviation). It determines reward per unit of risk. The higher the Sharpe ratio, the better the investment's historical risk-adjusted performance.

Short Squeeze Term used to describe a situation where a securities price rises and investors who have sold the security short are forced to buy back at higher prices.

Skewness A distribution table that has more observations in one tail.

Socially Responsible Investing (SRI) Investing based on social, moral or ethical guidelines.

Sovereign Debt A debt instrument guaranteed by a government.

Stable Value Fund A fund designed to maintain a stable net asset value. Stable value funds invest in a pool of guaranteed insurance contracts and fixed income securities.

Standard Deviation Measures volatility around the mean.

Stop Loss A sell stop order for which the specified price is below the current market price. It is designed to limit losses to a specific percentage.

Stop Order A market order to buy or sell a certain security if a specified price is reached or passed.

Style Sorting securities by characteristics such as price/earnings ratio, price-to-book ratio or earnings growth. Investment approaches can be broadly labeled as growth or value styles, large, mid, and small-cap.

Survivorship Bias The tendency for failed companies or mutual funds to be excluded from performance studies (since they no longer exist). Survivorship bias causes the results of some studies to skew higher because only companies or mutual funds which were successful enough to survive until the end of the period are included.

Systematic Risk Risk which is common to an entire class of assets and cannot be diversified away. Sometimes called market risk.

The Consumer Price Index (CPI) A measure of the average price level of a fixed basket of goods and services purchased by consumers. Monthly changes in the CPI represent the rate of inflation.

Third Party Administrator (TPA) A firm that specializes in providing unbundled recordkeeping services.

Time-Weighted Return A performance method measurement that calculates growth of a portfolio between each cash transaction and links those results together to create longer-term results. It eliminates the impact of cash flows.

Treasury Inflation Protection Securities (TIPS) A bond issued by the U.S. Treasury whose principal and coupon payments are adjusted to eliminate the effects of inflation.

Total Return Concept Having no preference for income over capital gains.

TPI Timber Performance Index.

Trade Date   The day a trade occurs, as opposed to settlement date.

Transparency   The ability to audit all transactions and positions of a fund or manager.

Treynor Ratio   A risk-adjusted performance measure developed by Jack Treynor. This is a measure of a portfolio's excess return per unit of risk, equal to the portfolio's rate of return minus the risk-free rate of return, divided by the portfolio's beta. This is a similar ratio to the Sharpe ratio, except that the portfolio's beta is considered the measure of risk as opposed to the variance of portfolio returns.

Trustee   An individual or firm that holds and/or manages assets for the benefit of others.

Unbundled Recordkeeper   Provides recordkeeping only. Compliance testing and regulatory reporting performed by other firms.

Venture Capital (VC)   Capital made available for startup firms and small businesses. Managerial and technical expertise are often also provided. VC is also called risk capital.

Wrap-Fee Product   An investment program that charges a single fee for a suite of services, such as brokerage, advisory, custody, and management.

Zero-Sum Game   Situation in which one investor's gain results only from another's equivalent loss.

Index